ROBALDO MOROZZO DELLA ROCCA 1904 | 1993

EXPERIMENTAL ATTITUDE

a book by
STEFANO PASSAMONTI

photography
FRANCESCA IOVENE

cover and design
ANDREA GIAMBELLI – FRANCESCA OPRANDI

QUART

Editor (concept and coordination)
Stefano Passamonti

Articles by
Carmen Andriani, Maria Carola Morozzo della Rocca, Valter Scelsi, Adam Štěch

Project management
Linus Wirz

Photographs
Francesca Iovene

Cover and design
Andrea Giambelli, Francesca Oprandi

Technical drawings
Stefano Passamonti with Carlotta Garavaglia

English translation
Violante Piccolomini Naldi Bandini

Text editing
Benjamin Liebelt

Archival images
Archivio Morozzo della Rocca, Archivio Storico Comune di Genova, SUE Comune di Genova

Printing and binding
Grafiche Veneziane, Venice

Lithography
Grafiche Veneziane, Venice

Typeface
Faktum, Self Modern

Paper
Munken Polar white 120 gsm / 300 gsm

Acknowledgements

Every project is the result of a collective effort, and I would like to extend my gratitude to several individuals whose substantial contributions made this book possible.

My deepest appreciation goes to the Morozzo della Rocca family, particularly Maria Carola, Angelica, Carla, Carlo and Donatella Morozzo della Rocca, for their unwavering support and kindness from the inception of this research.

Special thanks to my enthusiastic and careful PhD tutors, Carmen Andriani and Valter Scelsi.

I am also profoundly grateful to Leonardo Chironi, Carlotta Garavaglia, Andrea Giambelli, Francesca Iovene, Francesca Oprandi and Celeste Rampone, who played a crucial role in transforming the research into a book, generously offering their time, intellect and resources. I also deeply appreciate the dedicated work of Marta Copetti and Violante Piccolomini.

Thanks to Adam Štěch for accepting the challenge of framing Morozzo's figure from a different and broader perspective.

This book would not have been possible without the commitment and enthusiasm of Linus Wirz and the team at Quart Verlag. My sincere thanks also go to Filippo Ranchio and Grafiche Veneziane for their precision and accuracy in producing the book.

Moreover, this edition has greatly benefited from the advice and support of Michel Carlana, Carlo Gandolfi and Roberto Gargiani. I am also grateful to Jacopo Baccani, Lorenzo Bini, Andrea Canziani, Marco Fava, Giancarlo Floridi, Giovanni Galli, Antonio Lavarello, Angelo Lunati, Luigi Mandraccio, Natalia Moroni, Franco Passamonti, Katya Passamonti, Gregorio Pecorelli, Letizia Pella, Francesco Perrotta-Bosch, Emanuele Piccardo, Vittorio Pizzigoni, Francesco Rosadini, Giulia Ricci, Joseph Rigo, Giorgia Santilli, Marcos Sartori, Carlo Sciaretta, Giuseppe Spina, Guido Tesio, Francesco Testa and Federico Tranfa.

Finally, a heartfelt thank you to my parents, Giuseppina Moffa and Luciano Passamonti, for always believing in me and my passion.

Quart Publishers is being supported by the Federal Office of Culture for the years 2021–2024.

ISBN 978-3-03761-316-0

Index

This work originates from the PhD dissertation, defended at the University of Genoa in December 2022.

The research, titled *Professionismo e sperimentazione. Robaldo Morozzo della Rocca, Genova, il Novecento,* was supervised by Carmen Andriani and Valter Scelsi and benefited from the collaboration of Maria Carola Morozzo, Roberto Gargiani and Manuel Gausa Navarro.

Sponsored by:

ACG

BCC PIANFEI E ROCCA DE'BALDI
CREDITO COOPERATIVO ITALIANO

GrifoFinance

SFERA S.p.A.

Famiglia Morozzo della Rocca
Donatella, Carlo e Angelica
in ricordo di Robaldo

4

House for the lawyer Eugenio Chiappe
Alassio, Savona, 1929. Demolished.

Residence for the publisher Giuseppe Carabba and his wife Elena Muzzati
Ostia Lido, Rome, 1930. Demolished.

House for Carlo Reborati
Rapallo, Genoa, 1931–1934.

Proposal for a new railway viaduct
Bogliasco, Genoa 1946.
Competition, 1st Prize.

PLEASURE AND PAIN

A RATIONAL EXPRESSIONISM

Genesis

The architectural research surrounding the work of Robaldo Morozzo della Rocca constitutes a historical endeavour, aimed not merely at reconstructing the past but, above all, aspiring to be pertinent to the present.
This endeavour transcends the scope of a philological-historiographical operation concerning historical narratives. It extends beyond the "critical restitution" of a "minor" author, positioned at the periphery of debate, endeavouring instead to interpret the relevance of certain insights through a contemporary, post-ideological lens, without the presumption of being exhaustive.
From the career of this eccentric professional and thinker emerges an adherence to conventional (affirmed) historiographical categories that is consistently tempered by unconventional cultural references.
From Morozzo's artistic research – spanning the entire *Age of Extremes*,[1] from monarchical to republican Italy – emerges a constant methodological inquiry seemingly unscathed by the contingencies of Italy's significant historical events, such as the post-war reconstruction and the Economic Miracle of the boom, the working-class movement and the rise of Socialism, the *Sessantotto* Crisis, the era of collective action and radical cultures, the Compromise and the *Anni di Piombo*,[2] culminating just after the *Mani Pulite* scandal.

It is a territorial history, yet so expansive as to bequeath us a universal approach to architectural practice. Unlike the prominent figures of the "engaged" Italian architectural culture, selectively picked by historiography among those closely tied to politics, highly visible and militant, Morozzo appears as a character of impassioned detachment, refraining from systematic involvement in disciplinary debates, eschewing writing, abstaining from curating architectural exhibitions, hence neither propagating nor adjudicating it. **Morozzo exists beyond time while being moved by it simultaneously. He unites realism and vision, pragmatism and experimentation, the ability to engage with tradition alongside an impetus toward the future.** He amalgamates openness to questioning overly rigid canons, thereby engaging with fragments and heterogeneity, occasionally bordering on eclecticism or heresy, with a pursuit of unity that signifies not so much objectivity or objectification but a systematic orchestration of the manifold and the complex.

Thus, this book shares an idea of architecture, but above all, of how, through the art of construction, one can develop an autonomous path and a vision, simultaneously specific and universal, of the world.

1 See: Eric Hobsbawm, *The Age of Extremes: The Short Twentieth Century, 1914–1991*, London, 1994.
2 See: Paul Ginsborg, *A History of Contemporary Italy: Society and Politics, 1943–1988*, London, 1990; id., *Italy and Its Discontents. Family, Civil Society, State, 1980–2001*, London, 2001.

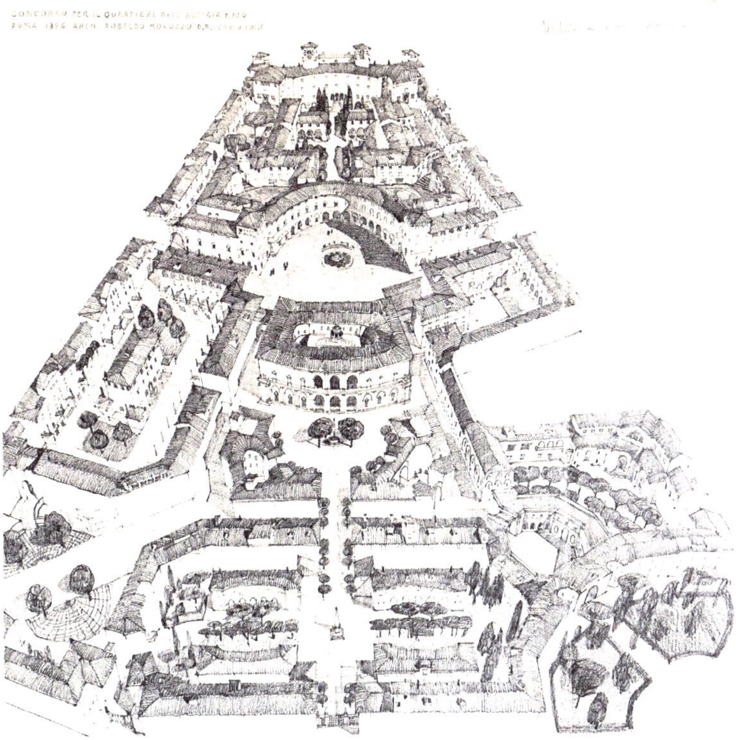

Robaldo Morozzo della Rocca
with Carlo Domenico Rossi,
proposal for the Artisan Quarter
Rome, 1925–1926.
Competition, 2nd Prize ex-aequo.

Study for a skyscraper of the Detailed
Master Plan for Piazza Dante
Genoa, 1931–1933.

Another Modern Movement

An architect and professional of undeniable quality, concurrently a sophisticated and profound architectural thinker, Robaldo Morozzo della Rocca (1904–1993) eludes and challenges, through his works, projects and writings, our immediate inclination to confine and reduce him within predetermined categories.[3]
An "irregular" figure, simultaneously stringent and capricious, intricate and contradictory, sophisticated and popular, Morozzo della Rocca is an architect *sui generis*. **He conceives and constructs profoundly diverse architectures, never constricted within a singular image – a disposition that renders him an unreliable subject for the militant historiography of his era.** Indeed, the diverse spectrum of his production is characterised by an irregular weave of progress and setbacks, professions of faith, and uncertainty, reflecting in an open and ambiguous manner the living substance of the context with which it engages.
Morozzo della Rocca, a pivotal figure essential for grasping the onset and subsequent evolution of European avant-gardes in Italy, stands as a key luminary within the framework of shaping the architectural culture of Genoa in the 20th century.
Modern, albeit a critic resistant to *modernist* expression and the idea of Modernism, and simultaneously an avid scholar of constructions from the past, Morozzo embodies an infinite array of ambivalences. These are shaped both by the historical transitional period in which he lived and by his distinct, remarkably multifaceted artistic personality. Endeavouring to reconcile, for instance, his role as a herald of modern enlightenment, the proponent of the rationality of "building anew", with the accusation of having created a *passé* and eclectic architecture, proves as inconclusive as seeking a middle-ground between his theoretical advocacy for the preponderance of "plastic creation" in architecture and his creations characterised by subdued and classicising tones.
For this reason, Morozzo merits a distinctive interpretation, positioned as an outsider within the avant-garde milieu and navigating a meandering course amidst the anomaly embodied by Italian Rationalism. Contradictions and ambiguities, far from diminishing the significance or allure of his exploration, instead rejuvenate its vigour and contemporary relevance.

Morozzo's undertakings unfold discreetly but prolifically throughout much of the 20th century, traversing from Futurism[4] to Neoplasticism[5], navigating the era of

3 The ensemble of Morozzo della Rocca's publications and writings, spanning almost four decades, does not constitute a unified and homogeneous corpus aimed at structuring a theory. The use of writing, employed sporadically to explore different themes, results in a collection of contributions completed at various times or initiated and concluded over an extended period. These writings are inspired by occasions of diverse nature and inevitably intertwined with personal and professional events. Among these, one may refer to:
"La Conservazione dell'Architettura Antica", in: *L'Architetto*, year VII, nos. 7–8, 1962, p. 30–37; *Una questione tecnica. La spaziatura degli scalini*, Genoa, 1966; *Modulazione sonora e visiva*, Genoa, 1966; "La Modulazione Architettonica nella Proiezione Ortogonale e nella Prospettiva", in: *Atti dell'Accademia Ligure di Scienze e Lettere*, year XXII, Genoa, 1966, p. 69–130; "Confronto critico tra i rilevamenti passati dei Palazzi della Strada Nuova", in: *Genova, Strada Nuova*, Genoa, 1967; "Architettura ed Economia", in: AAVV, *Documenti di Architettura*, no. 1, 1969.

4 See: Ezio Godoli, *Il Futurismo*, Rome-Bari, 1983, p. 74–75.

5 See: Bruno Zevi, *Poetica dell'architettura Neoplastica*, Milan, 1953.

Fascist rhetoric, and extending into post-war Italy with experiments involving the artisanal application of reinforced concrete.[6]

A profound connoisseur and scholar of mathematics and physics, adept in scenography, Morozzo, alongside Galeazzo Alessi, emerges as one of the most controversial and idiosyncratic figures in the architectural milieu of Genoa throughout history, with his most significant works materialising in Liguria. Rare are the instances where the endeavours of a singular professional have so decisively and indelibly shaped the reference points of a city, as is the case with Morozzo in Genoa. A seemingly peripheral urban context, marked by contradiction and dominated by latent historicism, Genoa was chosen by Morozzo as his personal field of action – a realm in which to experiment with alternative forms of reconciliation between art and technology and to identify diverse modes of growth for the seeds previously sown by the architects of the Modern Movement.

Having attended the Academy of Fine Arts and pursued studies in mathematics and physics in Genoa, Morozzo graduated in Architecture in Rome (1929).[7] Within the context of MIAR,[8] Morozzo staunchly positioned himself in the midst of the discourse surrounding the concept of Rational Architecture and its accreditation as a state-endorsed architectural approach, both on a theoretical and professional level. Before fully dedicating himself to independent practice, he served as the Director of the School of Scenography at the Teatro Carlo Felice in Genoa and held the position of Scenography Professor in Turin. Furthermore, he assumed the role of Architect Extraordinaire at the Superintendence for Medieval and Modern Art and served as a technical expert for the Municipality of Genoa.

In the 1930s, Morozzo participated in the V Triennale di Milano with a project for a steel-framed Dwelling. Additionally, he designed the Fiera del Mare, undertook the urban redevelopment of Piazza Dante and formulated the Eastern Expansion Plan for Genoa.

6 For the relationships between Novecentismo and Rationalism, see: Rossana Bossaglia/Paola Marescalchi, "L'ultimo Novecento", in: AAVV, *Anni Trenta. Arte e Cultura in Italia*, Milan, 1982, p.79–85.

7 Morozzo della Rocca graduated in 1929 under the guidance of Gustavo Giovannoni, alongside prominent figures in Italian and international 20th century architecture, including Rino Levi (1926), Adalberto Libera, Luigi Vietti (1928), Massimo Castellazzi, Mario Paniconi, Simeon Petroff, Mario Ridolfi (1929), Giulio Pediconi and Luigi Moretti (1930). The primary reason for his transfer was the swift recognition garnered by the Roman school. Inaugurated in 1920, the school was founded on the concept of the *integral architect*, developed by Giovannoni in 1916 with the aim of educating professionals capable of intervening with both technical and artistic competence in urban transformations. This envisioned figure was meant to ensure that the modernisation of cities would not compromise the cultural heritage. To achieve this, education had to transcend the divide between technicality and artistry. While sharing certain points with the Bauhaus ideal of Gropius, this formulation of the *integral architect* lacked any avant-garde aspirations. The Italian *integral architect* was envisioned as an agent of pragmatic modernisation, faithful to classical tradition and operating within the confines of established Treaties.

See: Gustavo Giovannoni, "Relazione della Commissione per le Scuole di Architettura", in: Guido Zucconi, *Dal Capitello alla città*, Milano, 1977, p.127; Giorgio Ciucci, *Gli architetti e il Fascismo. Architettura e città*, Turin, 1989; Alessandra Muntoni, "1926–1928: dalla Scuola di Architettura di Roma alla I esposizione di architettura razionale", in: Francesco Garofalo/Luca Versani (Eds.), *Adalberto Libera. Opera Completa*, Milan, 1989, p.36.

8 Acronym for the Movimento Italiano per l'Architettura Razionale (Italian Movement for Rational Architecture). Emerging after the first Italian Exhibition of Rational Architecture organised in 1928 in Rome by Adalberto Libera and Gaetano Minnucci, it brought together around 50 young architects who, attentive to contemporary European experiences, advocated rationalist architecture in Italy. Besides the Milan-based Gruppo 7 and Alberto Sartoris, participants included Pietro Aschieri, Guido Cancellotti, Gino Capponi, Giuseppe Piccinato, Mario Ridolfi from Rome, Gino Levi-Montalcini, Giuseppe Pagano from Turin, and Mario Labò from Genoa. Initially tolerated by the Fascist regime, MIAR faced strong opposition after the 1931 Rome exhibition, which sharply criticised official academic architecture. The infamous "*Table of Horrors*" incident ensued, featuring a collection of passé works endorsed by the regime and selected by Pietro Maria Bardi as a provocative act against his own party. The association dissolved under the threat of expulsion by the Fascist architects' union, which subsequently organised the RAMI – Ragruppamento Architetti Moderni Italiani – RAMI (Grouping of Italian Modern Architects). Some MIAR members joined RAMI, but the majority continued their research independently, albeit participating in official initiatives. Following MIAR's failure, the regime vehemently disowned its ties to Rationalism. With the onset of World War II, Fascist architecture definitively aligned itself not with "abstract classicism", but rather with "monumental Romanity".

See: Michele Cennamo (Ed.), *Materiali per l'analisi dell'architettura moderna. Il MIAR*, Naples, 1976; particularly see Chapter II: "La costituzione del MIAR", p.75–93.

Engaged in post-war reconstruction, notably through the INA Casa programme,[9] Morozzo secured noteworthy commissions such as the redesign of the new Foce Square in Genoa and the Nuovo Teatro Regio in Turin. He proceeded to construct some of the most significant works of 20th-century Genoa, including the Palace for the Ligurian Activity Society, the apartment building Ollandini Hoffer, the Headquarters of the Istituto Nazionale delle Assicurazioni in the Piccapietra district, the INA Casa Ansaldo and Unit C of the INA Forte Quezzi housing complex. Towards the end of his career, he dedicated himself to the pedagogy of subjects pertaining to history, styles, drawing and restoration at the Faculties of Engineering and Architecture in Genoa. Here, he seamlessly integrated his passion for antiquity and anecdotal erudition in decoration, as evidenced by his contributions to entries in the Treccani encyclopaedia.[10]

Due to the breadth of his thoughts and actions, Morozzo stands as proof of how the history of 20th-century architecture still offers numerous and accessible avenues of investigation.
It also underscores how the robust modelling of certain critical positions from the recent past has, through choices that now appear anachronistic, yielded analyses exhausted by the ideological thrust of a particular architectural culture. This culture has often been mistrusting of specific historical periods or, worse, deemed figures unsuitable for representing the "cultivated" professional model of the organic intellectual.[11]
The absence of a comprehensive and exhaustive critical framework for Morozzo della Rocca underscores his inherently challenging nature, one that defies easy categorisation and is only fully comprehensible when approached through a

9 In February 1949, the Italian Parliament approved Law No. 43, which pertains to measures aimed at increasing blue-collar employment. The initiative, entitled "Housing for Workers", marked the commencement of a substantial construction programme in various Italian cities. Termed the *Fanfani Plan* after its architect Amintore Fanfani, who served as the Minister of Labour in the government led by Alcide De Gasperi at that time, the plan sought to address the challenging employment situation arising from the aftermath of World War II. The objective was to boost the country's economy through residential settlement plans. In its early stages, INA Casa functioned as a subsidiary of the Istituto Nazionale Assicurazioni (National Insurance Institute), with financial coverage for the plans provided by the state, employers and employees through a wage deduction – essentially, a form of social fund in solidarity with the unemployed. Two committees were established: the Implementation Committee (chaired by Filiberto Guala), responsible for issuing regulations and financial contributions, and the Management Committee, which concurrently oversaw the development of the plans from a construction perspective, monitored peripheral entities and contributed to appointments (chaired by Arnaldo Foschini). The latter committee included representatives from the labour sector, both employers and workers, as well as government officials (Ministries of Treasury, Labour and Public Works). Competitions were organised to identify professionals and technicians for inclusion in the project lists.

See: Giuseppe Samonà, "Il Piano Fanfani in rapporto all'attività edilizia dei liberi professionisti", in: *Metron*, no.33–34, 1949, p.14; Luigi Beretta Anguissola, *I 14 anni del Piano INA Casa*, Roma, 1963; Paola Di Biagi, *La Grande Ricostruzione. Il Piano dell'Ina Casa e l'Italia degli anni '50*, Roma, 2002.

10 See: Robaldo Morozzo della Rocca, encyclopaedic entries: *Caryatid, Compluvium, Cordonata, Cord, Doccia, Downspout, Drapery, Beacon, Finial, Dripstone, Throat, Eaves, Gutter*, in: *Enciclopedia Italiana Treccani*, Rome, 1931.

11 For Gramsci, the communist intellectual, as an organic figure to the class tasked with constructing the new world, is not merely a man of thought but also an organiser and a political leader – someone who takes a stance. In the post-World War II era, the political left would achieve cultural hegemony in many sectors by applying a Gramscian strategy. The thesis of the organic intellectual is a critical response to the thesis of the independent intellectual, of which Morozzo could be considered an example. If the traditional intellectual is the humanist, the man of letters, the orator, the new intellectual, on the other hand, embodies both a specialist (or technician) and a politician. In his political role, he can find no other arena for the exercise of his expertise than the party, the sole place where the synthesis between theory and practice can be realized. In the 1960s, a series of groups of intellectual architects formed, convinced of the need to stand "against from within" neoliberal capitalist development through a rigorous political stance. A discourse to which Morozzo seems not to belong at all, for demographic and biographical reasons, as well as his reluctance towards the political relevance of architecture.

See: Antonio Gramsci, *Gli intellettuali e l'organizzazione della cultura*, Turin, 1955; Manfredo Tafuri, "Per una critica dell'ideologia architettonica", in: *Contropiano*, no.1, 1969, p.31–79; id. "Lavoro intellettuale e sviluppo capitalistico", in: *Contropiano*, no.2, 1970, p.241–281; id., *Progetto e utopia. Architettura e sviluppo capitalistico*, Rome/Bari, 1973; Alberto Asor Rosa, "Critica dell'ideologia ed esercizio storico", in: *Casabella*, no.619–620, 1995, p.28–33; Marco Biraghi, *Progetto di Crisi. Manfredo Tafuri e l'architettura contemporanea*, Milan, 2005; *Pier Vittorio Aureli, The Project of Autonomy. Politics and Architecture within and against Capitalism*, New York, 2008.

multifaceted lens. Without purporting to deem him a "master", the analysis seeks to shed light on the legacy of a distinctive poetics, firmly entrenched within the building culture of the 20th century but, above all, metahistorical in nature and manifested within a unique and specific context. Within the framework of a broader reassessment of the Western canon of 20th-century architecture, this endeavour aims to contextualize certain pivotal junctures in his career, constituting valuable material for reinstating an accurate placement of his figure within the narratives of architectural history. Despite occupying a position of evocative significance in the architectural panorama of 20th-century Genoa, Morozzo, paradoxically, finds mention only at the periphery of discourse. He is often portrayed as a traditionalist offspring of the conservative Roman culture, deemed by many as regressive and obscurantist in the face of the innovative trends of European Rationalism.[12]
The prolonged critical neglect towards figures like Morozzo della Rocca can be partially elucidated by the dual consequence of practising the profession within a context deemed "lesser" compared to the international architectural discourse. Additionally, it is a result of the shadow that has shrouded a substantial portion of Italian architecture during and after the Fascist era.

The "Morozzo predicament" resides in what could be characterised as a determination to be modern on one's own terms – devoid of the rhetoric and propaganda of avant-gardes, free from subjugation to various rationalist doctrinal frameworks, and resisting dissolution into the standardised and globalised image of the International Style.
This "unforgivable" quest for identity is constructed not only on the values of figurative abstraction, acknowledged as the conquest of a new expressive freedom, but also on a historically informed interpretation of classicism (the progenitor of such abstraction), thereby rendering it an aesthetic product within the semantic realm of the Modern Movement.

This identity is so potent, so deeply ingrained that, despite oblivion, it remains a reference point amid the current crisis in Italian architecture.[13]

12 See: Bruno Zevi, "La vicenda Italiana", in: *Storia dell'Architettura Moderna*, Turin, 1950, p. 185–187.

13 On the subject, see: Vittorio Gregotti, "Decadenza dell'architettura italiana", in: *Casabella*, no. 580, 1991, p. 2–3; Pierluigi Nicolin, *Notizie sullo stato dell'architettura italiana*, Turin, 1994; Italo Rota, 1844–1994. "Centotrent'anni d'architettura venti anni di altro", in: *Domus*, no. 764, 1994, p. 95; Pippo Ciorra, *Senza architettura. Le ragioni di una crisi*, Bari, 2011; Francesco Garofalo (Mario Lupano, Ed.), *Cosa è successo all'architettura Italiana*, Venice, 2016; Valerio Paolo Mosco, "Eclettismo nella continuità. L'insospettabile vitalità dell'architettura italiana contemporanea", in: *Industria delle costruzioni* no. 470, 2019, p. 12–19; Aslı Çiçek, "Stance through acceptance", in: *Area*, no. 185, 2022; Alberto Ferlenga, *Architettura. La differenza italiana*, Roma, 2023.

The Italian architectural landscape

In 1959, Reyner Banham, with what he terms the "Italian withdrawal from modern architecture",[14] identifies an "anomaly" in Italy. In the notorious altercation with the director of *Casabella-Continuità,* Ernesto Nathan Rogers, Banham vehemently rejects the notion that contemporary architectural culture could have roots in the past. He opposes the retrieval of the artisanal dimension melded with compositional exploration and attention to detail introduced by Neoliberty.[15] In opposition to Rogers' thesis in *Continuità,*[16] Banham perceives *Crisis* with the past as the sole solution to the future of the discipline, overlooking, however, that nearly every new artistic phenomenon in Italy stems from a profound attenuation through pre-existing and deeply ingrained content and expressive forms. In Italy, cultural factors intrinsic to various regional realms deform the conditions underlying original phenomena. This occurs in the Renaissance, heavily influenced by Christianity, and in Neoclassicism, where nostalgic reference to the classical world coexists with industrialisation. One thing is certain: the anomaly highlighted by Banham concerning Italy is a subject of reflection that cannot be disregarded. **Eclecticism within continuity[17] is the oxymoron that could encapsulate the events of an architecture in which tendencies and authors intertwine, disappearing and reappearing from alternative perspectives, artfully transforming the essence of original cultures.**

The trajectory of the Modern Movement, born elsewhere but imported into Italy, is emblematic. Much like how Gothic architecture acquired distinct traits that delineate Italian Gothic, or how the phenomenon of Liberty – originating in England with Arts and Crafts and in France and Belgium with Art Nouveau – was purified of political and social components in Italy to become a pure floral style, similarly, the Modern Movement, transitioning from Europe to Italy, adopted its specific physiognomy, allowing for the identification of an autonomous movement: Rationalism.

Italian architects harbour a sentiment towards the Modern Movement that, while on one hand is akin to an "epiphany", on the other, bears a subtle scepticism influenced by tradition and its "immutable principles". The young architects of the 1930s, such as Morozzo, were ready to swear by the validity of rationalist dogmas and then "betray" them in pursuit of an exploration that does not rigidly tether form to function.

14 See: Reyner Banham, "Neoliberty. The Italian Retreat from Modern Architecture", in: *The Architectural Review*, no. 4, 1959 (now in Reyner Banham, *Architettura della Seconda Età della Macchina*, Milan 2004, p. 54–61 [trans.]).

15 See: Paolo Portoghesi, "Dal neorealismo al neoliberty", in: *Comunità*, no. 65, December 1958; Roberto Gabetti, (entry) "Eclettismo", in: *Dizionario Enciclopedico di Architettura e Urbanistica*, Vol. II, 1968, p. 211.

16 See: Ernest Nathan Rogers, "L'evoluzione dell'architettura. Risposta al custode dei frigidaires", in: *Casabella Continuità* no. 228, 1959, p. 4.; id., "Continuità o Crisi", in: *Casabella-Continuità* no. 215, 1957, p. 3–5.

17 See: Valerio Paolo Mosco, "Eclettismo nella continuità. L'insospettabile vitalità dell'architettura italiana contemporanea", op. cit.

A distinctive attribute characterising Rationalism is that of classicism, not confined to scholastic historical classifications but conceived beyond the constraints of time and hierarchical chronology. It embodied a pervasive, enduring inclination to seek organisation, order, measure and a design of mouldings that render architectural organisms distinctly perceptible in the harsh light of the Mediterranean sun. In this sense, we can discern a substantial vein of classicism in Italian Romanesque, Gothic and Baroque, where even Francesco Borromini can be deemed classical for the superb imagination and freedom of his forms that align within an autonomous order of compatibility.
Antidogmatism, classicism and rationality – as timeless characteristics – formed the essence of the most vibrant aspect of Rationalism until it lost its propulsive force entirely: a convergence of factors wherein the balanced relationship between form and content[18] was systematically disregarded, an ellipticity that, fundamentally, enriched national expressions with nuances.
Ambitions of continuity and discontinuity animated the era of Rationalism, always teetering between Futurism and Metaphysics.[19] In Italy, continuity often feeds off its antithesis, exhibiting a propensity to hybridise with it.

Rationalism, nonetheless, begot one of the most successful architectural civilisations, wherein the etymons introduced by the Bauhaus underwent a figurative twist significant enough to alter their original meanings. Thus, a language that was conceived as abstract, anti-figurative, if not iconoclastic, and emulative of the machine civilisation, in Italy transformed into a transitive language – profoundly figurative and imbued with connections to spontaneous localism and the past, elements that the European avant-garde had sought to sever.

It is within this framework and in the context of the architectural culture of Genoa that Morozzo's poetics should be placed as an anomaly nestled within the folds of the Modern Movement. Profound internalisations and alterations of original impulses take on distinctive nuances in the meandering trajectory of Morozzo della Rocca's *alternative modernity*,[20] demanding a unique narrative for his unconventional approach.

18 De Sanctis analyses the connection between content and form with the aim of reconstructing the cultural and moral world from which the great works would later emerge. He regards art as the "living", that is, the "form", believing that there is no dissociation between form and content because they are interwoven with each other.

See: Francesco De Sanctis, *Storia della letteratura italiana*, Bologna, 2006.

19 Ambitions of continuity and discontinuity also animate the militant work of Bruno Zevi, who, on the one hand, envisions the advent of an architecture in Italy that is fundamentally distant from our tradition (organic architecture), while on the other, he retrieves Italian Rationalism to the point of considering, foremost among them, Terragni, Pagano and Persico as masters of the Modern Movement with international stature in only an apparent contradiction.

On this matter, see: Bruno Zevi, "La vicenda Italiana", in: *Storia dell'architettura moderna*, op. cit., p. 188–220.

20 On dissident modernities and the revision of the architectural canons of the past century see: Colin St John Wilson, *The Other Tradition of Modern Architecture: The Uncompleted Project*, London, 1995; Kenneth Frampton, *The Other Modern Movement: Architecture, 1920–1970*, New Haven, 2022.

Genoa and 20th-century architectural culture

Genoa or *La Superba*[21] is a peculiar city, a constrained archetype.[22] Morozzo della Rocca makes a formidable metaphor out of it, a unique vantage point for observing reality, the primary reference for his formal exploration in the field of architecture. Indeed, it is his architectural creations that, above all, accentuate the *forma urbis*[23] of the city, its topographic and panoramic nature as a compressed agglomeration nestled between the sea and the hills.
The architectural culture of the region of Liguria references a latent historicism throughout the 20th-century. In Genoa, the major city, various opportunities arose to renew significant urban areas according to rationalist forms. The late spurt of architectural discourse found its *raison d'être* in a bourgeoisie that persisted in representing itself through historical eclecticism, lagging behind its European counterparts and even in comparison to Italian trends. The bourgeoisie wearily embraced, on a merely superficial level, first the Liberty style and then the Avant-garde. Caution and, in certain terms, the insularity of Genoese citizens thus constitute the primary reason for the persistence of that conventional, eclectic and historicist spirit subtly and latently pervading much of Genoa's architecture in the 20th-century. Ultimately, this spirit determined the city's aura. The industrial and

economic development failed to contain the city's stance of artistic closure, nor did it overcome the cultural provincialism ingrained within the city. Despite its inherent openness stemming from its historical vocation as a maritime and port emporium, Genoa remained relegated to a marginal position, progressively slipping into a historical-critical oblivion that seems, to this day, to dictate a phase of stagnation.

The absence of disciplinary discourse, of journals and, for many years, an institution, resulted in a delay and a lack of quality in construction.[24]
Yet even in Genoa, Italy's foremost port and apex of the nation's most industrialised area, the avant-garde gradually made its appearance, emerging from the administrative invention of Grande Genova, the "metropolis" born from the union of the city centre with the delegations of nineteen surrounding

21 Francesco Petrarca already described the city of Genoa as the Superba in 1385. See: Francesco Petrarca, *Guida al viaggio da Genova alla Terra Santa*, Milan, 2018.

22 In this regard, Edoardo Sanguineti's words are significant: "*Posso dire che l'universo, che altrove si squaderna, è qui raccolto, miniaturizzato come si vede. Ma questo accade perché Genova è un po' una replica del mondo, e un po' è un suo archetipo ristretto, una specie di modellino ristretto*" (I can say that the universe, which unfolds elsewhere, is gathered here, miniaturised as you see. But this happens because Genoa is somewhat a replica of the world, and somewhat a restricted archetype of it, a kind of scaled-down model).

See: Edoardo Sanguineti, *Genova per me*, Naples, 2004.

23 See: Piero Barbieri, *Forma Genuae*, Genoa, 1938. A collection of 24 black and white plates, folded format 64 x 25 centimetres, open format 64 x 50 centimetres, numbered from I (Genova zero) to 24 (1937), representing the urban development of Genoa in the area between San Benigno and Punta Vagno, at a scale of 1:10,000.

24 Re. the architectural culture and urban development of Genoa, see: Ennio Poleggi/Paolo Cevini, *Le città nella storia d'Italia. Genova*, Bari, 1981; Ennio Poleggi, *Paesaggio e immagine di Genova*, Genoa, 1982; Giuseppe Marcenaro, *Genova, il Novecento*, Genoa, 1986; Francesca Balletti/Bruno Giontoni, *Una città tra le due guerre: culture e trasformazioni urbanistiche*, Genoa, 1990; Ermanno Ranzani, "Genova", in: *Domus* no. 727, 1991; Massimo Razzi, *L'ulivo sul tetto 1892–1992. Cent'anni di edilizia genovese tra storia e ricordo*, Genoa, 1992; Paolo Cevini, "Genova", in: Francesco Dal Co, *Storia dell'architettura Italiana. Il secondo Novecento (1945–1996)*, Milan, 1997; Ennio Poleggi, *Genova. Guida all'architettura*, Turin, 1998; Gianluca Cristoforetti/Hilda Ghiara, *Genova. Guida di architettura moderna*, Florence, 2004; Silvia Barisione/Matteo Fochessati/Gianni Franzone/Andrea Canziani, *Architetture in Liguria dagli anni Venti agli anni Cinquanta*, Milan, 2004; Giovanna Franco/Stefano Musso, *Architetture in Liguria dopo il 1945*, Genoa, 2016.

municipalities.[25] Moreover, the influx of professionals from other regions injected hints of quality into the city; yet these isolated leaps forward failed to coalesce into a system and instead, remained sporadic exceptions.[26]

In the Thirties and Forties, private construction relied on proven formulae and the repetition of tired historicist templates, while public construction, representing the official culture, more immediately reflected the contradictions of official power: on one side, avant-garde architecture and its varying degrees of rigorous Rationalism, and on the other, the reaction of neoclassical historicism. This landscape of works, an expression of the regime, was characterised by a great variety that sees a coexistence between Umbertine and neo-mannerist buildings alongside radical avant-garde expressions. Despite the public commission works carrying a historicist tone, it was precisely some of these, designed by municipal technicians, that solidified the affirmation of Rationalism in the Ligurian capital. Erected from 1933 onwards, these buildings[27] seemingly remained oblivious to any programmatic statement, with the exception of certain cases such as Piazza della Vittoria[28] on one side and Piazza Rossetti on the other. Here, the two tendencies declared themselves and antagonised each other, ultimately under the direction of the same mind: Marcello Piacentini.[29]
The authority established by Piacentini in Genoa, following the construction of Piazza della Vittoria, soon intertwined with the transformation of Piazza Foce. Thanks to his "consultancy", this transformation was carried out by one of the most active Genoese designers, Luigi Carlo Daneri,[30] subverting the outcome of

25 An administrative decision more than an urbanistic one, strongly endorsed by the Fascist regime under Benito Mussolini to address the disproportion between the demographic and territorial limits of the city and the wealth derived from its commerce and activities. Royal Decree-Law of January 14, 1926, no.74: Aggregation of 19 neighbouring municipalities to the city of Genoa.

26 Genoa attracted architects from diverse origins to establish their professional activities: Tuscany (Gino Coppedè, Mario Angelini, Giulio Zappa, Mario Braccialini, Alfredo Fineschi, Claudio Andreani), Piedmont (Eugenio Fuselli, Luigi Vietti, Robaldo Morozzo della Rocca), Lombardy (Carlo Nicoli, Beniamino Bellati), Veneto (Giuseppe Crosa di Vergagni), Emilia Romagna (Paride Contri) and Campania (Camillo Nardi Greco). This illustrates how Genoa, despite its presumed peripherality, evolved into a vibrant territory for intellectual exchange.

27 Among the noteworthy buildings, it is worth mentioning: the flower market (Paride Contri, 1934), Albaro pools (Paride Contri, 1935), fish market (Mario Braccialini and Municipal Technical Office, 1933) and student house (Mario Angelini and Mario Braccialini, 1934).

On the subject, see: Paolo Cevini, "Architettura razionalista e architettura di «regime»: il ruolo del Comune di Genova", in: *Genova Anni '30. Da Labò a Daneri*, Genoa, 1989.

28 See: Giuliano Forno, "La Sistemazione della Piazza della Vittoria", in: Giuseppe Marcenaro, *Genova, il Novecento*, Genova, 1986, p.320–331; "L'Arco trionfale ai Caduti genovesi e alla Vittoria italiana", in: *Genova*, no.6, 1931, p.417–458.

29 Marcello Piacentini (Rome, 1881–1960) was an extremely adept "strategist", capable of navigating within the dictatorship, opportunistically adhering to it without ever becoming overly loyal, using politics as a tool. Piacentini's was an unparalleled professional power. In a historical moment where governance extended to architecture, Piacentini stands as the professional who, with a significant number of realisations, most influenced the history of the discipline. If architecture served as an instrument of political consensus and an effective identity device, it also contributed to the "anthropological revolution" of the state. His exceptional intuition and chameleon-like ruthlessness correspond to the variety of stylistic directions that oscillate between modernity and tradition to opportunistically align with the political sentiments, compromising with his current interlocutor.
Similar to what occurred with Piazza Dante and Piazza della Vittoria, Piacentini offered his "consultation" to the podestà and remained crucial for the city's future. It seems that Daneri himself in 1936 convinces Marcello Piacentini to draft a letter reassuring Podestà Bombrini that his project is the most suitable for the city, inspired by new concepts capable of reconciling practical and aesthetic needs.

On the figure of Marcello Piacentini, see: Mario Lupano, *Marcello Piacentini*, Rome-Bari, 1991; Franco Purini/Simonetta Lux/Giorgio Ciucci (Eds.), *Marcello Piacentini architetto 1881–1960* (Conference Proceedings), Rome, 2010; Paolo Nicoloso, *Marcello Piacentini. Architettura e potere: una biografia*, Udine, 2018.

30 Luigi Carlo Daneri (Borgo Fornari 1900–Genoa 1972), four years senior to Morozzo della Rocca, completed his two-year engineering programme at the University of Genoa and concluded his studies in Rome, earning his degree in 1923 from the School of Application for Civil Engineers, Architecture section. Upon returning to Genoa, after an apprenticeship at Gino Coppedè's (1866–1927) studio, Daneri embarked on a rich professional career. Although predominantly centred around the city and its surroundings, his career, characterised by an initial brief period of eclectic influence, consistently demonstrated an openness to grasp the evolution of international architectural culture. Daneri emerged as a sincere interpreter and adept implementer of these influences. An active member of the Italian group of CIAM and the Movimento Studi Architettura, Daneri served as a lecturer at the Faculty of Engineering in Genoa. Recognised as a skilled and pragmatic professional–entrepreneur, Daneri adeptly navigated the terrain of professional and political relationships from the outset. He remained faithful to the pre-war Rationalism and avant-garde ideals, showcasing a continuity that many interpreted as a sign of personal and valorous coherence (Manfredo Tafuri, *Storia dell'architettura italiana 1944–1985*, Turin, 1986, p.61–62).

On the figure of Daneri, see: Pietro Patrone, *Daneri*, Genoa, 1982; Francesco Rosadini, *Luigi Carlo Daneri. Razionalista a Genova*,

the competition won by Morozzo.[31]
The events at Piazza Rossetti succinctly encapsulate the state of modern architecture in Liguria: **the contrast between Morozzo and Daneri serves as a potential key to frame not only the characteristics but also the fate of the architectural culture of the 20th century in Genoa. It could be argued that Morozzo is to Galeazzo Alessi[32] what Daneri is to Carlo Barabino:[33] visions and attitudes so divergent that they illustrate how a single city, often in confined patches of land,[34] within the folds of the same etymology, conceals authentic and radical differences in the interpretation of architecture.**[35] Until today, with rare exceptions, historiography and criticism have been inclined to equate the Modern in Liguria with the work of Daneri, relegating other figures to a subordinate role. Neither an ideologue nor an innovator, through media influence and entrepreneurial and relational skills, Daneri became the most prolific professional and the one with the most recognisable style in the city's rationalist scene.

A broader and non-programmatic reading highlights how, despite its marginal geographic and cultural position, Genoa became a fertile laboratory of ideas, a central ground for a re-evaluation of 20th-century architecture and its canons. Within the vibrant discourse stemming from a profound internalisation of avant-garde movements, Daneri was not the sole protagonist; other voices gathered in this city of contrasts. Affinities and analogies emerged between Morozzo and Eugenio Fuselli,[36] as well as between Morozzo and Giuseppe Crosa di Vergani.[37] Clear differences arose not only in comparison to Daneri but also with Mario Labò, an attentive cultural mediator engaged in historiographical studies, art criticism and politics.[38]

Rome, 2003; Warner Sirtori, *Una vicenda razionalista italiana. L'architettura di Luigi Carlo Daneri*, Milan, 2013; Elisa Boeri, *Luigi Carlo Daneri. 1900–1972. Abitare il paesaggio*, Cinisello Balsamo, 2024. Moreover the articles: Bruno Zevi, "Organic in Italy", in: *Architectural Review* no.6, 1985, p.89; Gian Antonio Bernasconi, "Razionalismo di Daneri", in: *Casabella* no.325, 1968, p.58.

31 See: Cesare Marchisio, "Il Nuovo Piano Regolatore del Centro di Genova", in: *Genova. Rivista Municipale*, no.2, 1932, p.143–168; "Concorso per un progetto di sistemazione edilizia della Nuova Piazza della Foce. Relazione della Giuria", in: *Genova. Rivista Municipale*, no.6, 1934, p.477–484; Mario Paniconi, "Concorso per la Sistemazione della Piazza Foce a Genova", in: *Architettura – rivista del sindacato nazionale fascista architetti*, no.11, 1934, p.672–678.

32 On the figure of Galeazzo Alessi, see: AAVV, *Galeazzo Alessi e l'architettura del Cinquecento*, Genoa, 1975.

33 On the figure of Carlo Barabino, see: Emmina De Negri, *Ottocento e rinnovamento urbano. Carlo Barabino*, Genoa, 1977.

34 The singularity of these contrasts involves the following buildings: Palazzo Custo (Morozzo, Via Mura di Santa Chiara, 1937–1938, for Giovanni and Nicolo Custo) and the Carignano Building Complex (Daneri, Corso Podesta, 1963–1969, for the Carignano Real Estate Society); Palazzo del Sole (Morozzo, Via Amendola, 1948–1953) and the Salvi-Roncallo (Daneri, Via Piave, 1927) buildings; the Mura degli Angeli (Morozzo, Via San Bartolomeo del Fossato, 1949–1951) and Porta degli Angeli (Daneri, Via Mura degli Angeli, 1954–1956) INA Casa neighbourhood; the Vitruvio (Morozzo, Via Pozzo, 1952, for the Vitruvio Society) and Sanguineti (Daneri, Via Fasce, 1953, for the Vernazzola Society) buildings; the Ollandini Hoffer (Morozzo, Via San Vito, 1953–1956) and Elios (Daneri, Via Trento, 1948–1951, for the Fasce Society) buildings; the INA Insurance Building (Morozzo, via XII Ottobre, 1948–1952) and the AMGA Headquarter (Daneri, Via dei Santi Giacomo e Filippo, 1949–1952); Unit C (Morozzo, Via Fea, 1957–1966) and Unit A (Daneri, Via Loria, 1956–1968) of the INA Casa Forte Quezzi Complex.

35 The analogies between Galeazzo Alessi and Morozzo della Rocca, as well as between Carlo Barabini and Luigi Carlo Daneri come frome a conversation with Valter Scelsi.

36 On the figure of Eugenio Fuselli, see: Guglielmo Bilancioni, *Eugenio Fuselli. Poesia e Urbanistica*, Bologna, 1994.

37 See: AAVV, *Giuseppe Crosa di Vergagni 1886–1962*, Genoa, 2014.

38 Mario Labò (Genova 1884–1961), CEO of DIANA (Decorazioni Industrie Artistiche Nuovi Arredamenti), a company specializing in the manufacturing and trade of art and furniture objects, the architect officially embraced Rationalism in 1931, marking his commitment with participation in the second exhibition of MIAR. At this juncture, he emerged as an advocate for innovative construction, contributing both as an editor for *Casabella* and as a designer. Throughout his career, in collaboration with Enrica Labò, he played a pivotal role in translating seminal texts for architectural discourse into Italian. Among these translations were Sigfried Giedion's *Space, Time and Architecture: The Growth of a New Tradition* (1941, trans. for Hoepli between 1950 and 1954; 2nd ed. 1965), Lewis Mumford's *The Culture of Cities* (1938, trans. for Edizioni di Comunità in 1953), and Nikolaus Pevsner's *An Outline of European Architecture* (1st ed. 1943, trans. after the 7th edition for Il Saggiatore in 1966).

On the figure of Mario Labò, see: Tomaso Lanteri Minet, *Mario Labò. Architetto e intellettuale*, Rome, 2021.

Among these authors, Morozzo della Rocca was the most singular, for whom process and reality determined works made of pure sensations, magnetic architectures that reveal a love for the curve and contain an implicit note of expressionism. **More than any other, Morozzo materialised in Genoa an alternative image of "modern" architecture, opposing the aesthetic of the machine with the visceral sensitivity of the Baroque, articulated through a rich compositional repertoire of forms and materials, proposing a profound paradigm shift.**

Left: Luigi Carlo Daneri, Luigi Vietti (coordinators) with Luigi Ferrari, Alfredo Fineschi, Renato Haupt, Robaldo Morozzo della Rocca, Giacomo Carlo Nicoli, Giuseppe Crosa di Vergagni, Aldo Viale, Giulio Zappa, Typical Steel-Structured Dwelling for the V Triennale di Milano, Milan, 1933. Rebuilt with alteration in Riccione.

Right: Robaldo Morozzo della Rocca with Luigi Carlo Daneri, Luigi Ferrari, Aldo Viale, Luigi Vietti, Giulio Zappa, Master Plan for the eastern areas of Genoa Genoa, 1931–1932. Competition, 1st Prize. Motto: Genova 1950.

Project for the Capurro restaurant and café at the Foce Genoa, undated.

Professional debut and stylistic exploration

Robaldo Morozzo della Rocca was born in Turin on May 16, 1904 into a noble family, among the oldest of the Piedmontese aristocracy, where he spent his youth. During World War I, he moved to Liguria with his family, where he completed his secondary studies with a Classical High School Diploma. Between 1921 and 1923, he attended the Ligurian Academy of Fine Arts, obtaining an Intermediate Diploma, and pursued a two-year course in Physics and Mathematics at the University of Genoa, intending to complete his higher education with a degree in Civil Engineering.[39]

During this period, Morozzo frescoed the walls and ceilings of a hall in the Abbey of Santa Maria del Castello (1668), one of the family properties in Rocca de' Baldi, with a cycle of Allegories of Virtues (1922). Simultaneously, his interest in scientific disciplines culminated in two publications, *La unità del moto* and *Memorie intorno alla ipotesi di unità del moto.*[40]

To harmonise humanistic aspirations with scientific rigour, he chose to enrol in the newly established Regia Scuola di Architettura di Roma (1919),[41] attending from 1924 to 1929. He graduated with top honours under the guidance of Gustavo Giovannoni, presenting a design thesis focused on a New National Library on the Oppian Hill.[42] This experience later informed his essays on the architecture of "modern" libraries, published in the journal *Architettura e Arti Decorative.*[43]

Even before completing his degree, he embarked on several competition projects: one for an Artistic Boarding House with a Library (1927, with Mario Ridolfi), another for a new district in Rome (1925–1926, with Carlo Domenico Rossi),[44] for the Master Plan of Novara (1928, with Aldo Morbelli), and for a Lighthouse

39 See the interview contained in the article: Mariapaola Gerbaz/Paolo Bandini/Fabio Postani (Eds.), "Architetto a Genova: 60 anni di professione", in: *AL – Architetti Liguria*, no.9–10, 1990, p.10–15.

40 *The Unity of Motion* and *Memoirs on the Hypothesis of the Unity of Motion.*

See: Robaldo Morozzo della Rocca, *La unità del moto*, Casale Monferrato, 1940; id., *Memorie intorno alla ipotesi di unità del moto*, Genoa, 1952.

41 Concerning the establishment of the *Royal School of Architecture in Rome* (the first initiated in 1920–1921, followed by others between 1926 and 1933 in Venice, Turin, Naples, Florence and Milan), see: Loredana Compagnin/, Maria Luisa Mazzola (Eds.), "La nascita delle scuole Superiori di Architettura in Italia", in: Silvia Danesi Squarzina/Luciano Patetta (Eds.), *Il Razionalismo e l'architettura in Italia durante il Fascismo*, Milan, 1976, p.194.

The regulations of the Royal School of Architecture in Rome, the first to be established, were confirmed by Royal Decree on June 2, 1921, no.1255. It granted the title of "civil architect", simultaneously abolishing the Advanced Course in Architecture at the Institute of Fine Arts in Rome. The school, dedicated to the training of the comprehensive architect, spanned five years and included teachings from three branches: the scientific, the artistic and the technical. The provisional location was set at the Institute of Fine Arts on Via Ripetta and only in 1932 were the new faculty headquarters inaugurated in Valle Giulia, designed by Enrico del Debbio. The first dean was Manfredo Manfredi, succeeded in the academic year 1926–1927 by Gustavo Giovannoni.

42 See: "Progetti di Laurea", in: *Annuario della R.S. di Architettura di Roma, 1929–1939*, 1930; "Lavori di laurea nella Scuola Superiore di Architettura in Roma", in: *Architettura e Arti Decorative*, Vol. 1, file no. II, year X, 1930–1931, p.61–89.

43 See: Robaldo Morozzo della Rocca, "Architettura delle biblioteche Moderne", in: *Architettura e arti decorative*, Vol. 2, file no. XII, year VIII, 1929, p.529–551; id., "Particolari e attrezzature delle biblioteche Moderne", in *Architettura e arti decorative*, Vol. 2, file no. VIII, year IX, 1930, p.337–360.

44 This concerns the competition for the Quartiere dell'Artigianato (Artisan Quarter, 1926) in Rome, within the area encompassed by Via Marmorata, Via di Porta San Paolo and Viale Aventino. The competition, announced by the National Institute of Popular Houses, under the direction of Alberto Calza Bini, on the initiative of the Governorate of Rome and the Artistic Association among Architecture Enthusiasts, was won by the group led by Pietro Ascheri. Morozzo and Rossi secured the second prize ex-aequo.

See: Roberto Papini, "Il Concorso per il quartiere dell'artigianato in Roma", in: *Architettura e Arti Decorative*, Vol. 1, file no. II, year VI, 1926, p.67–86.

in Santo Domingo (1929, with Luigi Vietti).[45] The first project reflects a Barochetto style, signifying the inclination to recapture the features of the anonymous Roman minor construction with a baroque influence, showing a keen attention to the environmental context. The second, resembling a Tower of Babel, embodies a solution characterised by potent gigantism, still adhering to a historicist and academic vision, which, up to that date, the two designers were not yet inclined to relinquish.

Morozzo's professional debut unfolded amid a tumultuous historical juncture within Italian architectural culture.[46]
In the 1930s, the quest for liberation from academic constraints intertwined with the pursuit of new content for the avant-garde. This movement was grounded in social issues stemming from a Marxist perspective and the cultural recontextualisation of the Mediterranean "myth".

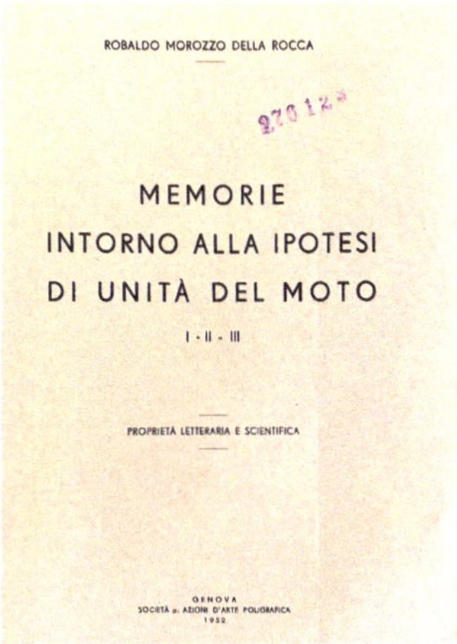

Physics books.
The Unity of Motion (La unità del moto), 1940.
Memoirs on the Hypothesis of the Unity of Motion (Memorie intorno alla ipotesi di unità del moto), 1952.

It is about overcoming the "cultural delay"' generated by a *beaux-arts* education, and about reformulating the relationship between form and content of the avant-gardes, aiming to secure authoritative approval and practical outcomes. Ultimately, it is about deciding whether spontaneous construction should serve as the benchmark for modern architectural language or whether it represents a repertoire of forms to draw upon in the quest for a new style rooted in Italian construction tradition. One of the most effective palliatives considered by most professionals to address this "delay" and resolve the issue of identity was the concept of Mediterraneanism. This notion, to which Rationalism's destiny was intended to be linked, was sufficiently tied to official myths to constitute a safe harbour (or a trench) for the

45 The proposal features a base of stepped buttresses that would reappear later in the scenic drum of the Teatro Regio in Turin.
See: Plinio Marconi, "Mostra Romana del Concorso per il Faro alla Memoria di Cristoforo Colombo", in: *Architettura e Arti Decorative*, Vol. 1, file no. II/III, year VIII, 1929, p. 100–135; "Concurso del Faro de Colòn", in: *Arquitectura. Revista Oficial de la Sociedad Central de Arquitectos*, no. 6, edited by the *Jurado Internacional*, 1929.

46 Critical literature on the subject is extensive and in-depth; see for example: Silvia Danesi/Luciano Patetta, *Il Razionalismo e l'architettura in Italia durante il Fascismo*, op. cit.; Cesare De Seta, *La cultura architettonica in Italia tra le due guerre*, Bari 1972; Enrico Mantero, *Il razionalismo italiano*, Bologna, 1984; Giorgio Ciucci, *Gli architetti e il Fascismo. Architettura e città*, op. cit.; Rosario De Simone, *Il razionalismo nell'architettura italiana del primo Novecento*, Bari, 2011; Sergio Poretti, *Modernismi italiani. Architettura e costruzione nel Novecento*, Rome, 2008; Roberto Gargiani, *Razionalismo emozionale per l'identità democratica nazionale 1945–1966. Eretici italiani dell'architettura razionalista*, Milan, 2021; id., *Razionalismo retorico per il regime fascista 1914–1944. Eretici italiani dell'architettura razionalista*, Milan, 2021.

pursuit of official recognition by political authorities and the conquest of the no man's land between tradition and avant-garde, alternating according to the course of debates, artificially seeking alignment with one of the two terms.[47]
It is not coincidental that during these years, two protagonists of architecture, characterised by radically different positions, Marcello Piacentini and Alberto Sartoris, respectively published *Architettura d'oggi* (1930) and *Gli elementi dell'architettura funzionale* (1932), aiming to define the trajectory for contemporary architectural culture and provide guidance for new designers.

During the latter phase of his stay in Rome, Morozzo gradually embraced the Rationalist Movement, drawing from the energies unleashed in meetings with young university colleagues: Vietti, Minnucci, Ridolfi, Libera, Piccinato, Cancellotti, Susini and others who significantly shaped the Movement. He shared a house on Via Margutta with Vietti, which became a pivotal venue for the *Movement's establishment,*[48] while also becoming an assistant at the university together to Moretti.[49]

In December 1930, when the Movimento Italiano per l'Architettura Razionale was officially established, Morozzo joined its Roman section, with Gaetano Minnucci as secretary, alongside Luigi Vietti, Eugenio Fuselli and Ernesto Puppo. However, while registered with the Roman group, Morozzo maintained close ties with the Turin section.[50] Here, he engaged with the futurists Nicolaj Diulgheroff and Alberto Sartoris, as well as Ottorino Aloisio, Umberto Cuzzi, Gino Levi Montalcini, Aldo Morbelli, Giuseppe Pagano, Edoardo Persico and Ettore Sottsass.

Through the MIAR, Morozzo significantly fuelled the heated debate surrounding the concept of rational architecture and its endorsement within the Regime, both theoretically through articles like *Architettura Razionale. Valore di una parola*[51] and *La Polemica sull'Architettura,*[52] (1931) and practically through the construction of

47 This gives rise to an ambiguous debate, not unfamiliar to the practice of proceeding in linguistic alienation, through slogans or stereotyped formulas that permeate many statements and writings in which the concept of Mediterraneanism intertwines with that of tradition, which, precisely due to its compromising connotations, never becomes a target for the conservative right of Ugo Ojetti and Gustavo Giovannoni or for the progressive centre of Marcello Piacentini. Essentially, two trends emerged in Italy from the debate on Mediterraneanism, summarised as neorealist and idealist or purist. While the former considered the "lesser" architecture of the Mediterranean coasts as a theme of inspiration, a spring component, an original stimulus of Rationalism, proof of its indigenous origins, and a useful source of typological models, in a perspective of mediation and compromise, the latter, generally more radical, advocated a non-literal interpretation of Mediterraneanism, admitting the possibility of an Italian path to Modernism, identifiable in the characteristics of classicism and Mediterraneanism to be understood, however, in spirit, and not in forms and folklore.

See: Giuseppe Pagano, "Case rurali", in: *Casabella,* no.86, 1935, p.8–15; id., "Architettura rurale italiana", in: *Casabella,* no.96, 1935, p.16–23; id., "Documenti di architettura rurale", in: *Casabella,* no.35, 1935, p.18–25; Giovanni Michelucci, "Fonti della moderna architettura italiana", in: *Domus,* no.56, 1932, p.460–461; Enrico Peressuti, "Architettura mediterranea", in: *Quadrante,* no.21, 1935; Gio Ponti, "Una piccola Casa ideale", in: *Domus* no.138, 1939, p.40–45; Paolo Cevini, "La quarta Triennale (1930) e l'affermazione del Razionalismo. I «genovesi» Robaldo Morozzo della Rocca e Luigi Vietti", in: *Genova anni '30. Da Labò a Daneri,* op. cit.; Silvia Danesi, "Aporie dell'architettura italiana in periodo fasciata- Mediterraneità e purismo", in: Silvia Danesi/Luciano Patetta (Eds.), *Il razionalismo e l'architettura italiana durante il fascismo,* op. cit., p.21–28; Andrea Maglio/Fabio Mangone, Antonio Pizza (Eds.), I*mmaginare il Mediterraneo. Architettura Arti Fotografia,* Naples, 2017, p.205–214; Jean Francois Lejeune, Michelangelo Sabatino, *Modern Architecture and the Mediterranean,* Abingdon, 2016.

48 See: Carlo Belli, "Origini e sviluppo del Gruppo 7 dalla costituzione del MIAR alla seconda esposizione di Architettura Razionale", Rome, 1931, in: *La Casa,* no.6, 1959 (now in Michele Cennamo (Ed.), *Materiali per l'analisi dell'architettura moderna. Il MIAR,* op. cit., p.83–84).

49 With Luigi Moretti, he serves as an assistant at the chair of History and Styles of Architecture (1927–1929), a course directed by Vincenzo Fasolo, within an academic context dominated by the figures of Gustavo Giovannoni, Arnaldo Foschini, Manfredo Manfredi and Marcello Piacentini.

50 See: Michele Cennamo (Ed.), *Materiali per l'analisi dell'architettura moderna. Il MIAR,* op. cit. – in particular the chapter II: "La costituzione del M.I.A.R.", p.75–93.

51 *Rational Architecture. The Value of a Word.*

See: Robaldo Morozzo della Rocca, "Architettura Razionale. Valore di una parola", in: *Il Giornale di Genova,* May 22, 1931 (now in: *Materiali per l'analisi dell'Architettura Moderna. Il MIAR,* op cit., p.382–384).

52 *The Architecture controversy.* See Morozzo della Rocca's direct involvement in the debate between Piacentini and MIAR, documented

several successful villas.[53]
On Gustavo Giovannoni's recommendation, Morozzo left Rome and, from 1930 to 1934, took on the role of Extraordinary Architect at the Soprintendenza all'arte Medioevale e Moderna per il Restauro dei Monumenti e gli argomenti urbanistici,[54] both at the Siena Superintendence and its detachment in Genoa. Here, he oversaw significant restoration projects[55] and engaged in urban planning.[56] Additionally, he had the opportunity to make impactful interventions in the city's design, acting as an Advisory Consultant to the Municipality's Urban Planning Commission in approving the Detailed Plan of Piazza Dante (1931–1933). In this context, he transcended both Giovannoni's stagnation and Piacentini's lack of moral impetus,[57] devising a new spatial breakthrough for the square by introducing the tower typology. Drawing inspiration from American models and from their local analysis[58], filtered through imaginative interpretations of skyscrapers by Piero Portaluppi and Renzo Picasso[59], Morozzo's innovative vision for the city's new administrative centre emerged as a captivating interpretation of the tall building motif.[60] Of the four towers, only two were realised through the demolition of the ancient village and the flattening of the hill: one designed by Giuseppe Rosso (1935–1937) and the South skyscraper, conceived by Angelo Invernizzi and Marcello Piacentini (1937–1941).[61] Morozzo's vision for this new entrance to the city was pivotal in interpreting a theme foreign to the Italian context. The final result was a porticoed and stepped solution that tapers upwards. His enduring interest in urban planning, entwined with architecture, is further evident in collaborations with the Gruppo Ligure:[62] Genova 1950 (1931–1932) or the Levante Master Plan and the prototype of a Typical Steel-Structured Dwelling for the V Triennale di Milano (1933). In the former, besides improving longitudinal mobility and establishing direct connections among the former municipalities admitted

in his article published in the Roman newspaper *Il lavoro fascista*, June 2, 1931, "La Polemica sull'Architettura" (both referenced by Bruno Zevi, in: *Storia dell'Architettura Moderna*, Turin, 1961 (IV edition), p.644–649, and further elaborated on with slight modifications and additions by Michele Cennamo, in: *Materiali per l'analisi dell'Architettura Moderna. Il MIAR*, op. cit., p.221.

53 These initial works, namely Villa Chiappe and Palazzina Muzzati Carrabba, garnered a degree of critical acclaim, marked by their participation in the Second Exhibition of Rationalist Architecture at the Galleria di Pietro Maria Bardi in Rome, as well as their inclusion in the Fourth Triennial Exhibition of Decorative and Modern Arts in Monza.

See: *36 Progetti di Ville di Architetti Italiani*, edited by the Esposizione Triennale Internazionale delle Arti Decorative Industriali e Moderne di Monza, Milan/Rome, 1930.

54 Superintendence for Medieval and Modern Art for Monument Restoration and Urbanistic Matters.

55 The restoration projects for Palazzo Ducale, the Sant'Agostino Convent, the Church of San Giovanni della Commenda di Prè and the Church of San Gerolamo degli Incurabili at the Ospedale dei Cronici di Quarto exemplify a commitment to the meticulous preservation and enhancement of historical architectural treasures in Genoa.

56 Urban Plan for Oregina (1930).

57 See: Paolo Portoghesi, "La mano di Piacentini", in: *Marcello Piacentini architetto 1881–1960*, op. cit., p.149–167.

58 See: Luigi Vietti, "Grattacieli", in: *Architettura*, no.4, 1932, p.189–201; from the same author see the Leon Pancaldo's Skyscraper project (Savona, 1938).

59 See: the Torre della Pace project by Renzo Picasso (Genoa, 1917) and the S.K.N.E. Skyscraper project by Piero Portaluppi (New York, 1920).

60 See: Eugenio Fuselli, "Il Piano Regolatore di Genova", in: *Architettura – rivista del sindacato nazionale fascista architetti*, no.12, 1932, p.687–700.

61 The building is a thirty-storey tower, standing over 120 metres tall. Unlike the case in Brescia, where Piacentini adheres to a strict celebratory programme aligned with the grim and crude rhetoric of the Fascist regime, in Genoa the compromise with history is less apparent. The *Littorio* style is tasked with confronting the advanced modernity of the skyscraper, which, in the meantime, had penetrated the superficial pretensions of the *Regime* and the provincial, middle-class character of the city. It presents itself as a homage to confused aspirations of renewed grandeur. This is an "Italic" version of the American skyscraper – the very same that, in 1923, Piacentini had deemed entirely unsuitable for the aesthetic and economic conditions of Italian cities, when he reviewed the competition for the new *Chicago Tribune headquarters* in the pages of the magazine *Architettura*.

See: Marcello Piacentini, "In tema di grattacieli", in: *Architettura e Arti decorative*, Vol. II, file no.8, year II, 1922–1923, p.311–317.

62 The group of Modern Ligurian architects was composed of architects Luigi Vietti, Luigi Carlo Daneri and Giuseppe Crosa di Vergagni, with Luigi Ferrari, Alfredo Fineschi, Renato Haupt, Robaldo Morozzo della Rocca, Giacomo Carlo Nicoli, Aldo Viale and Giulio Zappa.

to the historical city of Grande Genova, the objective was to partition the region into zones, each allocated a suitable manufacturing criterion corresponding to the landscape elements.[63] In the latter, the theme of tall buildings was addressed from the perspective of a compact city by the sea, emphasising the concept of density: a steel structure that could be rapidly constructed, capable of reaching significant heights.[64]

In this context, Morozzo constructed his initial designs – the Villa for the lawyer Eugenio Chiappe in Alassio and the residence for the publisher Giuseppe Carabba and his wife Elena Muzzati in Ostia Lido – projects that converged in a particular synthesis, encapsulating the issues suggested by the picturesque, the neoplastic and the classical. These creations breathed life into a form of Rationalism less functionalist and deterministic, capable of embracing the development of symbolic themes and generating substantial references for the collective imagination.[65] From these initial works, it became evident how the union of opposites, Rationalism and Spontaneity, was attainable: both rationalist architecture and spontaneous architecture were composed of essential elements.

The Villa Chiappe (1929), a remarkable synthesis of reverential spontaneity and rationalist elements, stands at the top of a cliff along the seaside promenade of Alassio. The villa, spread across three levels, can be accessed both from land and sea. The stringent constraints posed by the challenging building area were overcome by the creation of a grand arch and a system of terraces that anchor the building to the very cliff side. The house presents a compelling and pioneering image of a villa perched atop the sea – a figure that holds a contemporaneous essence, simultaneously domestic, abstract and Mediterranean in its flavour.[66]

The Palazzina Carabba Muzzati (1930) is situated on one of the lots identified by Gustavo Giovannoni's urban plan.[67]

63 See: "I progetti per il Piano Regolatore della Zona Orientale", in: *Genova. Rivista Municipale*, no.4, 1932, p.383; "Il Piano Regolatore della Zona compresa tra il Torrente Sturla e il confine orientale del Comune", in: *Genova. Rivista Municipale*, no.8, 1932, p.801–826.

64 Re. the group of Ligurian architects and the typical steel-framed dwelling constructed by the Servettaz Basevi Mechanical Workshops, see: Attilio Podestà, "V Triennale di Milano. La Mostra dell'abitazione", in: *La Specola delle Arti*, no.31, 1933; Luigi Carlo Daneri, "I Liguri alla V Triennale di Milano. Il Padiglione degli Architetti", in: *Genova. Rivista Municipale*, no.10, 1933, p.855–862; Ignazio Bartoli, "(Nuove Architetture) La casa in acciaio", in: *Quadrante*, no.20, 1935, p.22–27; "Il padiglione degli architetti liguri alla V Triennale di Milano", in: *Rassegna di Architettura*, no.11, 1933, p.481–483; Roberto Camus, "Abitazione tipica a struttura d'acciaio", in: *Edilizia Moderna*, no.10–11, 1933, p.48–51; "Luigi Carlo Daneri con Luigi Vietti (Gruppo Ligure)", in: *Architettura – rivista del sindacato nazionale fascista architetti*, special dossier, 1933, p.64–65; "Abitazioni tipiche. Padiglione di Elementi d'abitazione a struttura d'acciaio, del Gruppo degli Architetti Liguri", in: *Domus. L'Arte nella Casa*, no.70, 1933; "La casa a struttura di acciaio alla V Triennale", in: *La Specola delle Arti*, no.7, 1933.

65 Maria Antonietta Crippa, "L' "altra" modernità. Esplorazione di possibili significati", in: Marina Docci/Maria Grazia Turco (Eds.), *L'architettura dell' "altra" modernità* (Proceedings of the XXVI Congress of Architectural History), Rome, April 11–13, 2007.

66 Defined among the finest examples of modern architecture, Villa Chiappe earns the praises of Gillo Dorfles and stands among the architectural exemplars highlighted by Walter Gropius in the essay *Functional Architecture*. Plinio Marconi positions the house as a Mediterranean model among the best and small villas. It was presented at the Second National Exhibition of Rational Architecture at the gallery of art critic Pietro Maria Bardi in Rome in 1931, alongside other distinguished designers of the contemporary scene such as Ascheri, Bottoni, Libera, Ridolfi, Terragni, De Renzi, Sottsass, Pagano, Figini, Pollini, Lingeri, Minnucci, Paniconi, Pediconi and others.

See: Plinio Marconi, "I recenti sviluppi dell'Architettura Italiana in rapporto alle loro origini", in: *Architettura e Arti Decorative*, Vol. 4, file no.15, year X, 1931, p.761–817; Gillo Dorfles, "La II Mostra di Architettura Razionale Italiana", in: *Le Arti Plastiche*, year VIII, no.16, 1931, p.12, (now in Letizia Tedeschi (Ed.), Gillo Dorfles, *Scritti di Architettura 1930–1998*, Mendrisio, 2000); Walter Gropius, "L'Architettura Funzionale", in: Luigi Colombo said Fillia (Ed. by), *La Nuova Architettura*, Turin, 1931, p.218–219.

67 In 1916, on the site, a subcommittee of the Artistic Association among the Adherents of Architecture, composed of Vincenzo Fasolo, Tullio Passarelli and Marcello Piacentini, drafted the new General Urban Plan (PRG) under the signature of Gustavo Giovannoni. The plan aimed to fulfil a diverse programme, serving as the location for the (never realised) seaport of Rome, simultaneously a charming seaside hamlet and a modern urban district, contributing to the necessary decentralization of the population in the Urbs. Guided by principles inspired by international themes of the "garden city", this urban instrument placed a special emphasis on the morphology of the terrain, configured as a succession of three dune systems arranged parallel to the coastline and a system of roads following the contour lines. The constructions primarily adopted an extensive character, with the predominant typology being that of the single-family villa.

An inevitable comparison arises between Morozzo's building and those nearby, designed by Adalberto Libera and Luigi Moretti, revealing profound differences from the climate of renewal induced by the avant-garde.[68] Moretti's schemes with neoclassical symmetries and Libera's nautical style diverge from Morozzo's Neoplasticism, appearing as a median solution amidst the plastic-volumetric abstraction of some European works.[69]
Proportionality of masses and adherence of forms dictate the volumetric articulation of the building, resulting in sophistication even in the selection of materials.[70]
For Ostia, there were the projects for social housing and some prototypes of seaside villas.

Following the assignment at the Superintendence, Morozzo's professional growth continued away from Rome, dividing his time between Liguria and Piedmont. He became a Professor of Scenography at the School of Architecture in Turin (1930–1932). Morozzo maintained a main office in Genoa[71] and a detached one in Turin,[72] alongside his friend Aldo Morbelli, where they pursued several projects, including the unfinished masterpiece of the Teatro Regio.

Caught between public employment and private practice, Morozzo navigated within a city like Genoa, inclined to leverage acquired positions, attempting to introduce avant-garde ideas and new technologies. This effort started with the demands of an aristocratic clientele with a penchant for eclectic styles or a public patronage that imposes the rhetoric of the Lictorian style. Morozzo's response is marked by stylistic flexibility and an introspective humanism that allowed him to transcend from one style to another with ease, without exclusively adhering to either academic rigidity or avant-garde notions.
In Liguria, Morozzo stood among the culturally most engaged and well-integrated architects in the construction sector. These aspects enabled him to complete several significant works starting from the mid-1930s, where projects distinctly reflecting modernist influences alternated with those centred on the simplification of classical elements.

68 Moretti began working on the design of some villas from 1928 for the Lido di Ostia Cooperative, developing an initial project for an area near the Basilica di Regina Pacis square. A competition in 1932, organised by the Tirrena Real Estate Society for the development of 15 elegant villas along the Caio Dulio Promenade, within the framework of the general revision of the General Urban Plan (PRG), identified solutions by Mario Ridolfi, Vincenzo Monaco and Adalberto Libera. The latter, through the three Villas A-B-C, contributed to "updating" the town's architectural style with rationalist architecture with a "nautical flavour", distancing itself from the prevalent eclecticism of already constructed civic buildings: the Railway Station (Marcello Piacentini,1922), the Church of Regina Pacis (Giulio Magni, 1928), the Governorate Palace (1926), the Ex Colonia Marina Vittorio Emanuele (Vincenzo Fasolo, 1927–1930), the Palazzo del Pappagallo (Mario Marchi, 1929) and the Post Office Building (Angiolo Mazzoni, 1933).

69 For example: Villa Moissi (Adolf Loos, Venice, 1923), Casa Wittgenstein (Paul Engelmann, Vienna, 1928), Villa Allegond (JJP Oud, Katwijk, 1928) and Maison Mallet-Stevens (Robert Mallet Stevens, Parigi, 1927), among others.

Parallelepiped volumes aggregated in an asymmetric composition seemingly originating from within, terrace roofs articulated at various levels, and constructive elementalism are all elements that evoke the theme of introspection in Mediterranean architecture, even as the narrative enchantment persists (observe the interiors, particularly the representation through the window of the beach with cabins), reminiscent of "magical realism" and the lyrical, suspended atmospheres of the 20th century.

70 The walls are covered in slightly undulating pearlescent plaster, finished with exposed brickwork and faced with peperino rock slabs. Dark pink pivoting drapes project from the windows for light control. The roofing of the volumes creates a dynamic sequence of terraces. The highest one is surrounded by an extensive suspended garden bed replacing the parapet. Window fixtures are sliding or pivotable on a horizontal axis. The woods are nitrocellulose-varnished, and the metals are either varnished or chrome-plated. The villa is featured in the publication *36 Progetti di Ville di Architetti Italiani* (op. cit.), curated for the IV International Triennial Exhibition of Modern Decorative Industrial Arts, which premiered at the Villa Reale di Monza in April 1930, becoming a highlight of that triennial edition. The organising Directorate comprises Alberto Alpago-Novello, Mario Sironi, and Gio Ponti, the latter also overseeing the volume edited by Casa Editrice d'Arte Bestetti e Tuminelli, Milan/Rome.

71 In Genoa, the office changed locations four times: Corso Mentana, Corso Paganini, Salita Pollaioli, and finally, Via Jacopo Ruffini.

72 Offices on Via Santa Teresa and later on Corso Duca di Genova.

Morozzo's fusion of new technologies and spatial rationality with bourgeois taste is evident in his Villa Reborati for Carlo Reborati in Rapallo (1931–1934) and the villa I Ciliegi, built for Senator Paolo Orlando in San Michele di Pagana (1932–1936). In the former, modern in design and settlement strategy, the Mediterranean essence takes on a picturesque taste, resonating with echoes of a Baroque-like aesthetic internalised as antiquarian consciousness. In the latter, asymmetrical organisation, sudden folds due to the topography, precisely calibrated spaces orientated to harness sunlight, unusually expansive windows, and irregularities in the façade layout unveil its rational matrix, concealed within the body of a classically-inspired building.
With these villas, Morozzo combined the scenic with the prevailing taste. An example is represented by the expansion of the property of Marquess Carlo Bombrini in Genoa, known as Paradisetto (1935), a neoclassical building wherein the rules of Alessian architecture are expertly unfolded, from the cubic volume to the mouldings, betrayed only by a few hints, such as the green shutters of the windows.
This series also includes the Villino Daneri in Levanto (1938), a villa on the island of Elba (undated).

Simultaneously with these rational yet nostalgic works, Morozzo did not relinquish avant-garde aesthetics, which surface not only through collaborations with the Gruppo Ligure, but also in projects like the Fiera del Mare and the Villaggio Balneare (1931–1934). Additionally, evidence of his individual prowess can be found in the design for the Capurro Restaurant (undated), the Consortial Power Plant (1938), and the Workers' Houses at the Port (1939).

During these years, Morozzo engaged in the national stylistic debate through public competitions, such as those for the Florence Station (1933–1934, with Riccardo Haupt), the Postal Palaces (1933–1934) and the Deputy Police Headquarters in Rome (1934),[73] the headquarters of the San Paolo Institute in Turin (1937).
At a local level, affiliation with the National Fascist Party and the Fascist Union of Architects[74] yielded various commissions and appointments, including the

73 These are the competitions organised by the Ministry of Communications and Transport for the Santa Maria Novella Station, won by the Tuscan Group led by Giovanni Michelucci (Pistoria, 1891 – Fiesole, 1990), and for the postal buildings in the Appio and Milvio neighbourhoods and the Vice Questura of the Appio district in Rome.

See: "Il Concorso per la stazione di Firenze", in: *Architettura – rivista del sindacato nazionale fascista architetti*, no. 4, 1933, p. 201–230; Gaetano Minnucci, "Il Concorso Nazionale per i Palazzi Postali di Roma", in: *Architettura*, no. 10, 1933, p. 603–630; id., "I Concorsi per le Vicequesture di Roma", in: *Architettura*, no. 4, 1935, p. 227–237.

74 From a typewritten list entitled *Architects enrolled in the Registry and Union of the Province of Genoa* (Archivio Beniamino Bellati, Genoa), a massive enrolment in the National Fascist Party is noted in the early Thirties: 19 out of 31 enrolments (out of a total of 44 enrolments in the Registry and Union) are after 1932. Mentioned are Bifoli, Castello, Crippa, Dazzi, Fuselli, Ginatta, Mazzoni, Morozzo, Vietti, Daneri, Barbieri (the last two engineers also enrolled in the Registry of Architects). Among the early enrollees were Severi and Rosso. In 1925, Angelini, Bellati, Multedo, Nicoli and Zappa followed. There were 13 architects not enrolled in the National Fascist Party, including Haupt, Labò, Ravinetti, Oddini, Orzali, Noce, Rovelli, Sappia. Among the non-enrolled was also Crosa di Vergagni, who held important positions both in trade unions and public offices. Enrolments in the National Fascist Party (at least those in the thirties) seem almost exclusively dictated by political expediency. Regarding the union, enrolment was practically mandatory, as, since 1923 (Law of June 24, 1923, no. 1935), the unions were effectively replacing the professional orders.

In addition to the control exercised over competitions, the power of the union was expressed – usually through personal and confidential channels – by appointing members to design and consultancy assignments for public bodies. More often, it involved appointments to municipal building commissions, study commissions for master plans and public works, arbitrations, etc. The designated individuals were usually the most active members of the union: often with the secretary (Del Debbio), the members of the Directorate itself: Barbieri (master plans), Bellati (residential buildings, public buildings), Daneri (any topic), Morozzo della Rocca (master plans, public buildings), Rosso (residential buildings, public buildings), Vietti (residential buildings, public buildings, master plans, furnishings).

Information now in: Paolo Cevini, *Genova anni '30. Da Labò a Daneri*, op. cit., p. 155–157.

Residence Carabba Muzzati
Ostia Lido, Rome, 1930.

26 Villa Chiappe
Alassio, Savona, 1929.

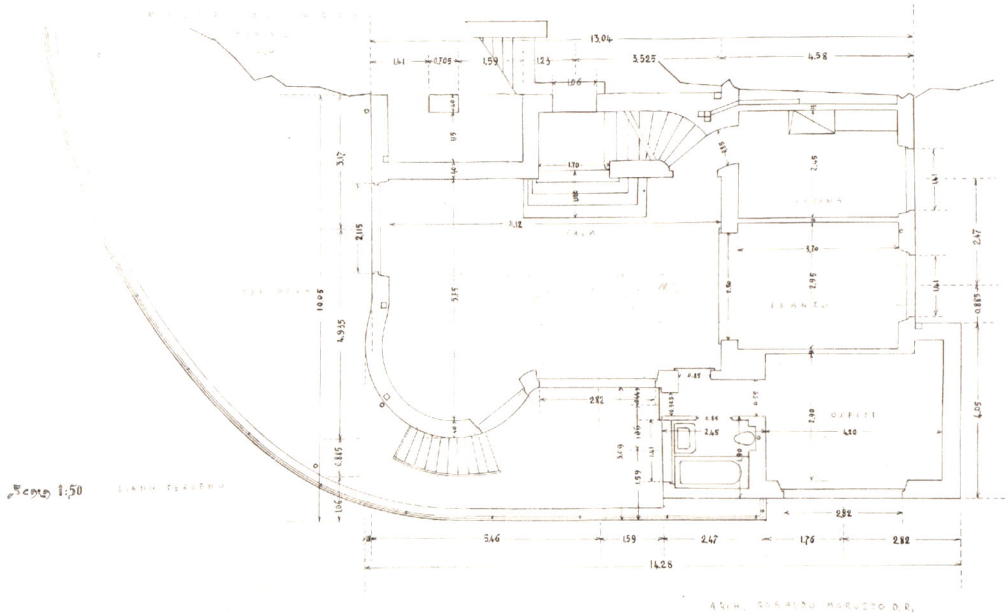

Residence Carabba Muzzati
Ostia Lido, Rome, 1930.

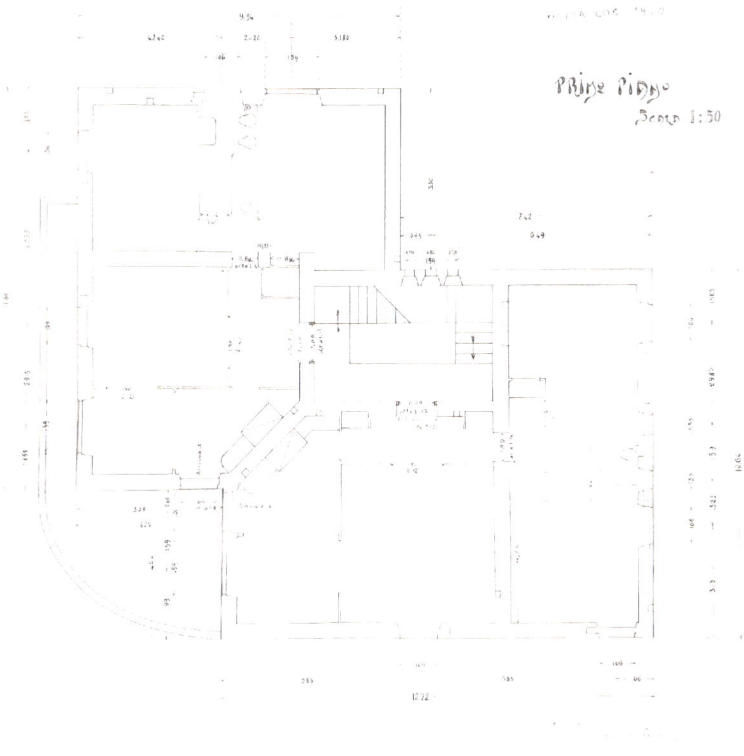

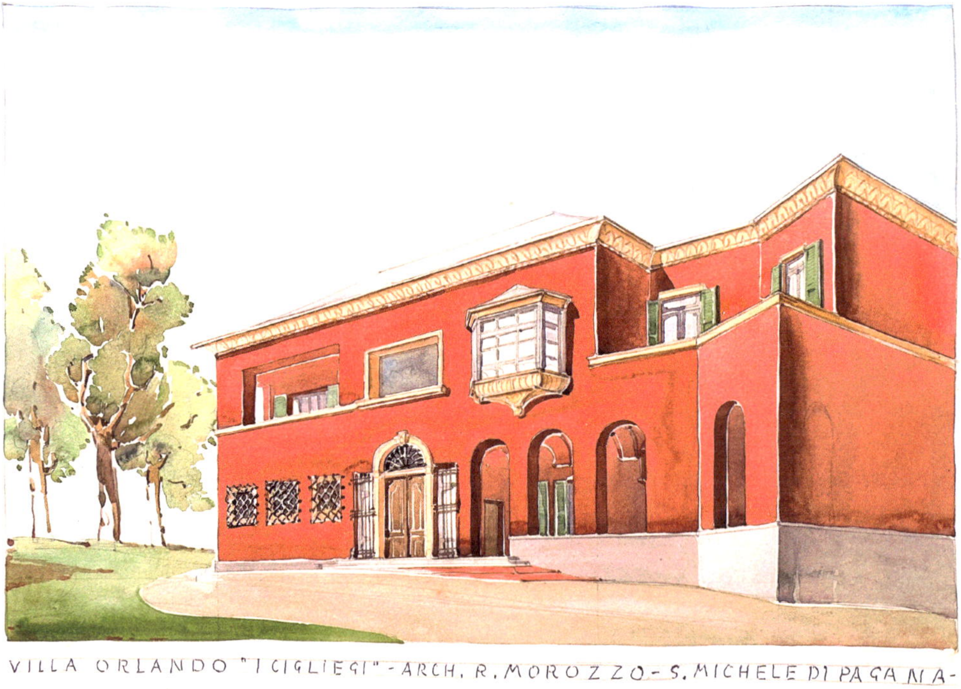

Above: Private villa "I Ciliegi" for Senator Paolo Orlando
San Michele di Pagana, Genoa, 1932–1936.

Below: Apartment building for the contractors Giovanni and Nicolò Custo
Genoa, 1937–1938. Invited competition, 1st Prize.

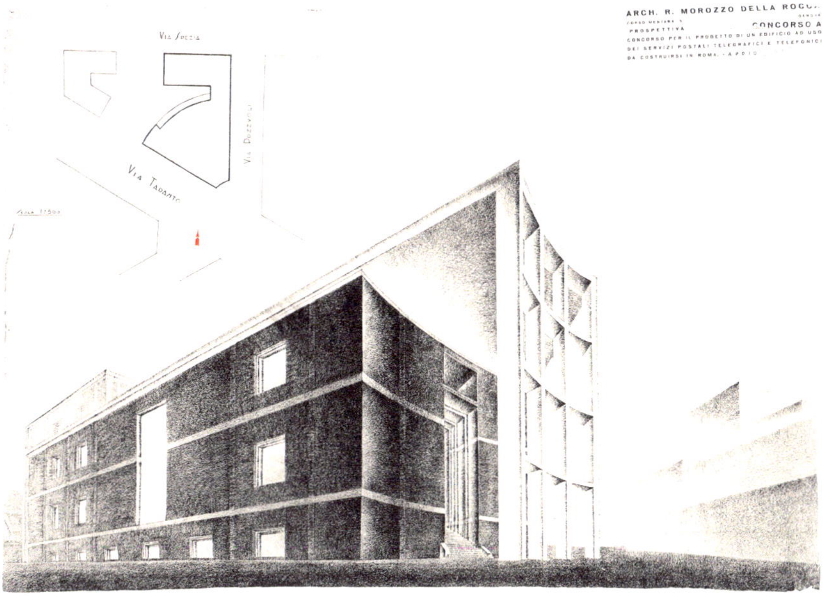

Proposal for the Postal Palaces Rome (Appio), 1933–1934. Competition, honorable mention.

Proposal for the Postal Palaces Rome (Milvio), 1933–1934. Competition, honorable mention.

Proposal for the Deputy Police Headquarter Rome, 1934. Competition, finalist.

transformation of Villa Boccanegra (1931–1939), Palazzo Fieschi (1932), Palazzo Orlando (1932), the headquarters of the Genoa Savings Bank (1934–1936, with Luigi Daneri),[75] the Centrale del Latte in Rivarolo (1933–1934),[76] the restyling of the Palazzo Nafta in Piazza della Vittoria (1934), the Municipal Office Building on Via Garibaldi (1935), the Fascist Union of Industry Headquarters in Lagaccio (1935–1936), the building for the Silos Company (1936), the Casa del Balilla in Sampierdarena (1937), Palazzo Custo Mazzarino (1937–1938), the competition for the New Theatre in Verona (1938–1939, 1st Prize, with Morbelli, Ettore Fagiuoli), the Triumphal Decorations for Political Events in the Port (1939), Palazzo Tallone (undated), the Ansaldo Workers' Quarter in Fegino (1940, with Aldo Morbelli),[77] which prophetically foreshadowed some insights of the post-war era (INA Forte Quezzi).
Starting from the reduction of the linguistic repertoire of Central European and Baltic tradition, Morozzo developed these projects with a strong synthesis: powerful spatial frameworks are defined through sturdy volumetrics and decisive icasticity. Rigorous urban integration, appropriate angular characterisation of the block, the plasticity and depth of building envelopes, and mastery of grand scale are the foundations of these proposals imbued with a 20th-century fervour. The potency of *chiaroscuro* contrasts with an accentuated movement of masses and confronts the new lifestyles and typologies.

One of the most controversial projects of this period, reflecting considerable uncertainty in style, was the proposal for the Villaggio dei Pescatori alla Foce in Genoa (1935).[78] It anticipated and presaged subsequent settlement developments that would culminate in the invention of the *Tourist Village*. Unlike Vietti, who constructed the building based on a Mario Braccialini scheme, Morozzo favoured, instead of the linear house formed by a main body and two lateral wings, a single compact and permeable agglomeration, composed of precise sequences of public and private spaces. In addition to the traditional architectural features – the square, alleys, arcades, loggias, terraces and diverse paving of streets – the project, simultaneously rigorous and plastic, accentuates the sense of overall unity, elementary constructiveness, volumetric synthesis and the sense and rhythm of proportion, arranging two rows and articulating them around a square.

Two striking episodes marked Morozzo's career from the 1930s onwards, altering his professional trajectory and affecting critical success.
During the mid and late decade, Morozzo triumphed in two significant competitions in cities closely linked to him: alongside Bruno Ferrati, he won the competition for the

75 See: "La cassa di risparmio di Piazza della Vittoria. Il progetto degli architetti Daneri-Morozzo della Rocca", in: *Il Lavoro. La Cronaca di Genova*, February 21, 1936, p.5.

76 The Rivarolo Milk Plant. Re. the project, see: Pasquale Carbonara, "La Centrale del Latte di Genova", in: *Architettura – rivista del sindacato nazionale fascista architetti*, no. 11, 1938, p.677–679.

77 See: Aldo Melis, "Il Nuovo Quartiere Ansaldo di Abitazioni per i Dipendenti della S.A.Ansaldo a Fegino (Genova)", in: *L'Architettura Italiana. Periodico Mensile di Architettura Tecnica*, no.6, 1941, p.171–185.

78 *Fishermen's village at the Foce*. Re. the project, see: "La casa dei pescatori", in: *Genova-Rivista Municipale*, no.7, 1936, p.85–86; Mario Badano, "La nuova attività costruttiva dell'Istituto Provinciale Fascista per le case popolari. La 'casa dei pescatori' alla Foce", in: *Genova-Rivista Municipale*, no.7, 1939, p.45–51; Plinio Marconi, "Casa dei Pescatori a Genova", in: *Architettura – rivista del sindacato nazionale fascista architetti*, no.12, 1939, p.730–31; Silvia Barisone/Valter Scelsi, *Luigi Vietti. Architetture Liguri*, Genoa, 1999, p.61–63.

redevelopment of Piazza Foce in Genoa (1934)[79] and, with Aldo Morbelli, secured the reconstruction project for the Teatro Regio in Turin (1938).[80]

In the former, originating from the plan-volumetric framework devised by municipal technicians Aldo Viale and Giulio Zappa[81], within the framework of the Piano Regolatore della Aree Centrali,[82] the objective was to renew the city-sea relationship. This endeavour entailed an aesthetic exploitation of the marine backdrop by crafting a monumental square, incorporating the beach along one-quarter of its sides. In this way, the Foce district acquired a distinctive character, functioning as a hub for spring and summer social life.
The competition, chaired by the Podestà Carlo Bombrini,[83] witnessed the participation of seven groups, with only four being awarded.[84] However, following the awarding phase, a cunning strategy was orchestrated by Daneri, leading the municipality to overturn the commission's verdict and assign the project to himself, rather than to the Morozzo-Ferrati duo.[85] Daneri, as a landowner through his shares in the Città Nuova company, persuaded Marcello Piacentini to draft a letter reassuring Podestà Bombrini that his design was the most suitable for execution. Daneri's plan as a builder-architect envisioned all residential buildings within the development, without favouring any specific one, resting

79 See: "Concorso per un progetto di sistemazione edilizia della Nuova Piazza della Foce. Relazione della Giuria", in: *Genova. Rivista Municipale*, no.6, 1934, p.477–484; Mario Paniconi, "Concorso per la Sistemazione della Piazza Foce a Genova", in: *Architettura – rivista del sindacato nazionale fascista architetti*, no.11, 1934, p.672–678.

80 See: Gabriele Manfredi, "Il Teatro Regio", in: *Rassegna Municipale Torino*, no.12, 1937; "Il progetto premiato degli arch. A. Morbelli ed Morozzo D.R.", in: *L'Architettura Italiana. Periodico Mensile di Architettura Tecnica*, no.1, 1938; "Il Concorso per la Ricostruzione del Teatro Regio a Torino", in: *L'Architettura Italiana. Periodico Mensile di Architettura Tecnica*, no.3, 1938.

81 Giulio Zappa (Livorno 1895 – Genoa ?) was a pivotal figure in the development of 20th-century Genoese architecture. As a dedicated civil servant, he skilfully applied his professional expertise for the benefit of the community within a public framework. After earning his architecture diploma in 1921 from the Royal Institute of Fine Arts in Rome, he began his service with the Municipality of Genoa in 1924, where he spent his entire career. Zappa coordinated some of the city's most significant plans and projects in collaboration with the Ligurian Group. A meticulous and perceptive designer, Zappa was particularly responsive to avant-garde movements. Nevertheless, his contributions were somewhat overshadowed by his engineer superiors, such as Mario Braccialini and Aldo Viale, as well as by the dominant personality of Daneri.

82 Central Areas Master Plan.

83 The jury of the competition is chaired by Podestà Carlo Bombrini and composed of Raffaello Fagnoni (National Institute of Urban Planning), Luigi Noce (National Fascist Union of Engineers), Giuseppe Rosso (National Fascist Union of Architects), Antonio Gallino (Fascist Regional Union of Engineers), Lorenzo Castello, Giuseppe Mazzoni (Fascist Interprovincial Union of Architects), Carlo Piaggio, Giovanni Aula (Municipal Consultation), Ugo Nebbia (Office for the Monuments of Liguria), Tomaso Badano (Public Works), Aldo Viale (Chief of Planning Service), Orlando Grosso, Rosolino Multendo (Office of Fine Arts), Alcibiade Anselmi (Office of General Affairs).

Referring to the themes of the competition, the jury identified the following judgment criteria: the planimetric and altimetric arrangement of the square (40 points); the utilisation of covered areas (20 points); the aesthetics of the square and the beach (20 points); the exhibition palace (10 points); the sports palace (10 points).

84 Eugenio Fuselli and Ernesto Puppo (*San Pietro*, 4th Place), Beniamino Bellati (*La Vela*, 3rd Place), Luigi Carlo Daneri (*Città Nuova*, 2nd Place), Robaldo Morozzo della Rocca and Bruno Ferrati (*Zena Foxe*, Winner).

85 Daneri, through a series of skilful strategic moves, aimed to secure for himself not only as a professional but effectively as an entrepreneur, the implementation of the building initiative. Similarly to what happened with Piazza Dante and Piazza della Vittoria, Piacentini offered his "consultancy" to the Podestà and still proved crucial for the future of the city: it seems that Daneri himself in 1936 convinced Marcello Piacentini to draft a letter comforting Podestà Bombrini that his project is the most suitable for the city, inspired by new concepts capable of reconciling practical and aesthetic needs. Simultaneously, Daneri forged a financial alliance with his brother-in-law and a circle of individuals, allowing him to control the ownership of a large portion of the areas designated for the square's construction through the formation of the real estate company Città Nuova. Another significant aspect is that the Piazza della Foce operation, like those of Piazza Dante and Piazza della Vittoria, involved the alienation of areas to private entities. The buyer of six of the eight lots into which the plan is divided was the real estate company Città Nuova itself, as of 1936. Luigi Carlo Daneri, along with Paolo Codeglia, Tancredi Spinetta and Vincenzo Gagliardi (close to him in friendship), Anna Pia Daneri (sister of Luigi Carlo), and Umberto Musante (spouse of Anna Pia), was (from February 1938) a shareholder and main administrator. The company admitted as its corporate purpose "the purchase, sale and exchange of building land and areas, specifically the construction and reconstruction, on its own and on behalf of third parties, of houses to be built on the four areas in the Foce region in Genoa". Having obtained the opportunity to build this new part of the city through a skilful political financial and entrepreneurial action, Daneri only had to focus on perfecting the urbanistic aspects of his project. The construction, entrusted to the historical Genoese firm Garbarino & Sciaccaluga, saw the first buildings completed in 1937. The war period slowed down the works, which resumed only after 1945, concluding in 1958. The current complex, predominantly residential, contradicts the initial direction of being a mixed-use hub with commercial, hotel and exhibition functions.

See: Paolo Cevini, *Genova anni '30. Da Labò a Daneri*, op. cit., p.158–166; Pietro Patrone, *Daneri*, op. cit., p.65–73; Francesco Rosadini, *Luigi Carlo Daneri. Razionalista a Genova*, op. cit., p.90–91.

upon a communal porticoed platform that opened toward the sea. He adopted the U-shaped layout from the regulatory plan but proposed an increased building height using a volume compensation formula. Conversely, the winning proposal by Morozzo-Ferrati did not include residences but focused on public buildings organised around a central square: an exhibition palace with an auditorium, a hotel featuring a cinema-theatre, and a stadium with a pool. A service and parking square was planned behind the Palazzo dell'Arte, placed in a baricentric position. While Daneri's reference model was the lamellar tower house, Morozzo was inspired by historic Italian *piazzas* and *palazzi*. For the area destined to become the new centre of social life, Daneri's subdivided areas were highly exploitable for real estate market demands, while the Morozzo-Ferrati project entailed a partial sacrifice of these areas, a critical factor leading to manipulation of the results.[86]
The events at Piazza Foce shed light, on the one hand, on the character similarities between Daneri and Piacentini – both being unscrupulous, persuasive and adept at systematically uniting the links in a chain of relationships with decision-making levers and influential circles. They did not hesitate to strategically align themselves with individuals from entirely different backgrounds and objectives, yet with whom they could share common motivations. On the other hand, it underscores the profound divergence between Daneri's commercial attitude and allegiance to rationalist orthodoxy and the aristocratic refinement in Morozzo's urban project.

The saga of the Teatro Regio in Turin represents an equally contentious narrative, demanding a substantial historical-critical revaluation.

The uncertainty surrounding the theatre's reconstruction,[87] destroyed by fire in 1936, was short-lived. Despite proposals for a wholly free reconstruction on the same or different areas, the following year saw the announcement of a competition for a theatre equipped with services suited to the times.
From the initial 27 groups, the competition was narrowed down to ten in the second stage, culminating in the victory (December 1937) of Aldo Morbelli and Robaldo Morozzo della Rocca, both natives of Turin and friends since their days at the School of Architecture in Rome.[88]

86 See: Marco Brandolisio/Marco Vido, "Luigi Carlo Daneri. Edifici alla Foce Bisagno", Genova, in: *Domus* no. 718, 1990, p. 80–88.

87 The original structure of the Teatro Regio (1740) was conceived by Benedetto Alfieri Bianco of the Counts of Cortemilia and Count Giuseppe Nicolis di Robilant, commissioned by Carlo Emanuele III. It underwent restoration (1838) following the French occupation, carried out by Pelagio Pelagi in neoclassical canons of stylized craftsmanship. The theatre underwent substantial modifications (1904) by the engineer Ferdinando Cocito, on behalf of the municipal administration. This transformation adhered to regulations aimed at safeguarding public safety and the principles of equality, seeking to eliminate the division of the audience based on caste or socio-economic status.

88 Aldo Morbelli (Orsara 1903 – Turin 1963) primarily conducted his activities in Turin. After a year of courses at the Faculty of Architecture in Turin, he continued his studies at the newly established Royal School in Rome, where he graduated in 1926. Upon returning to Turin, he collaborated with Annibale Rigotti, and from 1930, for a few years, he served as an Assistant at the Faculty of Architecture. Between 1932 and 1933, he worked on restoration projects for the Superintendent of Monuments in Piedmont. In 1934, he left Rigotti's studio for that of Giuseppe Momo, with whom he collaborated, not only on numerous competitions but also on the realisation of the Apostolic Palaces in the Vatican.
In 1938, following his success in the previous year's competition for the Teatro Regio, Morbelli opened his own studio, marking the beginning of a tumultuous chapter. This period led Morbelli and Morozzo to develop seven projects for the Regio, the last and definitive one in 1962 (abandoned by the municipality in 1963, after his death, in favour of the one eventually realised and entrusted to Carlo Mollino). In the 1930s, Morbelli worked on the renovation of family properties in Orsara Bormida, as well as on villas, funeral chapels and furnishings, primarily in Turin. During the war, he developed studies and consultations for the Urban Development Plan of Aosta, following Marcello Piacentini's guidance.
From 1950 to 1961, he collaborated with Roberto Graziosi and Franco Mancini, realising numerous villas in the Biella region, Aosta Valley and the province of Turin. They also worked on residential buildings in Turin and Biella, interior furnishings and funeral shrines. Among Morbelli's post-war works in Turin, notable projects include the Alexandra Cinema (1947) and Ambrosio Cinema (1954), the Rai Auditorium (1952, with Carlo Mollino), the Sip Offices (1952) and the Rai Offices (1962–1963, with Domenico Soldiero Morelli).

The outbreak of war initially and the uncertainties of the client later on, the conflicting pressures of public opinion, the obstacles posed by military regulations, and the persistent requests for modifications – sometimes from the Ministry of Public Instruction, sometimes from the Ministry of Public Works, and at other times from the planners of the local zoning regulations – turned the intentions of the two architects into an agonising ordeal of continual revisions.
Already in the year of approval, the Higher Council of Public Works requested modifications and additions, and only in late spring deemed it worthy of procurement. Morbelli and Morozzo were tasked with the construction in June 1938, although the works, already commenced, were suspended due to the war in May 1940. After the hostilities ceased, the municipality decided to proceed with the reconstruction.
Following the new Urban Development Plan for the Cultural Area of the city, amidst fiery controversies in newspapers and the challenges faced by the Military Engineering Corps in acquiring new areas, the situation led, in November 1958, to the submission of a sixth proposal. This encompassed an underground theatre and additional supplementary works.
Upon the Ministry's official endorsement, the municipality assumed full responsibility for the outcomes. An *ad-hoc* commission was appointed by the municipality to examine these aspects.[89]
In 1963, following Morbelli's premature passing, the municipality reaffirmed Morozzo's role. The construction began in September of the same year. By the initial months of 1965, the load-bearing structures reached the first above-ground floor. With the demise of Mayor Giovanni Carlo Anselmetti, a previous advocate for the Morbelli-Morozzo project who had also served as the Public Works Councillor, the new Mayor Giuseppe Grosso, considering the severe economic downturn, decided to curtail expenses by initiating the study of a new, smaller-volume and cost-effective theatre. This time, in the subsequent assignment, directly commissioned, Morozzo was the only one replaced. The engineers Marcello and Adolfo Zavelani Rossi, Gino Sacerdote and Carlo Graffi were reappointed alongside the new architect, Carlo Mollino,[90] who completed the project over eight years (1965–1973).

Within a broader historical examination, a close comparison seems inevitable between the figures of Daneri in Genoa and Mollino in Turin with that of Morozzo della Rocca, who was essentially overshadowed both by the entrepreneurial profile

89 The committee was comprised of Marziano Bernardi, Felice Casorati, Carlo Mollino and Alberto Bruni Tedeschi.

90 Mollino is not entirely detached from the design developments of the new Teatro Regio, as he had already been involved (November 1955) as a member of the architectural subcommittee for the theatre's reconstruction alongside Aloisio, Dezzutti, Melis, Moretto, Musso, Ricci and Viale. Then, in the autumn of 1960, we find him as a member of the committee for the new theatre concerning the aesthetic and architectural aspects of its exterior, tasked with forming an opinion on the Morbelli-Morozzo project. The higher council of the Ministry of Public Works indeed delegated the City of Turin to decide on the external appearance of the project itself.

The Italian architect and designer Carlo Mollino (Turin 1905–1973) graduated in 1931 at the Superior School of Architecture of the Accademia Albertina of Turin, the city where he continued to work until his death (1973) and to which he was always linked by an intense, conflicted relationship. Photographer, writer, mountaineer, skier, inventor of engines, acrobatic pilot and Professor, Mollino shared in the particular cultural scene that developed in the Piedmont city during the two decades before World War II, but his independent research also drew on stimuli from the main European currents and Futurism. An ironic non-conformist, he worked passionately on design, mixing a love of detail with a taste for abstraction. Free from any rigid ideological position, he introduced elements of Surrealist art and culture into the Modern movement. Among other projects, he is the author of the Circolo Ippico equestrian centre (1936–1940, demolished), the RAI Auditorium (1950–1952) and the Chamber of Commerce (1964–1973) in Turin; the Casa del Sole in Cervinia (1945–1954), the Lago Negro ski lift in Sauze D'Oulx (1946–1947) and the Casa Cattaneo on the Agra plateau (1952–1953).

On the figure of Mollino, see: AAVV, *Carlo Mollino. 1905–1973*, Milan, 1989; Chris Dercon, *Carlo Mollino. Maniera Moderna*, Cologne, 2012; Napoleone Ferrari/Michelangelo Sabatino, *Carlo Mollino. Architect and Storyteller*, Zurich, 2021.

Robaldo Morozzo della Rocca with Luigi Carlo Daneri, proposal for the headquarters of the Genoa Savings Bank
Genoa, 1934–1936. Competition, 1st Prize ex-aequo.

Rivarolo Milk Plant.
Genoa, 1934–1935.

Above: Project for the Fascist Union of Industry Headquarters in Lagaccio
Genoa, 1935–1936.

Centre: Fishermen's village at the Foce.
Genoa, 1935. Invited competition, finalist.

Below: Robaldo Morozzo della Rocca with Aldo Morbelli, project for the Ansaldo Workers' Quarter in Fegino
Genoa, 1940.
Invited competition, 1st Prize ex-aequo.

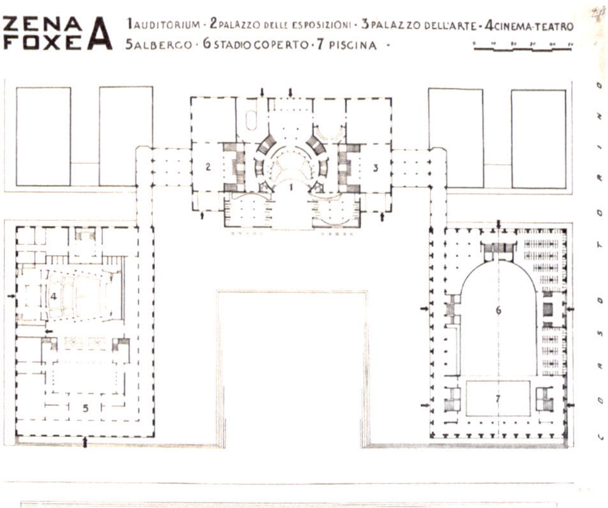

All images:
Robaldo Morozzo della Rocca with Bruno Ferrati, proposal for the redevelopment of Piazza Foce,
Genoa, 1934. Competition, 1st Prize.
Motto: Zena Foxe.

Built by Luigi Carlo Daneri between 1934–1958, following the overturning of the competition's results.

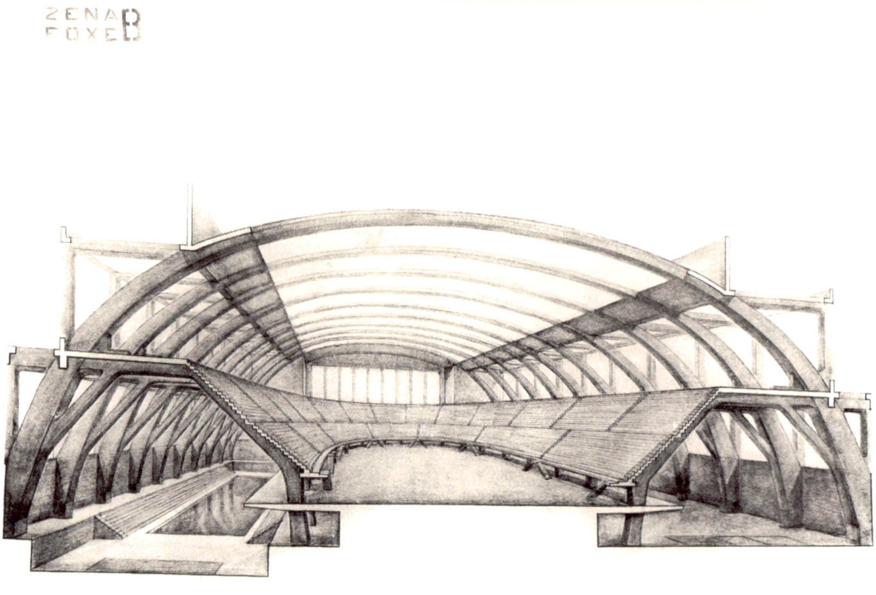

of the former and by the surrealistic wunderkind character of the latter. Political contingencies, relational power and profound character differences on one hand, and talent and design skills on the other, formed the delicate balance that consecrates the "success" of the former and the professional and critical oblivion of the latter. Hence, it becomes essential to evaluate the significance of Morozzo's work in the history of architecture in light of the decisive and compromising events in Genoa and Turin.

One of the works that chronologically concluded the period preceding World War II is the Tower Hotel for a Thermal Spa in Lurisia (1942), commissioned by Napoleone Coltelletti. The complex consists of a lower linear building and a 13-storey circular tower, whose volume gradually diminishes almost imperceptibly on each floor, creating a slight shifting of the columned elements in the surrounding peristyle. The setback is more pronounced at the penthouse. The tower is perforated at the centre by a courtyard, around which the service corridor to the rooms unfolds along its perimeter. Conscription during the period of World War II (1941–1942) led to a decline in activities, but did not prevent the acquisition of new professional assignments, such as the project for the Reconstruction of the Palazzo della Flotta Lauro (1942–1950). Over the remains of the palace commissioned by Nicolò Lomellini (1567) and purchased by the shipowner Achille Lauro for the offices of his Fleet, Morozzo executed a sophisticated stylistic invention by integrating new elements seamlessly into the overall image of the building. Through meticulous management of construction techniques and the use of creatively devised decorative elements, the reconstruction blurs the line between authenticity and inventive intervention, making it difficult to discern what is genuine from what is a product of invention.

Project for the Casa del Balilla at Villa Scassi
Genoa, 1937.

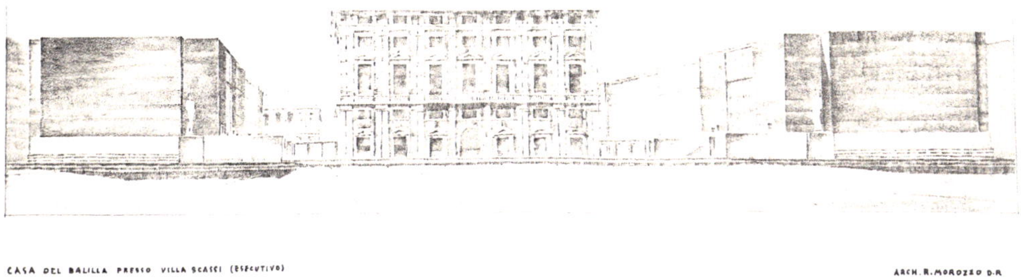

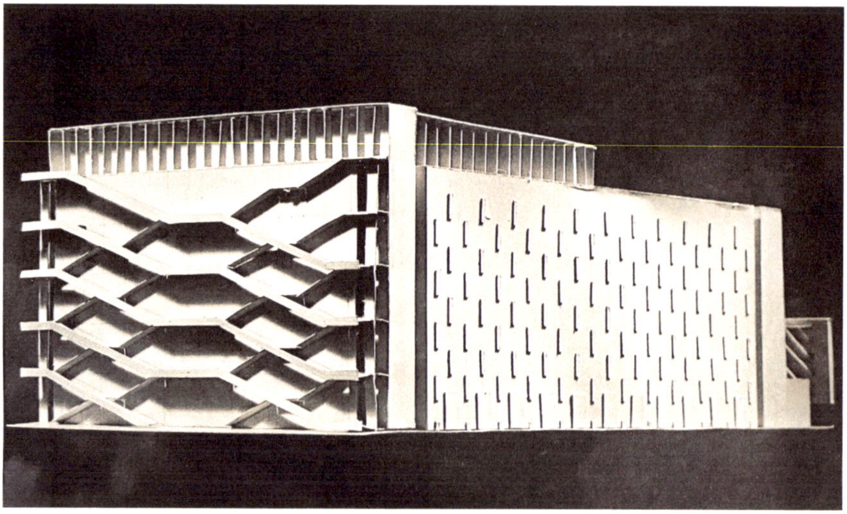

All images:
Robaldo Morozzo della Rocca with Aldo Morbelli, proposals for the reconstruction project of the Teatro Regio Turin, 1937–1964.
Two-stage competition, 1st Prize.

Completed by Carlo Mollino after the death of Morbelli and the dismissal of Morozzo from the position.

Projects four (1954), five (1956), six (1959).

Both images: Final design (7th version, 1963) for the new Teatro Regio, Turin, 1938–1964.

The post-war era and figurative experimentation

After the war, demographic, economic and political changes[91] intensified urban phenomena associated with the repositioning of steel and shipbuilding industries following wartime production.
In the climate of reconstruction urgency, the fact that Ligurian culture remained, in comparison to debates elsewhere, in the background of a poignant confrontation with the modernist legacy, does not equate to an absence of significant architectural works. For instance, Genoa boasts a quality production driven by substantial economic resources and its historical vocation as a maritime-port emporium. This production, often led by designers from external and local origins, although always educated elsewhere, was geared towards both the transformation of existing structures and the building of new holiday scenarios for Italy during the *boom*.
If the influence of Roman architectural culture remained a legacy of the pre-war era, often placed under the shadow of critique with architects like Morozzo, the relationship with Milanese culture, subtler and less pervasive in the pre-war period, intensified in the post-war period.[92] During this fruitful phase in Genoa, figures like Franco Albini[93] – with Caterina Marcenaro – and Ignazio Gardella[94] take

91 The turning point of 1948, marked by the defeat of the left-wing forces and the advent of centrist politics, signals the beginning of a developmental phase in which construction was called upon to play a fundamental role in economic reconstruction. In the initial municipal elections of 1946, the victory of the PCI (Italian Communist Party) and the Socialists is evident, with the DC (Christian Democracy) trailing in third place. Between 1946 and 1951, the city was led by two communist mayors, Giovanni Tarello and Gelasio Adamoli. However, this outcome was not confirmed in the subsequent three municipal elections of 1951, 1956 and 1960, where the DC emerged as the leading party in the city, followed by the PCI and the Socialists in third place. The mayor of Genoa for a 15-year span was the Christian Democrat Vittorio Pertusio, who guided the city through the intricate task of physical reconstruction and the delicate management of the post-war crisis.

92 See: Paolo Cevini, "Architettura a Genova e Liguria (1945–2015)", in: Giovanna Franco/Stefano Musso, *Architetture in Liguria dopo il 1945*, op. cit., p. 52–73.

93 If Milan served as his professional base, Genoa can be deemed the city of choice for Franco Albini (Robbiate 1905 – Milan 1977). His initial opportunities for intervention extended to urban planning, such as the detailed plan for the Angeli district in 1946 with Gardella, Palanti and Tevarotto. In the same year, a commission chaired by Daneri, and including Albini alongside Fuselli and Pucci, initiated studies for the Regulatory Plan, approved in 1948. In 1953, Albini drafted the Detailed Plan for the Piccapietra area, and in 1955, he participated in the competition for the Palazzo dell'Arte on Via XII Ottobre. Admitted to the second stage, he joined forces with Daneri to submit a joint project in 1959, approved in 1962 but left unrealised.

Genoa, in particular, is the city where Caterina Marcenaro (Genoa, 1906–1976), art historian and curator at the Municipal Department of Fine Arts, called upon Albini to renew the city's museum heritage. The collaboration between Marcenaro and Albini led to the transformation of Genoa's main historical and noble palaces into museums and exhibition spaces, significantly contributing to the modern concept of museums and the creation of the new civic museum centre: the renovation of Palazzo Bianco (1949–1951) and the restoration and transformation into the Museum of Palazzo Rosso (1952–1962). Albini designed the private apartment on the top floor of Palazzo Rosso (1954) for the curator. Under Marcenaro's mandate, Albini–Helg Studio works on the Treasure Museum (1952–1956), the Municipal Offices Palace (1950–1963) and the transformation into the Museum of the Cloisters of Sant'Agostino (1962–1984). In the later years, the studio inserted an octagonal staircase in the Bruzzo apartment in Palazzo Podestà (1966–1975) and created a complex for residences and offices clad in Silipol pink prefabricated panels, between Via del Colle and Via Fieschi in the Madre di Dio area (1969–1978). Additionally, under Marcenaro's direction, the Oriental Art Museum Edoardo Chiossone (Mario Labò, 1971–1988) was also realised, complementing the Strada Nuova museums.

See: Federico Bucci/Augusto Rossari, *I musei e gli allestimenti di Franco Albini*, Milan, 2005.

For a more comprehensive overview of the work of Albini-Helg, see: Studio Albini (Ed.), *Franco Albini – Architettura e design: 1930–1970*, Milan, 1980; Antonio Piva/Vittorio Prina (Eds.), *Franco Albini 1905 – 1977*, Milan, 1988.

94 Ignazio Gardella (Milan 1905 – Oleggio 1999) was commissioned, from 1969 to 1972, to draft the *Detailed Plan for the Arrangement of the San Donato and San Silvestro Zone* in the historical city centre, with the collaboration of Silvano Larini, Jacopo Gardella, Gilberto Nardi and Daniele Vitale. The plan envisioned the integration of a university hub for humanities faculties in that portion of the historical nucleus already home to civic and religious institutions of the early Middle Ages. This plan activated a qualified instrument for reconnecting to the fabric of a lost space, fostering a dialogue between the old and the new. It is after this experience that Gardella proposed to a local developer, Mario Valle, to establish a design company, MVE (Mario Valle Engineering), to promote coordinated real estate development initiatives under a single direction to manage the growing complexity of the construction process. Gardella, as a consultant for this comprehensive design, was thus the one who initiated the entire construction of the Pineta di Arenzano for the Cemadis Society through MVE.

the lead, with Daneri standing as the sole local counterbalance to their impact. In this scenario requiring a strong impetus for change, Morozzo found himself in a position of relative "disadvantage" due to his connection with the recent past. Uninterested in aristocratically aligning with the most powerful groups, he affiliates with the Liberal Party,[95] representing a moderate right-leaning stance compared to the affluent classes in the capital. However, while excluded from the dominant groups that hold sway over institutions, Morozzo was a recognised and respected professional within the narrow field of Ligurian construction.

In the post-war period, the material culture of construction also underwent change. In the 1930s, within the most significant projects of the regime, the use of bold cement frames used for the coverage of vast spaces became prevalent. However, these sophisticated structures largely remained concealed by the building envelope, inspiring new architectural configurations only indirectly. It represented one of the experimental lines along which, within various Italian modernisms, there was a tendency to renew architectural language while not entirely departing from the tradition of masonry architecture. Morozzo, a dedicated interpreter, embraced this substantially non-tectonic use of structures with intriguing scenographic outcomes, a feature distinguishing Italian language from European Rationalism. Even after the war, Morozzo continued to exhibit commitment to this approach, evident in competitions such as the completion of Rome's Termini Station (1947, 3rd Prize, with Carlo Domenico Rossi), the Palace of Justice in Beirut (1948), and the reconstruction of the Carlo Felice Theatre in Genoa (1949).
A deep-rooted connection to masonry tradition, in fact, did not diminish even in the post-war era, where the desire to transform architecture into a narrative structure demanded concealing the structural "bones" beneath layers of coatings imbued with various meanings. Moreover, the persistent inclination towards the artisanal use of reinforced concrete within small construction sites – a direct consequence of leveraging the construction sector to combat unemployment – solidified this approach to mixed stone-cement construction entirely executed *in-situ*.[96] This method, developed during the years of autarchy, produced works marked by eccentric traits. Firmly entrenched within this Italian vein that maintains its distinctiveness from the international process of architectural industrialisation, while also distancing itself from the dominant current of constructive *realism* within the national discourse, **Morozzo exploited the extreme versatility of the Italian construction site to revitalise his research on plastic forms and spatial configurations that retain a figurative-abstract character.**
In apartment buildings and housing blocks, the framework was distorted to make it almost unrecognisable: the concrete framework is concealed and the "structure" of the "form" becomes the primary concern of the building, transforming it from a mere

See: Ignazio Gardella/Silvano Larini, "Genova: un progetto per la città antica. Piano particolareggiato per i nuovi insediamenti universitari nelle zone di San Donato e San Silvestro", in: *Controspazio*, no. 7, 1974; AAVV, *Ignazio Gardella. Architetture*, Milan, 1988; Marco Porta (Ed.), *L'architettura di Ignazio Gardella*, Milano, 1985; Marco Franzone/Gerolamo Patrone, *La Pineta di Arenzano. Architettura e paesaggio. Storia di un'utopia mancata*, Milan, 2010.

95 Membership of the Liberal Party is attested by the membership cards conserved at the Morozzo della Rocca Archive in Rocca de Baldi.

96 See: Adrian Forty, *Concrete and Culture: A Material History*, London, 2012; Carmen Andriani, *Le forme del cemento*, Vols. 1–4, Roma, 2008–2012.

Two apartment buildings in Quarto for the Society of Mario Braggion
Genoa, 1949–1953.

42 Foreground: Robaldo Morozzo della Rocca, apartment building for Selene Ollandini and Rodolfo Hoffer in Albaro, Genoa, 1953–1956.
Background: Luigi Carlo Daneri, apartment building with Cinema Elios for the Society of Eugenio Fasce, 1948–1951.

Above: Multipurpose building (housing, offices, shops) for the Attività Ligure Society
Genoa, 1936–1952.

Right: Restoration project for the Cathedral of San Michele
Albenga, 1966–1968.

"Elios" and "Selene" Villas for the construction company of Rino Bagnasco
Pineta di Arenzano, Genoa, 1968–1972.

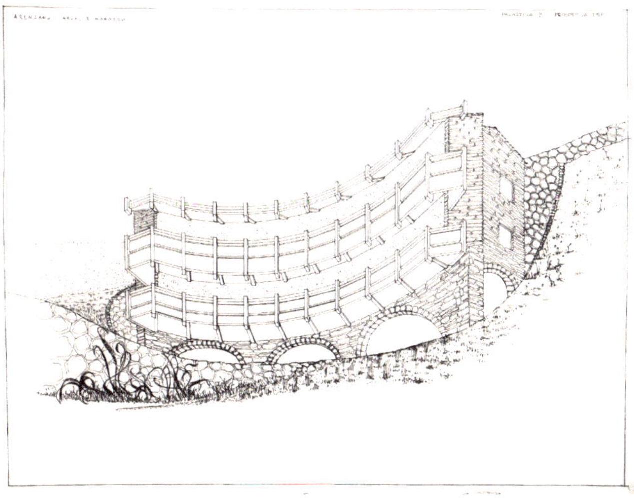

market product into a work of art. Reinforcing the rejection of the iterative logic of the frame and the subsequent dematerialisation of the claddings, the walls retain their material consistency but, through reliefs and grafts of membranes, acquire unexpected plastic qualities. The shapes do not originate from the laws of structural mechanics. Instead, they translate inspirations germinated within Morozzo's rich figurative repertoire, where the structure is required to adapt to the building's form rather than vice versa. Yet, within these tumultuous expressive dynamics, when the structure becomes the protagonist of the compositional strategy and partially or entirely emerges prominently, it assumes the characteristics of plastic form, of pure figure, primarily conceived for visual perception.
These are the years when the scientific approach of engineers, focused on optimising structural behaviour as a generating element of form, was countered by the formalist approach of architects. The latter tended to explore the horizons opened by the malleability of the framework, following the path of Le Corbusier's grand plastic and symbolic forms.[97]
In this framework, Morozzo navigated with freedom and originality, maintaining a strong connection with one of the foundational principles of Italian modernism – that of visionary structures. It is based on the duality between the figurative nature of architecture and the scientific sensibility of construction. **The outcome is a unique ambivalence between the fundamentally figurative genesis of the structure as an abstract form and its subsequently sought and rediscovered compliance with the laws of static behaviour.**

In the years following the war, devoid of public commissions, Morozzo primarily engaged with residential construction, both public and private, collaborating with real estate enterprises involved in developing the former Villa territories.[98]
Thus emerged works marked by brilliant lines and traits, distinguished by a vocabulary simultaneously rational and irrational. Morozzo interpreted this language with great freedom and bold compositional audacity, representing innovative yet mature linguistic choices – somewhat daring given the predominantly anti-modern and conformist Genoese context he navigated. These creations represented a highly personal taste that evolved and refined itself in seemingly precarious balances of forms and materials, embodying an ambiguous "unfinished" harmony. They were also the fruit of a distinct constructive instinct and an enthusiastic embrace of the abstract/concrete spirit of the era. His inventive brilliance and prejudice-free creativity led him, between 1948 and 1972, to construct new works and carry out transformations of existing structures. These are significant exemplars of private residential construction, such as the Palazzo del Sole (1948–1953) and two Palazzine in Quarto for the Braggion Society (1949–1953), the Palazzina Vitruvio for the homonymous enterprise (1952), the Palazzina Ollandini Hoffer[99] in collaboration with the historical Garbarino & Sciaccaluga firm (1953–1956) and the Elios and Selene Villas for the Bagnasco enterprise in the Pineta di Arenzano (1968–1972).

97 Re. forms of Rationalism, see: Roberto Gargiani, *Eretici italiani dell'architettura razionalista*, Vol. 1 – *Razionalismo retorico per il regime fascista 1914–1944* and Vol. 2 – *Razionalismo emozionale per l'identità democratica 1945–1966*, op. cit.

98 Re. the "invasion" of the suburban territories in the eastern and western parts of Genoa, see: Ermanno Ranzani, "La palazzina genovese tra tipo e figura", in: *Rassegna di architettura e urbanistica 89/90. La Palazzina*, May-December, 1996.

99 See: Lucia Oddone, "La Villa Ollandini a Genova", in: *L'Architettura. Cronache e storia*, no.37, 1958, p.454–457.

Other works of urban relevance include the Palace of the Ligurian Activity Society (1936–1952), along with the transformation of the Palazzo del Principe Doria Pamphilj (1937–1962) and the headquarters of the Istituto Nazionale delle Assicurazioni (1955–1964).[100] These constituted interventions straddling transformation, restoration and adaptation include the works for the Church of the Sacro Cuore e San Giacomo of Carignano (1963–1970), for the Cathedral of San Michele in Albenga (1966–1968), and for the Church of Santa Maria delle Grazie in Sampierdarena (1967).

Alongside the theme of housing, another central issue of reconstruction concerns infrastructure. For Morozzo, an example lies in the tender competitions, partnering with the Rutelli and Coltelletti enterprise, for the reconstruction of the Railway Viaducts in Recco and Bogliasco along the Aurelia highway (1946).

In 1949, the inaugural seven-year plan of INA Casa commenced. Morozzo was among the list of professionals available to the organisation, which emerged as a branch of the insurance institute. Leveraging his prior association with President Arnaldo Foschini, his mentor, and his connection with his former colleague and director of the technical department at INA, Adalberto Libera, Morozzo secured several assignments in public housing. Thus, *housing for all* became a significant theme in his endeavours, bolstered by synergies between INA Casa and Ansaldo, a relationship established even before the war.
In Genoa, the new INA neighbourhoods arose in decentralised, if not marginalised, areas, concurrent with the depopulation of the historical city centre. The residential complex of Mura degli Angeli, which emerged even before the Piano Fanfani, was brought to life through a collaboration between Morozzo and Levi Montalcini (1949–1951).[101] Other popular residential complexes include the residences for Ansaldo workers in Cornigliano (1956–1959)[102] and Unit C of the INA Forte Quezzi neighbourhood (1957–1966), one of the most significant and extensive interventions promoted by INA Casa. In this setting, the building structures undulate along the steep ridges of the hill, tracing the contour lines and asserting their presence in the cityscape as a new domestic fortress.[103]

There are many projects, infrastructures and plans that were only partially realised or unrealised. Among them, buildings for the Manufacture Francaise de Lingerie (Casablanca, 1953), the Palazzo of the Savona Province (1st Prize in a competition, with Marco Dasso, 1957), as well as the Nervi Skyscraper (undated) and the buildings for Morassutti (Genoa, 1959), Immobiliare BLC (1962), Fiorentino

100 *National Institute of Insurance.* Re. the Detailed Plan for the Piccapietra area and the INA building, see: Alessandro Christen, "Cronache urbanistiche: Sistemazione della zona di Piccapietra a Genova", in: *Urbanistica*, no.6, 1950, p.58–59; Mario Labò, "Il Concorso di Piccapietra a Genova", in: *Urbanistica*, no.4, 1950, p.36–41; Stefano Passamonti, *Ex Palazzo INA Piccapietra. Robaldo Morozzo della Rocca*, Genoa, 2022.

101 Initially designed by Albini and Gardella (with Palanti and Tevarotto, 1946), later modified in the implementation entrusted, from 1951, to Morozzo and Levi Montalcini for one part and to Daneri for the other.

See: Giovanni Astengo, "Nuovi quartieri in Italia. Mura degli Angeli a Genova", in: *Urbanistica*, no.7, 1951, p.29–30.

102 See: Marian Possevini, "Una casa per gli operai dell'Ansaldo a Genova", in: *L'Architettura. Cronache e storia*, no.57, 1960, p.164–167; Alberto Galardi, *New Italian Architecture*, New York, 1967, p.48–49.

103 Re. the INA Forte Quezzi see: Renato Bonelli, "Quartiere residenziale al Forte di Quezzi in Genova", in: *L'Architettura. Cronache e storia*, no.41, 1959, p.762–763; Gian Antonio Bernasconi, "Cronache di architettura italiana. Il Quartiere di Forte Quezzi, Genova", in: *Casabella*, no.325, 1968; Pietro Patrone, *Daneri*, op. cit., p.132–137; Paola Veronica dell'Aira, "Riflessioni sugli interventi residenziali di Forte Quezzi e della Foce del Bisagno", in: *Edilizia Popolare*, no.263, 1999, p.4–15; Federico Bucci/Marco Lucchini, ""La Casa per tutti": la Stadtkrone di Genova. Il Biscione, la lezione di Le Corbusier e il Piano Fanfani", in: *Casabella*, no.793, 2010, p.50–61; Paolo Cevini, "Il dopoguerra. La crisi del movimento moderno e la "corposa inerzia" di Daneri", in: *Architetture in Liguria dopo il 1945*, op. cit.

(1963–1966), as well as the headquarters of Esso Company (Genoa, 1965). Additionally, there are developments like the Pareto Spinola urbanizations (1952–1958) for the Public and Agricultural Real Estate Company (1956–1958), the INA Ansaldo residences in La Spezia (1959), the INA Ansaldo neighbourhood in Sestri Ponente (1962),[104] the Le Ginestre District developments and residences in Genoa (1963–1965) and the ISES district in Secondigliano (1965).

Morozzo's passion for set design and theatre remains vibrant even in the post-war period, evidenced by competitions such as the open-air theatre in Pescara (1958).[105] Here, the terraces, resembling a stylised seashell, are supported by V-shaped stands. Similarly, the competition for the Cagliari Theatre (1965, with Donatella Morozzo della Rocca) underscores this enduring passion for theatrical endeavours.

Maquette of the entry for an open-air theatre. Pescara, 1958. Competition, 3rd Prize.

Project for the headquarters of Esso Company. Genoa, 1965.

104 See: "Groupe de 200 Logements a Sestri Ponente", in: *L'Architecture d'aujour d'hui. Cités Nouvelles-Centres Urbains*, no. 101, 1962, p.47; Gio Ponti, "Per un nuovo quartiere", in: *Domus*, no. 393, 1962, p.9–10.

105 See: Pasquale Carbonara, "Concorso nazionale per un Teatro all'aperto a Pescara", in: *L'Architettura. Cronache e storia*, no. 35, 1958, p.322–327.

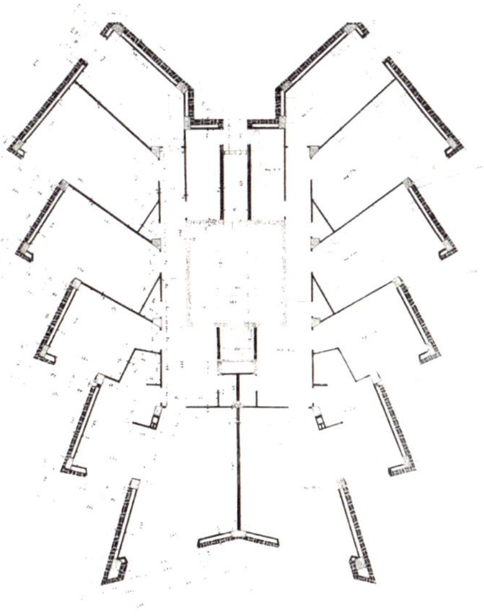

Typical floor plan of the apartment tower for the Ina Ansaldo neighbourhood
Sestri Ponente, Genoa, 1962.

Project for the Ina Ansaldo neighbourhood
Sestri Ponente, Genoa, 1962.

Apartment tower at Villa Maria for the Society of Gaetano Fiorentino
Genoa, 1963–1966.

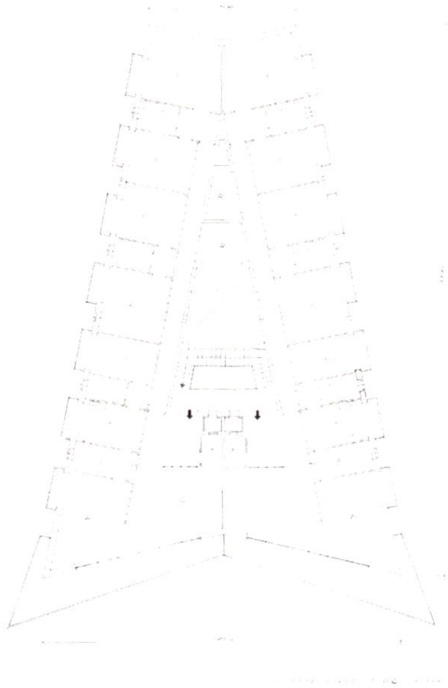

Typical floor plan of the apartment tower for the Society of Gaetano Fiorentino
Genoa, 1963–1966.

Morozzo in history

Within the realm of Italian architecture, Morozzo could be situated among those select few authors who generate interest due to their elusive personal trajectories, diverging in many aspects from canonical ones.

Among authors such as Gio Ponti,[106] Luigi Moretti,[107] Mario Ridolfi,[108] Luigi Caccia Dominioni[109] and Luigi Vietti,[110] for instance, Morozzo appears to have shared certain inclinations, particularly an omnivorous and vitalistic interest that urged him to contaminate his research with experiments and insight from various fields of knowledge, culminating in a de-ideologised architecture with a client-orientated approach. Among these designers emerged a continuous willingness to engage that brought them closer to some protagonists of the Italo-South American school, particularly concerning the shared inclination towards free forays into the realms of emotional Rationalism and expressionism.
In Morozzo, as with Caccia, Ponti and Vietti, one can discern the utilisation of morphologies and roots from abstract expressionism, along with a unique complicity with clients enabling him to practice a cultured architecture, never aloof from the client's expectations, blending rationalist spatiality and ornamentation. In particular, as for Caccia Dominioni, to Morozzo the project embodied "the pleasure of discovery". Both Morozzo and Caccia preferred taking risks, embracing the possibility of error, rather than seeking affirmation within conventional expressions. Consequently, they can both be characterised as experimentalists. For both individuals, human activities, more so than mere functions, served as sources of inspiration and morphological opportunities. The translation of movements and perceptions into architectural elements signifies peculiar aspects, exemplified by the utilisation of curves.
Like Moretti, he was drawn to mathematical scientific thought, pursued with an almost professional commitment. Both were directly involved in other visual arts, practised and lived as intrinsic to the architectural design. Similarly to Ridolfi, Morozzo found the genesis of formal expression rooted in "Baroque taste"[111] and an expressionist vein. Like Vietti, he identified the foundations for inventing a tradition in architecture without an author or in the practice of building in the city.[112]

106 See: Fulvio Irace, *Gio Ponti. La casa all'Italiana*, Milan, 1988; Ugo La Pietra, *Gio Ponti*, New York, 1995; Manfredo di Robilant/Manuel Orazi, *Officina Gio Ponti. Scrittura, grafica, architettura, design*, Macerata, 2023.

107 See: Salvatore Santuccio, *Luigi Moretti*, Bologna, 1986; Federico Bucci/Marco Mulazzani, *Luigi Moretti. Opere e scritti*, Milan, 2000; Cecilia Rostagni, *Luigi Moretti 1907–1973*, Milan, 2008; Bruno Reichlin/Letizia Tedeschi, *Luigi Moretti: razionalismo e trasgressività tra barocco ed informale*, Milan, 2010; Corrado Bozzoni (Ed.), *Luigi Moretti. Architetto del Novecento*, Rome, 2012.

108 See: Claudio D'Amato/Francesco Cellini, *Le Architetture di Ridolfi e Frankl*, Milan, 2005.

109 See: Gio Ponti, "Stile di Caccia", in: *Stile* no. 3, March 1941, p. 28–32; Giacomo Polin, "Un architetto milanese tra regionalismo e sperimentazione: Luigi Caccia Dominioni", in: *Casabella* no. 508, December 1984, p. 40–51; Maria Antonietta Crippa, *Luigi Caccia Dominioni*, Turin, 1996; Fulvio Irace/Paola Marini (Eds.), *Stile di caccia. Luigi Caccia Dominioni. Case e cose da abitare*, Venice, 2003; Elli Mosayebi, "Caccia Dominioni. L'invenzione della storia", in: Cino Zucchi/Nina Bassoli (Eds.), *Innesti-Grafting*, Vol. 2, Milano Laboratorio del Moderno, Venice, 2014, p. 50–57.

110 See: Paola Veronica Dell'Aira, *Luigi Vietti. Progetti e realizzazioni degli anni '30*, Florence, 1997; Marco Gramigni, *Luigi Vietti Architetto*, Novara, 2001.

111 Re. the influence of Baroque in 20th-century architecture, see: Gillo Dorfles, *Barocco nell'architettura moderna*, Milan, 1951.

112 See: Giorgia Sala, *Luigi Vietti e Venezia (1946–61). Modernismi e tradizioni*, Siracusa, 2023.

For all, there was a vivid and present attempt to embody the principle of the unity of the arts, where the art of construction intertwined with complex morphogenetic processes.
Biographical and character affinities found a meeting point in the pride of individuality, in living their own time without adhering to organised movements, intellectually aligning more with the clientele than with the professional category. These were authors who poured into their designs a profound understanding of the world and the savoir-faire they possessed due to their background and upbringing. Morozzo's almost conspiratorial relationship with his clientele marks his work in stark contrast to the ideological currents that contemporary Italian architectural culture was progressively developing. Such intellectual independence remarkably and unpredictably managed to express both the utmost formal rigour and, in other instances, the pinnacle of arbitrariness. Morozzo appears to demonstrate that only a markedly individualistic culture with strong autodidactic tendencies can embrace and nurture, within itself, classical-historicist skills and inclinations, at times antiquarian, alongside other modern cross-disciplinary competencies.
A syncretism seamlessly pervades the four decades of his activity, oscillating between urges for renewal and autarchic impulses toward preservation.

The other aspect that piques interest involves the apparent ease with which this talented personality traversed from one repertoire of architecture to another, mastering and equally favouring history, conservation, historical etymology citations, the application of classical lessons and avant-garde experimentation. He dedicated himself entirely to each aspect without becoming exclusively ensnared, unabashedly pursuing a subjective course of diverse thoughts, unencumbered by conformist reservations, even if not exclusively eclectic.
Thus emerged Morozzo's inclination to operate based on individual responsibilities, to be tested at each new opportunity, never relying on a constant simplifying rationalisation or adopting a code to remain faithful to. This reluctance towards any form of *a priori* adherence may be the origin of certain divergences found both in the figurative repertoires and in the varying levels of quality achieved in his different works. However, it is precisely this aristocratic indifference to ideological relevance that gave rise to the courage seen in some solutions. Morozzo seems to have recognised, as the only legitimate form of coherence, the fidelity, moment by moment, to one's immediate conviction and the continuity of one's own experience and judgment, attributing to every other choice the role of a variable at one's disposal.
Morozzo did not deploy specialised knowledge cultivated in a separate laboratory, nor did he assert demonstrative theses. Instead, he preferred direct engagement with the design commitments he faced and the city that welcomed them. With the city and the environment, he weaved a dialogue that privileged not so much his undeniable qualities as a specialist, but rather those of a man with broad, cross-disciplinary culture. In this way, his work can retain the unblemished value of splendid amateurism, an unprecedented response to existential needs, and occasionally attain that particular vividness often denied to specialisation.[113]

113 Re. this interpretation, see: Benedetto Todaro, "Moretti e i suoi fratelli. Complessità e contraddizioni di una elite", in: Corrado Bozzoni (Ed.), *Luigi Moretti. Architetto del Novecento*, op.cit.

This repertoire of styles, employed as much in the new as in the existing, places Morozzo within a broader discourse that transcends immediate temporal and geographical boundaries, encompassing him within a larger culture of design characterised by astounding authors such as Joseph Hoffmann,[114] Fritz Höger,[115] Jože Plečnik[116] and Hans Poelzig[117]. These designers compel a reinterpretation of the architectural canon, surprisingly close in attitude to certain masters of the past, such as Francesco Borromini[118] and Guarino Guarini.[119]

Able to encapsulate the entirety within its own order, Morozzo's work seems sub merged yet pulsatingly contemporary. It is difficult to explain that profound attention demanded by the panoramic images of the Ollandini building or those of the Municipal Offices, both culminations of the city's design, perspective figures overlooking the peripheral square which embodies the infinity of the sea.

Above: Project for the Morassuti building for housing and offices. Genoa, 1959.

Below: Project for the house Gregorini Tanas. Ceriale, Savona, 1953.

114 See: Christoph Thun-Hohenstein/Matthias Boeckl/Franz Rainald/ Christian Witt-Dörring, *Josef Hoffmann 1870–1956: Progress Through Beauty*, Basel, 2021.

115 See: Piergiacomo Bucciarelli, *Fritz Höger, maestro anseatico 1877–1949*, Venice, 1991.

116 See: Damjan Prelovcek, *Joze Plecnik (1872–1957)*, Milan, 2005.

117 See: Marco Biraghi, *Hans Poelzig. Architettura, ars magna, 1869–1936*, Venice, 1992.

118 See: Hans Sedlmayr, *L'architettura di Borromini*, Milan, 2002; Paolo Portoghesi, *Francesco Borromini*, Milan, 1990.

119 See: Harold Alan Meek, *Guarino Guarini*, Milan, 1991.

“Bourbonnaise” housing and factory project for the Manufacture Francaise de Lingerie society
Casablanca, 1953.

Robaldo and Donatella Morozzo della Rocca, proposal for the new municipal theatre
Cagliari, 1964. Competition, finalist.

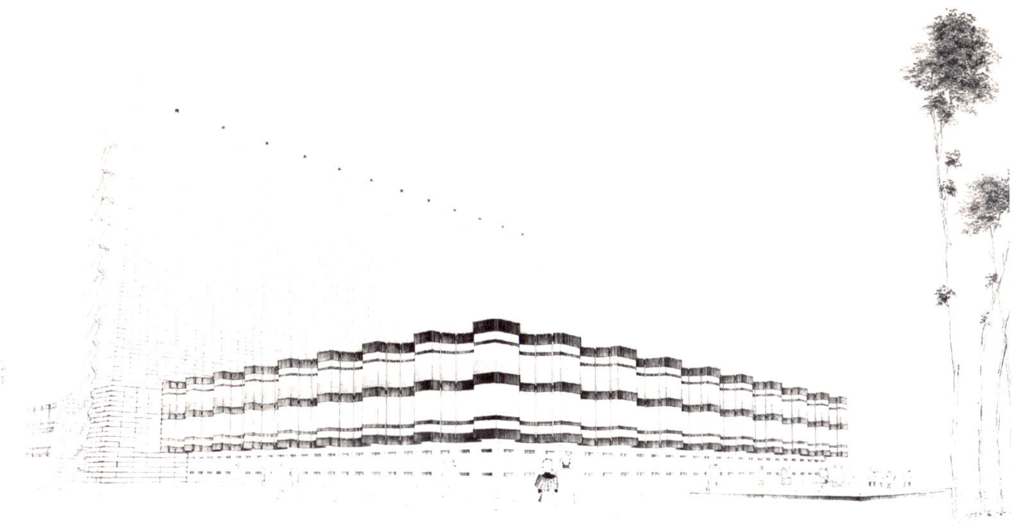

Morozzo's styles and the contemporaneity of the outdated

Morozzo passed away at the end of the last century, nearing the age of 90. Throughout his career, he bore witness to the trajectory of 20th-century Italian architecture, constructing an unparalleled synthesis that juxtaposed the personal against the universal. His volumetric movements, stemming from a Baroque sensitivity, fractured surfaces and planes, engaging in a *chiaroscuro* interplay that fragmented form across the three projections of space, while retaining the unmistakable features discernible within it.

Behind the reserved and seraphic figure lies a lively and inquisitive professional who leaves us with a kaleidoscopic repertoire of projects. These projects, drawn from diverse sources and languages, culled from the realm of art and developed with scientific-mathematical rigour, constitute endeavours that, without anticipating their outcome, liberate linguistic exploration from nostalgic constraints. They look towards both architectural traditions and the material cultures of spontaneous construction as tangible operational resources. **Morozzo's experimental nature infuses his research with a heterogeneous lexicon and eccentric, multiform and expressive works to the extent that they appear both popular**[120] **and simultaneously unsettling.**[121] This pronounced autonomy guides Morozzo towards an ungrammatical and blurred exploration, rendering him an enigmatic phenomenon. The absence of a formal, spatial, structural manner or relationship with the context results in entirely unique works that, despite their surprising differences, bear a semblance to one another. It is within this dissimilarity that one finds the hallmark of vivacity and vitality in his oeuvre.

Morozzo counterposes the heroic figure of the Total Architect[122] with that of the demiurge artist, a proponent of a work fragrant with originality, unlocatable within the canonical confines of codified historicist labels. He champions his own ambiguities, deflecting potential critical judgments and challenging the very notion of modernism as a rationalist and universal movement, introducing many of the elements that become central to post-modern architecture.[123]

120 The term popular in this context refers to the familiarity and ease with which, in the common Genoese perception, many citizens identify certain particularly "symbolic" works of the city's architectural heritage. Specifically, Morozzo della Rocca created two structures commonly denominated and colloquially identified through a caricatural appellation: the *Pianoforte*, namely, the Palazzina Ollandini Hoffer, the *Biscionetto*, namely, Building C in the INA Forte Quezzi Quarter and the *Interruttori*, namely, Grande INA Casa Ansaldo Coronata.

121 Something ostensibly concealed that instead surfaces, captivates and enchants due to its infrequently encountered characteristics. An object that amalgamates traits of alienation and familiarity into a sort of affective dualism.

See: Anthony Vidler, *The Architectural Uncanny. Essays in the Modern Unhomel*, Cambridge (USA), 1992.

122 See: Adam Caruso, "What is modern?", in: *Caruso St John's: Collected Works Vol. 2, 2000–2012*, London, 2023.

123 The rejection of the rationalist code, the opposition to the idea of progress and novelty enacted through an architecture that presents itself as unfinished and imperfect, foreshadows a distancing from the theoretical foundations of the modernist movement. The critical reclamation of traditions and linguistic conventions through sometimes ironic experiments is reflected in the eclectic revival of past stylistic elements, allowing for greater compositional freedom and a new openness to the symbolic and metaphorical meanings of the architectural image.

Of noble disposition and far removed from engaging in pressing political endeavours, Morozzo relies on a pragmatic methodology, devoid of upheavals or sudden paradigm shifts. The *contemporaneity of the outdated* in his poetics is grounded in an exploration that revolves around the same elements throughout his career: a glossary of "obsessions" that Morozzo reinvented through a sophisticated repertoire of elements (such as the dichotomy between façades, emptied angles, monumentalised staircases, inflections, displacements, etc.), aligning with *modern architecture* as a vanguard capable of renewing design culture only if understood as spirit rather than mere style.[124] Hence, the dimensions and attributes of Morozzo's work are rooted in a condition that could be defined as post-ideological[125] – a testament to the autonomy of the language to any external conditioning.

Evoking his architectures, from the *Pianoforte* (Palazzina Ollandini) to the *Biscionetto* (INA Forte Quezzi), from the *Interruttori* (Grande INA Casa Ansaldo) to the former building for INA, passing through the Municipal Offices Palace, there is no single image that could encapsulate them all, nor a stylistic signature that remains unaltered and identical, predefined in relation to the project. In Morozzo, compositional coherence is of a mental nature concerning the images it manifests, as if an original manner allows him to "conceal" his compositional processes within the body of the buildings.

The emotional nature of architecture, not reducible to purely logical parameters, and the peculiar interpretation of the concept of "function" in contrast to the canonical analytical version of Rationalism, lead Morozzo to conceive construction as a whole entity. The strict norm governing the genesis of form from function assumes an equivalent place to formal canons in ancient architecture. He works with deviations from the canon, where some architects perceive immutable norms for correct composition. Instead of an analytical and taxonomic approach to functionalism, Morozzo favours a profound assimilation. The "relentless discipline" of style is precisely what makes it impossible to "settle" on it, believing that one has achieved it. It needs continuous recreation. In this regard, an intriguing aspect of Morozzo's architectural practice is the emancipation from the obligatory duty of a purely rational awareness of one's design gestures and thoughts. It is an indispensable dimension to the creative act – a realm of freedom where the pursuit of multiple meanings explores and combines all possible languages, ultimately "ambiguously"' choosing the form while still preserving the mystery of its origin.
For these reasons, Morozzo deserves credit for not fully embracing the formalist and closed mannerist logic evident in the designs and construction of the *Pianoforte*, and for leaving to others the "pleasure of unveiling". This explains why the image of this building appears distinct from subsequent productions, yet at the same time, certain methodological traces originating in this architecture permeate his entire body of work. Evocative in this sense are the similarities in the

124 Robaldo Morozzo della Rocca, "Valore di una parola", in: Michele Cennamo (Ed.), *Materiali per l'analisi dell'architettura moderna. Il MIAR*, op. cit., p. 382–384.

125 No ideological operation exists that is not immediately verifiable in language. Post-ideological, in this context, refers to an autonomous and neutral reading that carries out a de-ideologised and depoliticised interpretation of historical testimonies. It avoids placing moral judgments and can influence the present in the disciplinary practice. This involves a morphological analysis, a phenomenal expression of the language and poetics unique to the author.

articulation between the top-floor plan of the *Pianoforte* and the morphology of the Palazzo in Via Mura degli Zingari.[126]

Morozzo embraces the division between content and form, between essence and appearance. Thus, it becomes possible to discuss form, free from pre-established meanings and internal obligations within the discipline, as an "abstract exercise", fervently invoked by avant-gardes and cherished by numerous Italian architects who were thus accused of formalism.[127]
Then let this "formalism" be sanctified or at least forgiven if it enables the revival of experiences deliberately forgotten in their time, such as those belonging to Italian Rationalism between the two World Wars and its post-war aftermath, of which Morozzo undoubtedly is a part.
For Morozzo, architecture is an act of invention rather than mere intuition, wherein all formal, structural, technical, functional, mnemonic, historical, cultural contents – those deeply rooted in our existence – integrate and coalesce within the unity of the whole, undergoing modification through their interplay, guided by the designer's free and subjective choices. This comprehensive integration imbues meaning and value to the entirety of the architectural work and simultaneously to each of its parts.

The "peculiar" figurative object represented by the *Pianoforte*, this scenic contrivance that constructs itself in the eye of the observer, traversing the coastal landscape from below, based on the dichotomous relationship between the "'stone crust" and the "glassy pulp" of its façade, represents possibly the most poetic and prophetic urban object envisioned during the era of highly modern and markedly non-rationalist projects. While remaining an architecture still overlooked today, within it we perceive the discerning critical spirit of Robert Venturi, who could have included it among the works that enable him to identify the pioneering features of that complex design method based on the "contradiction between signs", theorised almost 20 years later[128] – a method the Ollandini Building prophetically anticipates. *Contraria contrariis curentur*: concealed within this edifice lie some interpretative keys to the phases of transcending the experiences of the modern movement – or at the very least, its transformation from a quest for "pure unity" in the name of an ideological truth to an acceptance of opposing sign-based categories, where morphology holds no "formal obligation".

Morozzo consistently nurtured this ambiguity by combining modernism with his personal uninhibited figurative exuberance and a sense of the theatrical, thereby giving life to moments of invention, singularly prophetic, and creating authentic works of inspiration that are distinctly pre-emptively post-modern. The value of these design moments resides entirely in sensitive invention, in the courage to replace the reasonable evolutionary line

126 Observing the floor plans of the two structures reveals how both sinuous building masses bend to create a subtle convexity.

127 Morozzo rejected the old and tautological distinction between form and content, upon which architectural criticism had long been based. The distinction between form and content is tautological because form is merely one of the contents or "shaping" (*Formung*) of one of the parts that constitute the whole, that is, the architectural object. Stating that form is one of the contents does not imply a subordinate role; rather, it emphasises the weight and autonomy of form in the compositional process.

128 In his work *Complexity and Contradiction in Architecture* (New York, 1966), Robert Venturi contends that architecture primarily concerns form, not social action; one should scrutinise existing typologies and the city more closely; and cultural continuity is not necessarily something to be avoided at all costs. While Venturi is clearly a Europhile, *Complexity and Contradiction in Architecture* is written from an American perspective, rendering its viewpoint broader in scope.

of rationalist ideological architecture with the evocative and rhetorical power of vision, however arbitrary and unnecessary. Thus, buildings are liberated from the domain of "good" rules of distributive tradition to assume motivation and sense, a depth of meaning and memory. Morozzo thus endowed the "new architecture" with the quality of architecture finally freed from the constraints of function, to present itself to the city as urban and to its inhabitants as form. In this sense, based on a specific notion of *environment*,[129] the city of Genoa represents for Morozzo the primary opportunity to engage, a fertile ground for experimentation, an expressive laboratory for his artistic practice.

Stylistic abstraction, the reclamation of language autonomy, and an anti-"contextualism" transform place into something more than merely a "context" in which to "situate" one's buildings. Place is not something pre-existing and fully defined to which one adapts their architecture; rather, it is something that architecture contributes to re-establish, "to destroy judiciously",[130] to reconstruct as space, place and backdrop of dwelling. Architecture presents itself as a fundamental thought, an autonomous value capable of transforming place. Yet, without the determination of place, this kind of thought would not be possible; it would not transcend the confines of purely formal abstraction: the figurative abstraction through the construction of an element that establishes an unprecedented relationship with its surroundings, seemingly as if it has been there for eternity while also asserting its exceptional nature. **In Genoa, through imaginative works, Morozzo sought in architecture that imperfection, that rational expressionism, that material abstraction which will definitively prevail over the problem of function, translating normative and landscape-related issues into graceless plastic forms.** From these premises, Morozzo della Rocca signed some of the city's most significant and lyrical buildings – fragments that belong to collective imagination and that characterise Genoa's post-*modern* image, redeeming it from the conventional attribution of an eclectic and historicist aura. Morozzo della Rocca created a body of work that anticipated and prophetically represented the contradictions of our times – a historical era where architecture, unlike its avant-garde past, no longer embodied any utopian ideal capable of addressing society's traumas.

129 Referring to a nuanced set of factors that shape the original condition of the physical environment of the project: morphological features, the history of the place, settlement principles, physical consistency, materiality, significant episodes, etc.
See: Adrian Forty, "Context", in *Words and Building. A Vocabulary for Modern Architecture*, London, 2004.

130 "Every intervention presupposes a destruction. Destroy with wisdom."
See: Luigi Snozzi, "Viva la Resistenza !", in: Luigi Snozzi/Fabio Merlini, *L'architettura inefficiente*, Bellinzona, 2014.

Top left: Third proposal (1949) for the reconstruction project of the Teatro Regio
Turin, 1938–1964.

Top right: Robaldo Morozzo della Rocca with Marco Dasso, proposal for the new province headquarters
Savona, 1957. Competition, 1st Prize.

Centre left: Project for a skyscraper in Nervi
Genoa, undated.

Centre right: Robaldo Morozzo della Rocca with Gino Levi Montalcini, INA Casa Mura degli Angeli
Genoa, 1949–1951.

Bottom: Project for a spa hotel
Lurisia, 1942.

AN ITINERARY

GENOA AS A LABORATORY

1932–1936, Villa I Ciliegi, San Michele di Pagana, Genoa

see project info sheet – p. 196–199

1933–1934, Centrale del Latte, Fegino, Genoa

see project info sheet – p. 200–203

UFFICIO
TECNICO

1935, Villa il Paradisetto, Albaro, Genoa

see project info sheet – p. 204–207

14
EK 640FV
FE 385TC

FN 944AJ

1937–1938, Palazzo Custo, Carignano, Genoa

see project info sheet – p. 208–211

96

1942–1950, Palazzo della Flotta Lauro, Prè, Genoa

see project info sheet – p. 212–215

express
PARK

FLOTTA LAURO

1948–1953 (modified 1962), Palazzo del Sole, Albaro, Genoa

see project info sheet – p. 216–219

P

1949–1951, INA Casa Mura degli Angeli, San Teodoro, Genoa

see project info sheet – p. 220–223

116

1936 (1st project) – 1949–1952 (2nd project), Palazzo della Società Attività Ligure, San Teodoro, Genoa

see project info sheet – p. 224–229

Welt

1936–1962 (restoration and transformation), Doria Pamphily Palace, San Teodoro, Genoa

1949–1953, Palazzine Braggion, Quarto, Genoa

see project info sheet – p. 230–233

corso europa
autostrade

1952, Palazzina Vitruvio, Albaro, Genoa

see project info sheet – p. 234–237

DD 820PK

1953–1956, Palazzina Ollandini Hoffer, Albaro, Genoa

see project info sheet – p. 238–241

1955–1964, Palazzo dell'Istituto Nazionale Assicurazioni, Piccapietra, Genoa

see project info sheet – p. 242–245

SCAL

1956–1959, INA Casa Ansaldo, Cornigliano, Genoa

see project info sheet – p. 246–249

1957–1966, C Building of the INA Forte Quezzi, Marassi, Genoa

see project info sheet – p. 250–253

VIETATO

109

1963–1970, Completion of the Church of Sacred Heart and St. James, Carignano, Genoa

see project info sheet – p. 254–257

PATRIS ET FILII ET SPIRITUS

NOME DEL PADRE DEL FIGLIO
IN MEMORIA

1968–1972, Villini Elios and Selene, Pineta di Arenzano, Genoa

see project info sheet – p. 258–261

Apartment building Ollandini Hoffer
Genoa, 1953–1956.

Multipurpose building for the National Insurance Institute in Piccapietra
Genoa, 1955–1964. Invited competition, 1st Prize for Plot IV.

Apartment building for Ansaldo workers in Cornigliano, 1956–1959.

nit C of the INA Forte Quezzi neighbourhood Genoa, 1957–1966.

Above: Palazzo Custo.
Genoa, 1937–1938

Below: Palazzo della Società Attività Ligure
Genoa, 1949–1952

AN ARCHIPELAGO

BUILDING ATLAS

Villa i Ciliegi

1932–1936
Via Costantino Nigra, San Michele di Pagana, Genoa

The building occupies a plot located near Punta Pagana, set back from the entrance gate of the estate, positioned adjacent to the road cutting through the coastal promontory. The project was commissioned by Senator Paolo Orlando (1858–1943), an engineer hailing from Rapallo, whose professional journey commenced in the family shipyards in Livorno, later ascending to the roles of councillor and municipal assessor in Rome, where he played a pivotal role in the construction of the Ostia port.

The structure manifests as a compact, asymmetrical volume with protruding three-dimensional elements such as bay windows and recessed features such as loggias, bestowing upon it a significant plastic value. A concave cornice, adorned with ornamental friezes, precedes a hipped roof covered in slate slabs, contributing to its aesthetic allure.

The villa unfolds across four levels: basement, ground floor, mezzanine and noble floor. Accessible from the garden level, an atrium serves as the entry point, presided over by a double staircase. Following an initial straight ascent, the staircase gracefully winds to reach the first floor. Positioned in alignment with the atrium, the staircase not only functionally divides the house into two distinct realms, but also extends beyond the silhouette of the main volume, announcing its presence on the rear façade.

The northeast-exposed section of the house accommodates the garage and storage rooms at the ground level, while the upper floors house bedrooms and bathrooms. In the northwest part of the mezzanine, a secondary entrance leads to the kitchen. The ground floor features bedrooms and utility rooms, with the mezzanine hosting the master bedroom with a private bathroom, additional bedrooms and another kitchen. The first floor is dedicated to the prestigious spaces: a living room, a lounge with a loggia, an office, the master bedroom and a bathroom.

The house disregards many rules of "correct" classical composition, introducing numerous infringements of the rule on proportions between parts, both in plan and in elevation. The asymmetrical functional organisation is reflected in the plant morphology and the layout of the elevations.

In parallel with his avant-garde exploration, Morozzo's trajectory in the 1930s sees the emergence of a series of works executed in a stylistic manner, drawing from a historically determined morphological repertoire. This operational framework is justified both by the repeated reluctance of the clientele towards avant-garde architecture and by the relevance of specific urban planning regulations concerning the Ligurian coasts. In Villa Orlando, Morozzo departs from the sophisticated play of pure and candid stereometrics found in his earlier villas, indifferent to any need for theoretical foundation. Instead, he embarks on a "return to order" where modernity is achieved on moral and ethical grounds rather than aesthetic ones.

The stylistic neoclassicism permeating the entire project coexists with the generous spatiality of the interiors, made possible by the reinforced concrete structure, optimal orientation and rational organisation of internal functions. Classical architectural elements, such as decorative volutes or whimsical floral friezes, coexist and conceal distinctly modern elements and technologies, with the large windows facing the gulf being a testament to this coalescence.

1. Yacht garage for the boat show
Luigi Carlo Daneri with Pier Luigi Nervi | 1948–1950

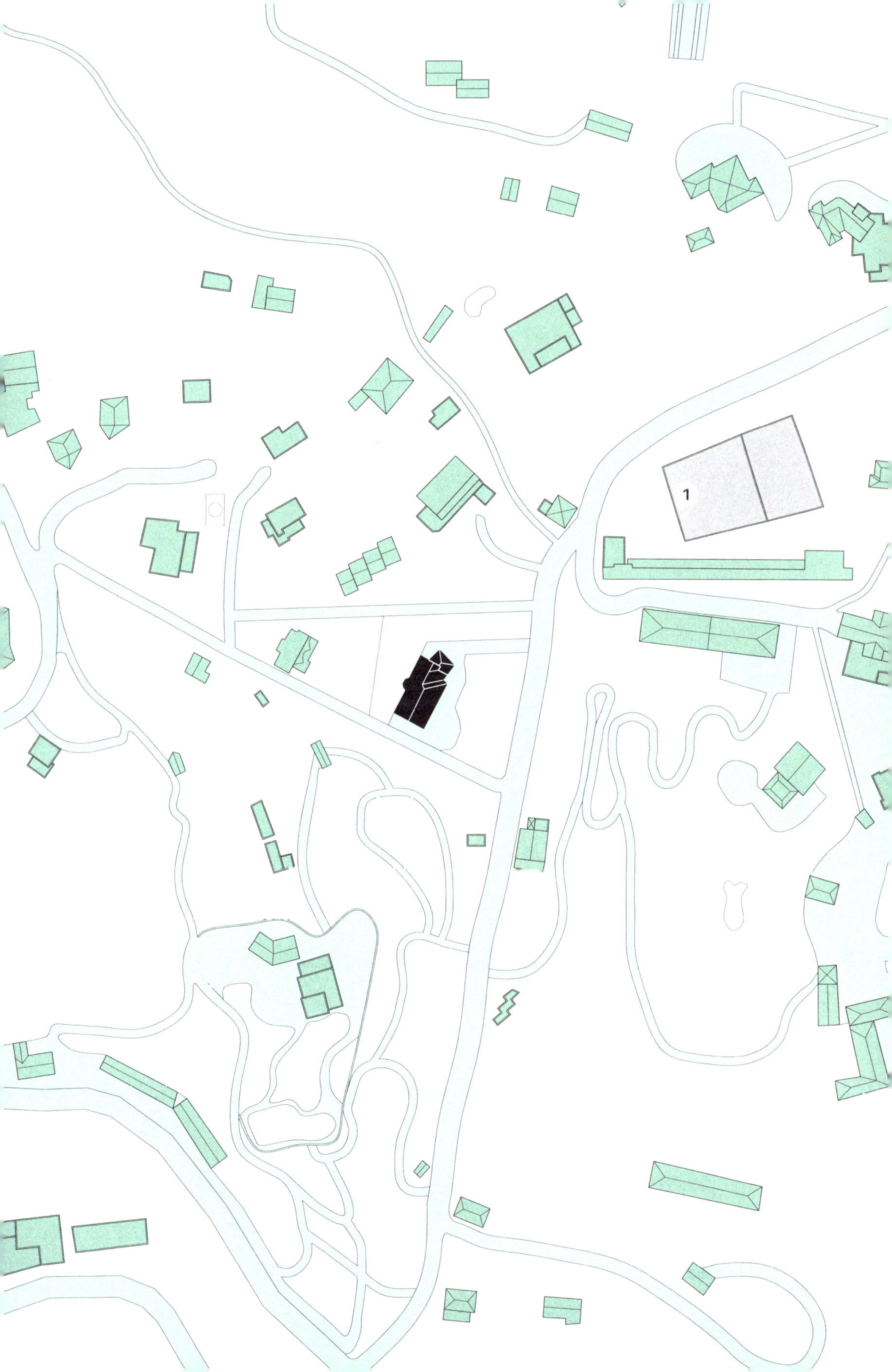
1

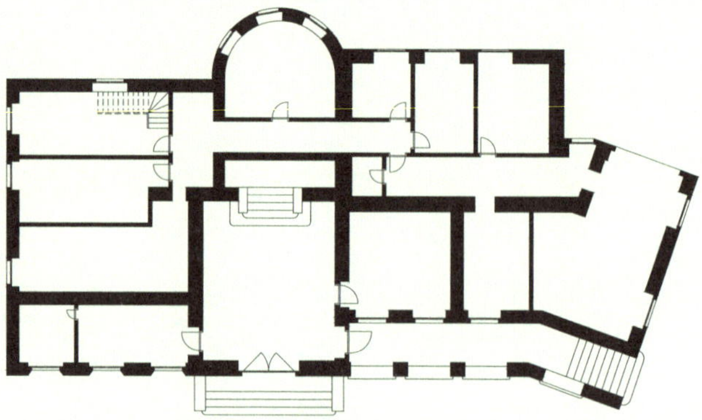

Ground floor plan

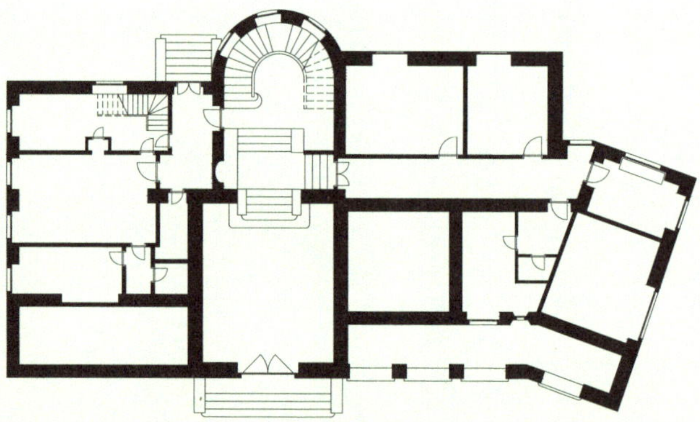

Mezzanine floor plan

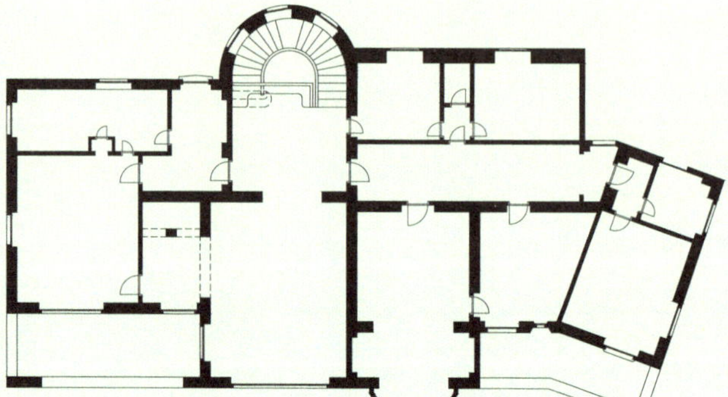

First floor plan

Scale 1:333

East façade

North façade

South façade

Scale 1:333

1933–1934

Piazza Fulceri Paolucci De Calboli, Fegino, Genoa

Centrale del Latte

The Fegino Dairy Plant is realised through the transformation of the former Ansaldo Pipe Factory, disused since 1935. Consequently, the project must contend with the existing building's architecture on one hand and the intricate system of machinery required for product processing on the other.
The structure, which served as the headquarters of the dairy until 2012, stands as one of the early notable examples of Rationalist Architecture in Liguria. Additionally, it ranks among the larger facilities of its kind in terms of size and stands at the forefront of technological advancement for its time.
The structure, with dimensions measuring 26 metres in height, 56 in length, and 45 in width, occupies a plot of 1.45 hectares and is surrounded by an extensive courtyard and additional areas supporting the main activities, including the cafeteria, staff recreation facility and warehouses.

The industrial complex, marked by a basilical layout exuding solemn aesthetics, is articulated into two distinct sections: a large "technical" body with pronounced horizontal development and the end building, devoted to administrative functions, distinguished by an eloquently defined three-dimensional façade.
The technical section is equipped with a system divided into four main areas: for the collection, control and treatment of milk; for the reception, washing and filling of bottles and containers; for the storage and subsequent distribution of bottles and filled milk containers; and for administrative offices and control laboratories.

All these components are arranged to ensure a unidirectional workflow, following a carefully established cycle, where the milk, upon arrival, is lifted only once and then proceeds by gravity. After undergoing thermal treatment, it passes through holding tanks, from which, through pipelines, it descends to the underlying bottling and capping machines. The section designated for receiving used bottles and containers consists of a platform opposite to the one receiving the milk, and is directly connected through roller conveyors to the section for the washing and automatic sterilisation of the containers, and from there to the filling section. Once sealed, the bottles are placed in baskets and, through one of the customary roller conveyors, admitted into the refrigeration chamber, located beneath the platform supporting the filters, pasteurisers and tanks.

In Morozzo's project, alongside engineers Ferrari and Ghezzi, a strong vein of the 20th century emerges, a characteristic feature of works from the Thirties. The numerous solutions devised for the definition of the front building are all articulated according to a tripartite scheme: entrance portal, façade, lateral wings. These solutions bear witness to the influence of Central European architecture, especially by Bonatz, Kampmann and Fahrenkamp, introduced to Italy through Marcello Piacentini's work *Architettura d'Oggi*. On the front of the building, the rigorous geometry and radical work of figurative simplification are shaken by sudden formal subversions and enriched with sophisticated compositional solutions: Morozzo organises an atrium with a staircase and a corresponding façade, characterised by a tall glass portal that illuminates the environment on both floors.

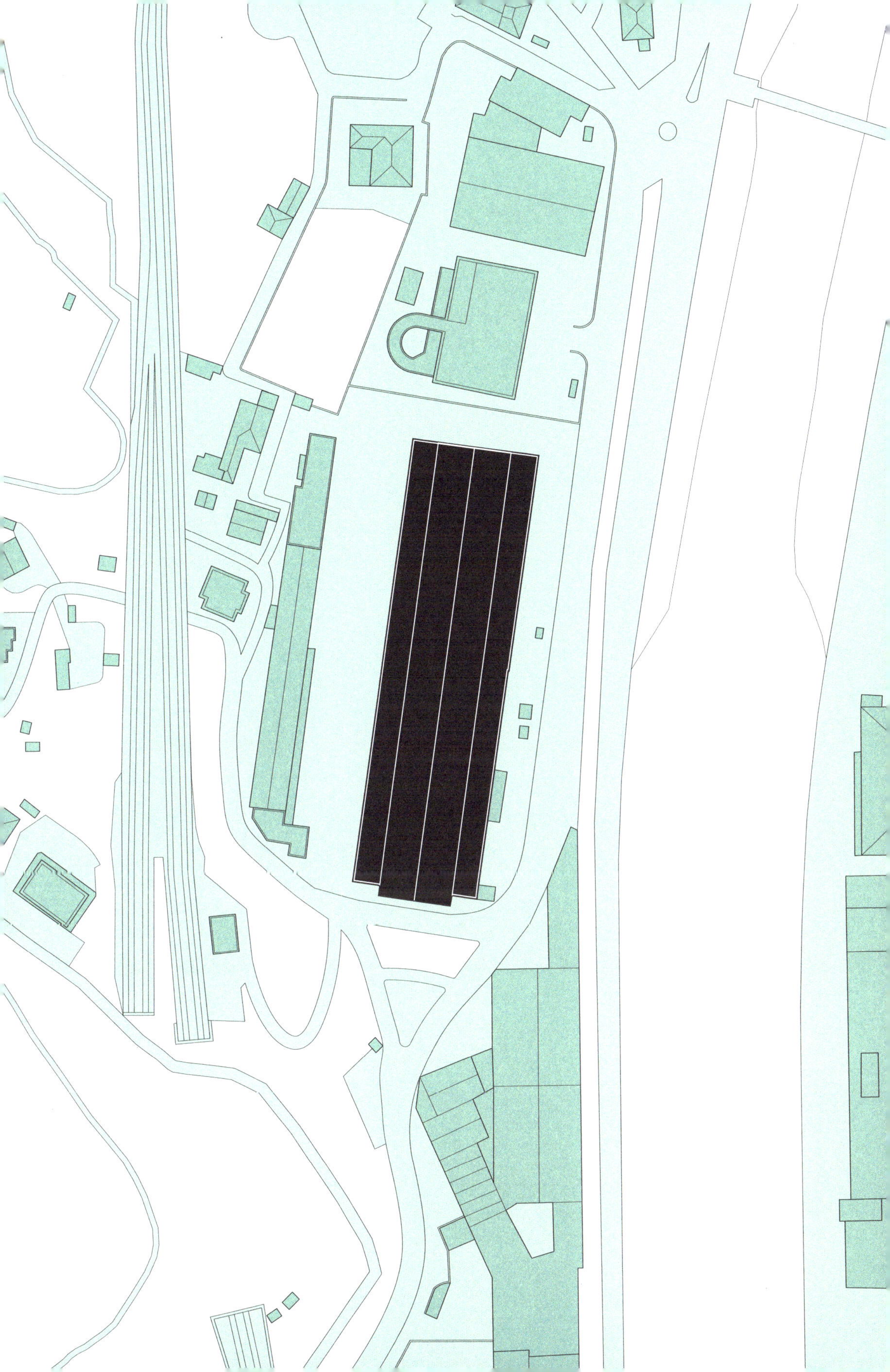

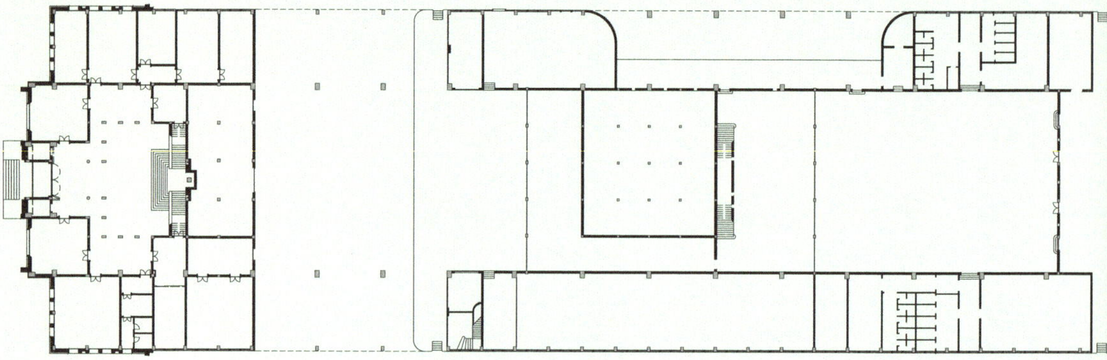

Scale 1:1000

Ground floor plans

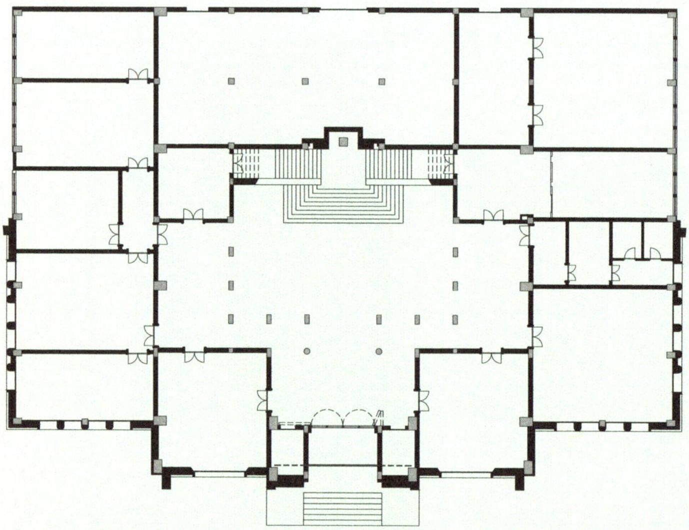

Scale 1:500

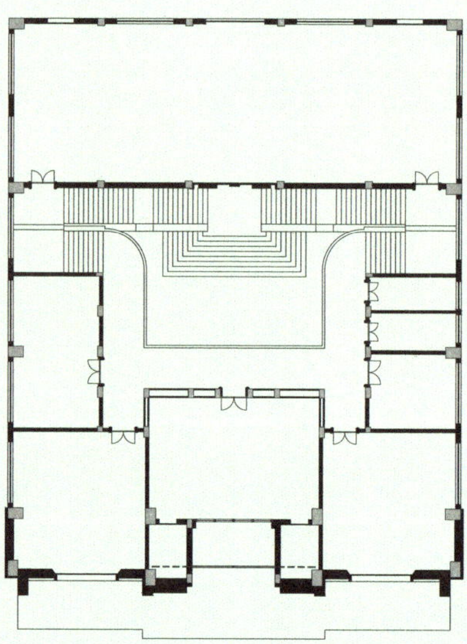

First floor plan

Scale 1:500

Scale 1:333

South façade

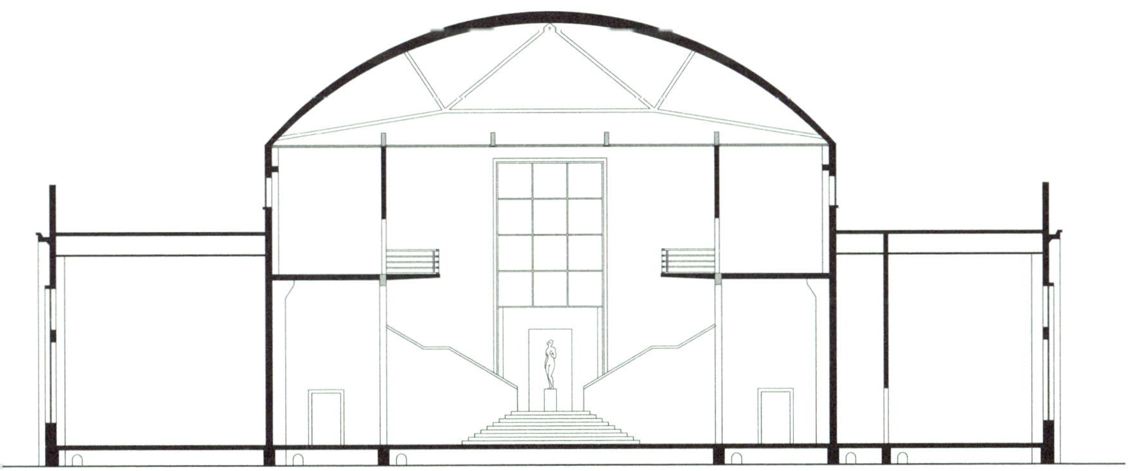

Transversal section

Villa Il Paradisetto

The edifice is situated on an elevation, strategically positioned to command a panoramic view, within the framework of a monumental setting: to the east, the villa borders the Monastery of the Sacramentine Sisters and is physically contiguous to the forest enclosed within the Park of Villa Saluzzo Bombrini, known as "Il Paradiso", from which its name is derived. The latter stands among the most noteworthy examples of pre-Alessian villas, characterised by a rectangular layout. Constructed at the end of the 16th century by Andrea Vannone for the Marquises Saluzzo, it earns the epithet "Il Paradiso" due to its exquisite location at the entrance of the Albaro hill and the panoramic view of the city offered by loggias that open like scenic backdrops on the rich façade. The monastery, on the other hand, originated from the initiative of Antonietta Celesia, who acquired lands for its construction, completed in 1884. The complex comprises two distinct structures: the convent and the church. The latter, destroyed during bombing in 1942, was reconstructed by Crosa di Vergagni in 1955. The convent consists of two separate sections: the large U-shaped building constructed at the end of the 19th century and an older structure dating between the 15th and 16th centuries, part of the estate purchased by the benefactor Celesia in the late 19th century. This section, originally intended as an adjunct to an adjacent villa, was later acquired by the Bombrini family and transformed by Morozzo della Rocca to create an 18th-century-style building, destined to accommodate the residences of their daughters.

Morozzo's design engages with the tradition of Genoese Baroque architecture to fulfil the client's wishes: above a massive, rusticated substructure, the architect arranges a palace composed of the superimposition of two grand bourgeois residences. This typological solution finds its roots in ancient examples such as Michelangelo's Farnese Palace (1546) or the palace built by Bartolomeo Bianco in Genoa for Giacomo and Pantaleo Balbi (1618), both characterised by the superimposition of two noble floors. Access to the building is granted from a lower level, passing through an ornate gate linked to a caretaker's residence, also designed in a stylistic manner, ascending through a small curvilinear slope. The classically composed floor plan reveals a functionally "modern" organisation: bedrooms and sanitary facilities are located on the north side, while the representation areas face southwest; the stairwell is positioned adjacent to the monastery, acting as a separating element. A small cloister provides light and air to the internal distributive gallery. An elaborate cornice precedes the hipped roof, sloping only towards three edges of the volume, featuring a sunbathing roof terrace facing east. The building boasts a mixed load-bearing structure, partly constructed with structural masonry of stonework and bricks and partly utilising reinforced concrete, including vaults, floors, lintels and the framework of the central loggia. Externally, there is no trace of the "modern" technology used for the building, completely concealed by decorative elements, except for the unconventional use of green shutters. Internally, vertically striped plaster coexists with modern glass-block surfaces used for skylights.

1. **Palazzina Vitruvio**
   Robaldo Morozzo della Rocca | 1952
2. **Palazzina Sanguineti**
   Luigi Carlo Daneri | 1953–1956
3. **Monastery of the Sacramentine Sisters**
   Giuseppe Crosa di Vergagni | 1955
4. **"Il Paradiso" or Villa Saluzzo Bombrini**
   Andrea Vannoni | late 16th century

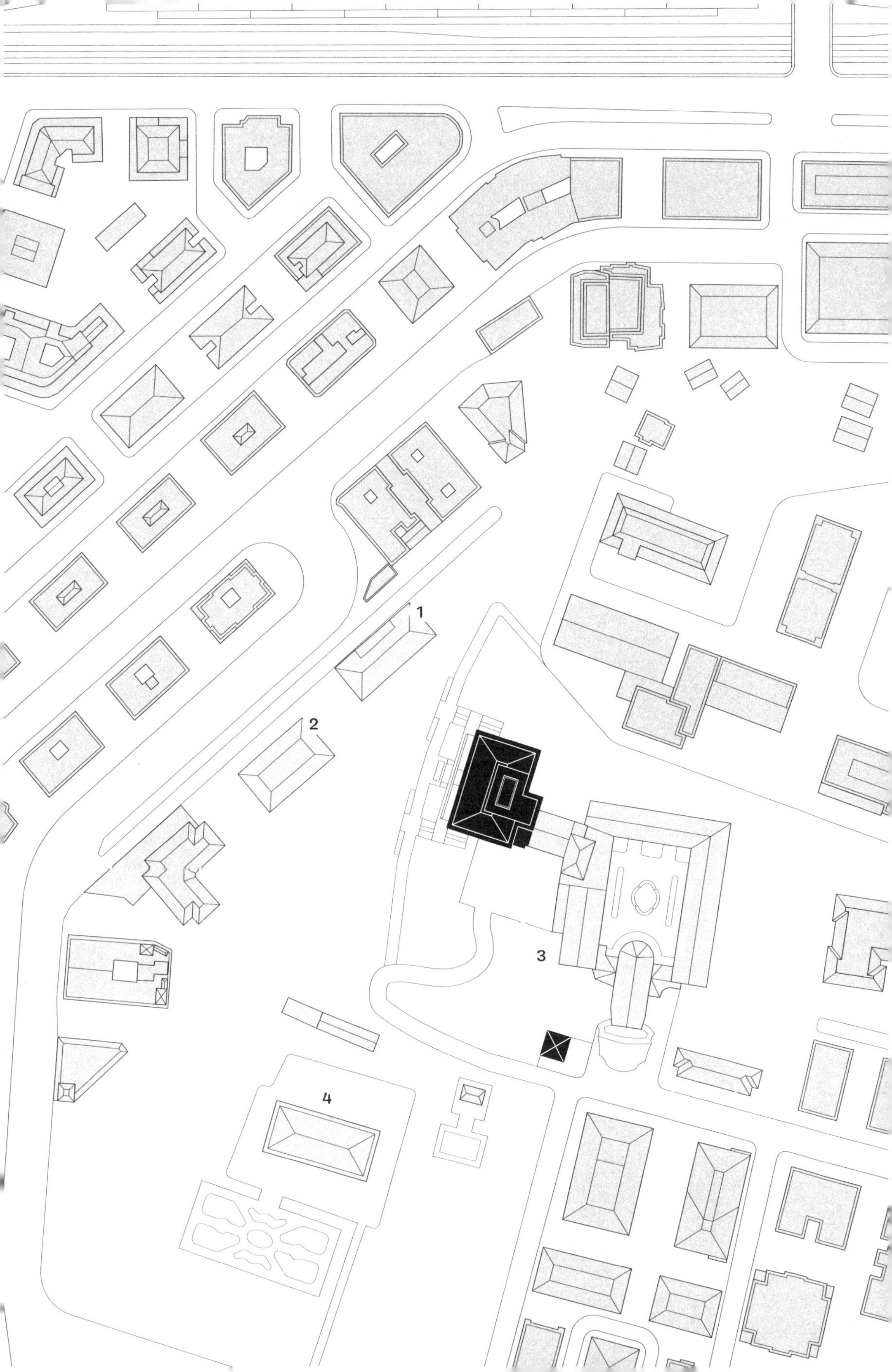
1
2
3
4

Scale 1:333

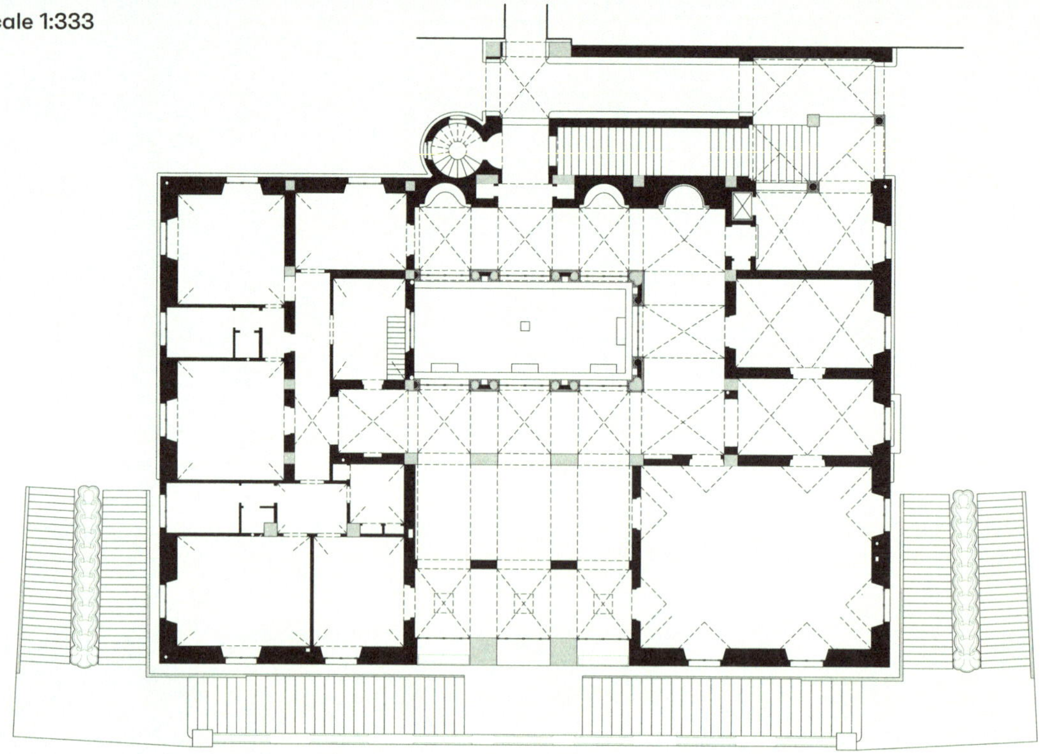

Ground floor plan

Typical floor plan

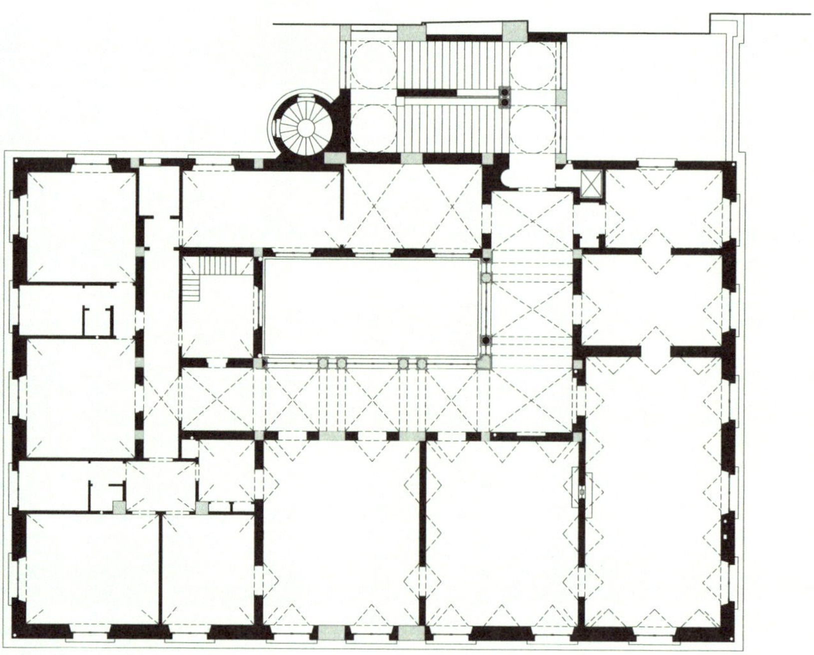

Scale 1:333

South façade

Transversal section

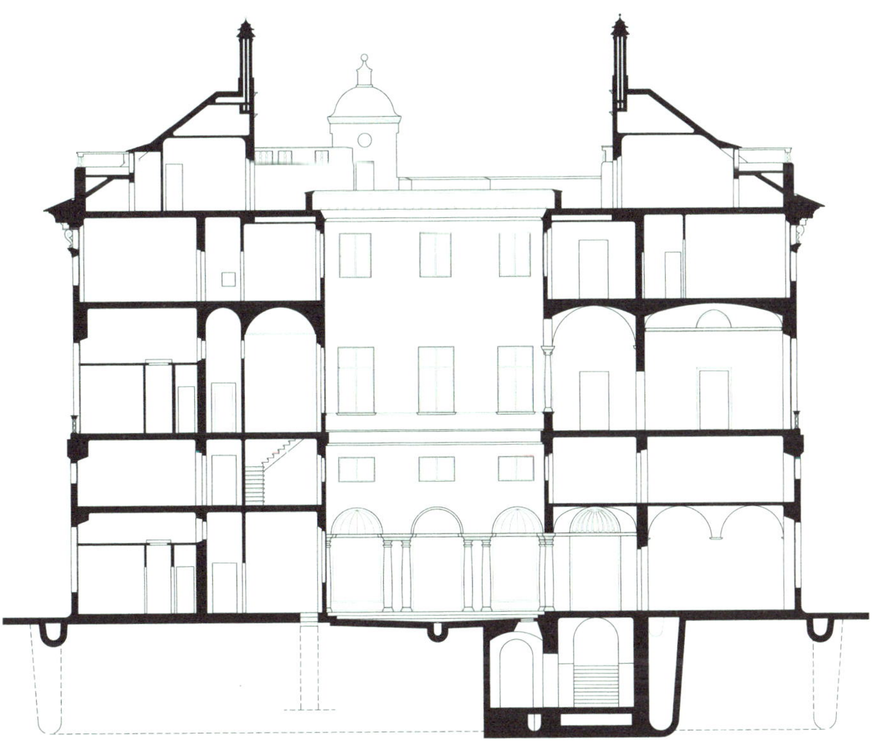

Palazzo Custo

The palace is located within the historical walls, on the site of the ancient Monastery of Santa Chiara (1644), variously transformed by, among others, Mario Labò. After the abandonment of the building and the municipal declaration of permission to build (1935), Giovanni Battista Custo sought the construction of a new structure under the supervision of the engineer Nicolò Custo. Given the panoramic significance of the site, two solutions were presented, one by Mario Labò and the other by Morozzo della Rocca. The latter was chosen for its "harmony" with the contemporary constructions of Piazza della Vittoria and Dante. The prominent position of the building, its visibility from the hilly areas, and the Bisagno plain would have made it a showcase for the capabilities of the enterprise.

The block has a rectangular plan and features two courtyards separated by a central body containing one of the two elliptical staircases serving the upper floors. Service and ancillary rooms overlook the courtyards, while representative spaces and master bedrooms face the external fronts, allowing for a uniform development of the façades visible from the street, characterised by an alternation of deep loggias and windowed surfaces. The rear façade is tripartite due to the presence of three columns of balconies in the central area. The building rises over six floors clearly articulated by the pronounced projection of the stringcourses, topped by a setback attic featuring three glazed verandas and concluding with an airy belvedere. The structure is composed of a load-bearing framework in reinforced concrete, with perimeter walls in split stone, a technique less common at the time of the building's construction, chosen to reuse material obtained from the excavation of a rocky area. Except for the grey granite base, the building is entirely clad in Verezzi stone, with slabs arranged in aligned joints, emphasising its nature as a pure facing.
Three portals provide access to the atrium. The central one serves pedestrian traffic, while the lateral ones facilitate the entrance and exit of automobiles, allowing passengers to disembark within the building.

The atrium, delineated through a subtly distorted, accelerated solid perspective, is arranged on three levels: at the lower level, two semicircular niches conclude its short sides, establishing a spatial axis orthogonal to the main entrance-stair axis. Upon reaching the first landing, the stairs split into two, proceeding orthogonally to the initial ramp until they reach the upper level of the atrium, divided into three bays. Four large marble pillars, paired with two each at the lateral openings, are closed toward the lower level of the atrium by two marble benches. Between the two groups of pillars, ground-level lights illuminate the vast space, accentuating the geometry of the surroundings. The transition from the atrium to the stairs is mediated by two spaces, distinct in shape and character. The left one is solid and enclosed, while the right one is linear and glazed, serving to reconcile the symmetry of the atrium with the asymmetric position of the stairs. The stairs wind in a spiral with fluid elegance; the elliptical shape of the enclosure is emphasised by the marble floor design, and the masonry parapet crowned with a wooden handrail accentuates the sinuosity of the spiral, while the windows mark the development of the ramp, adapting to its curvature.
With its structural masonry, stone cladding, the sculptural depth of the loggias, and the setback attic, the building anticipates the insights of Fernand Pouillon and exhibits some similarities with the contemporary works of Giovanni Muzio.

1. **ILVA building headquarters**
   Giuseppe Crosa di Vergagni | 1929–1930
2. **Galliera Hospital**
   Cesare Parodi | 1877
3. **Apartment building**
   Luigi Carlo Daneri | 1937
4. **Congregation of the Dominican Sisters Building**
   Giorgio Massardo and Giuseppe Fortunato | 1947–1949

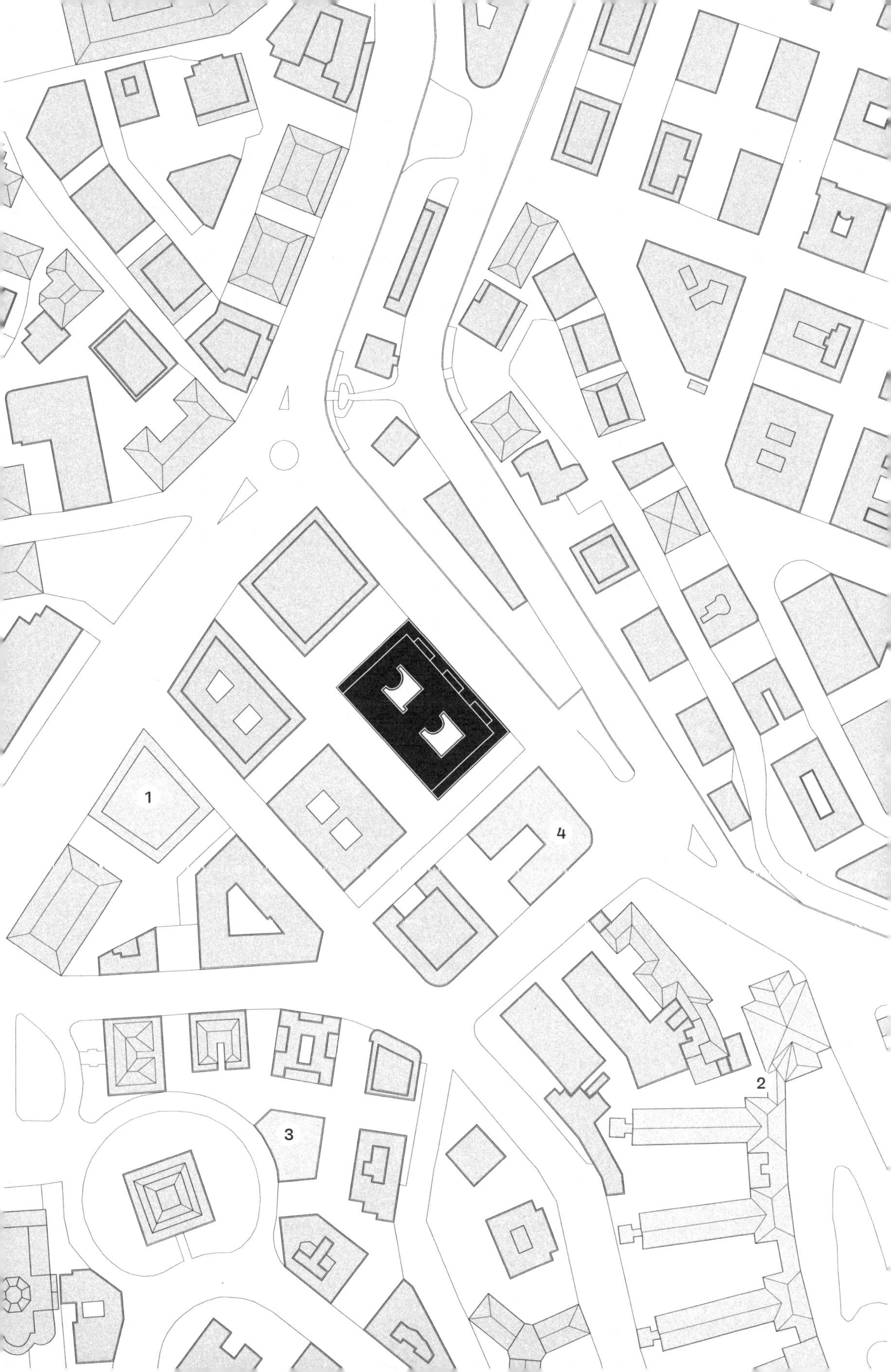
1
4
2
3

Ground floor plan

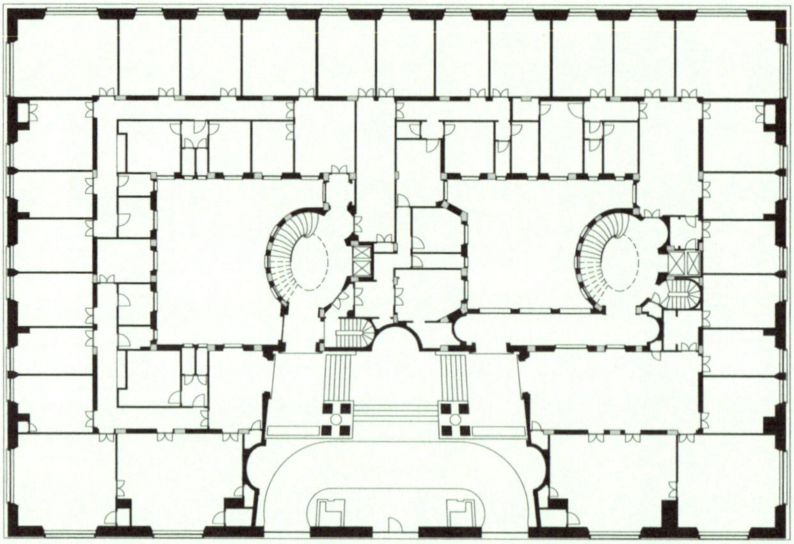

Typical floor plan

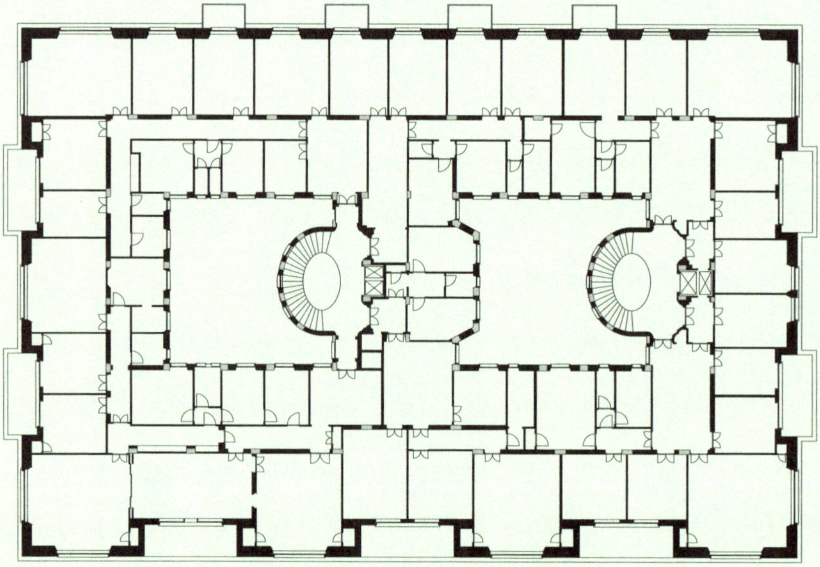

Scale 1:500

North-east façade

North façade

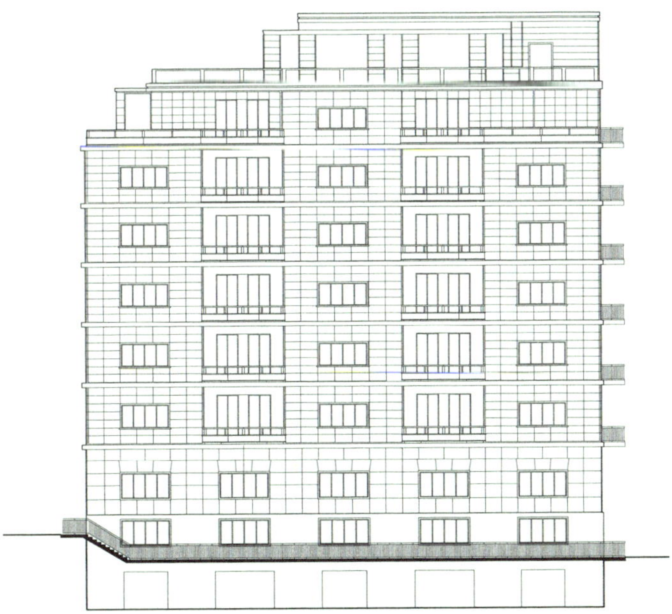

Scale 1:500

Palazzo della Flotta Lauro

1942–1950 Piazza della Nunziata, Prè, Genoa

The palace, commissioned by Nicolò Lomellini, who also sponsored the garden expansion in 1567, stands as an architectural testament to shifting ownerships and historical intricacies. Transitioning into the possession of Marquis Giacomo Durazzo, the edifice experienced a complex lineage in the 19th century, passing hands between the Durazzo and De Mari families.
Nestled within the urban fabric of the Strade Nuovissime, it occupies a pivotal position on Piazza della Nunziata, serving as a nexus between via Balbi (1601–1618) and via Nuovissima (via Cairoli, 1786). In its original conception, the palace represents a unique Genoese specimen, blending elements of 18th-century villa aesthetics into an urban context, where the animated mass of the structure is enlivened by two projecting bodies on the façade.

The ravages of bombing in 1942 and 1943 nearly obliterated the edifice. However, its remnants were safeguarded from complete annihilation until its acquisition by the Lauro Company, which spearheaded the reconstruction, a task initiated in 1949 and entrusted to Morozzo della Rocca by the new owner, shipping magnate Achille Lauro. The pre-war semblance of the building owes itself to late 19th-century modifications to an older structure, bearing vestiges of the 18th century. Morozzo della Rocca's design aspires to a stylistic unity within the entire urban ensemble, recognising the challenge of integrating a wholly new structure into the existing urban expanse. Hence, the decision was made to draw inspiration from the characteristics of the pre-existing structure, based on casts and surveys. In this context, Morozzo orchestrates a sophisticated endeavour, leveraging a profound understanding of ancient architecture as the foundation for a project that, while grounded in classical rules and criteria, ingeniously interprets the constraints. The outcome is a stylistic reconstruction that seamlessly integrates inventive elements into the overall building image, meticulously managing construction techniques and decorative features to blur the distinction between authenticity and invention.

The façade's original layout on the square is largely preserved, with a reconfiguration of shop openings to align with the rhythm of the windows above, alongside the conservation and restoration of the decorative ensemble on the upper floors. Nevertheless, novel elements are introduced, such as raising the ground floor and creating a new portal. A superstructure is added to the upper floor within the crowning frame, adapting it to its new office function while retaining its original features and harmonising it with the rhythmically aligned façades below. The project envisages advancing the main façade by one interaxial space, both to enhance the use of internal spaces and to mitigate the stifling effect of projections. Internally, a classically styled staircase unfolds in continuity with Genoese palace traditions, while at its centre, a grand circular hall capped by a dome constitutes the building's focal point. Within the same atrium, the frescoed ceiling is meticulously reinstated and the umbrella vault of the new atrium is adorned with a large fresco featuring angels and architectonic backdrops by Andrea Carlone. This artwork, recovered from the demolished Palazzo Grimaldi on Via San Luca, embellishes the stairwell that ascends to the top floor, open towards a patio adorned with walls featuring architecturally inspired decorations.

1. **Church Santissima Annunziata del Vastato**
   Taddeo Carlone with Domenico Casella and Giacomo Porta | 17th century
   Façade by Carlo Barabino | 1867
2. **Antonio Cattaneo Palace**
   Andrea Cerasola (Vannone) and Giovanni Battista Pellegrini | 1611–1785
3. **Giacomo and Pantaleo Balbi Palace**
   Bartolomeo Bianco | 1634–1638
4. **Gio Agostino Balbi Palace**
   Bartolomeo Bianco | 1618–1650

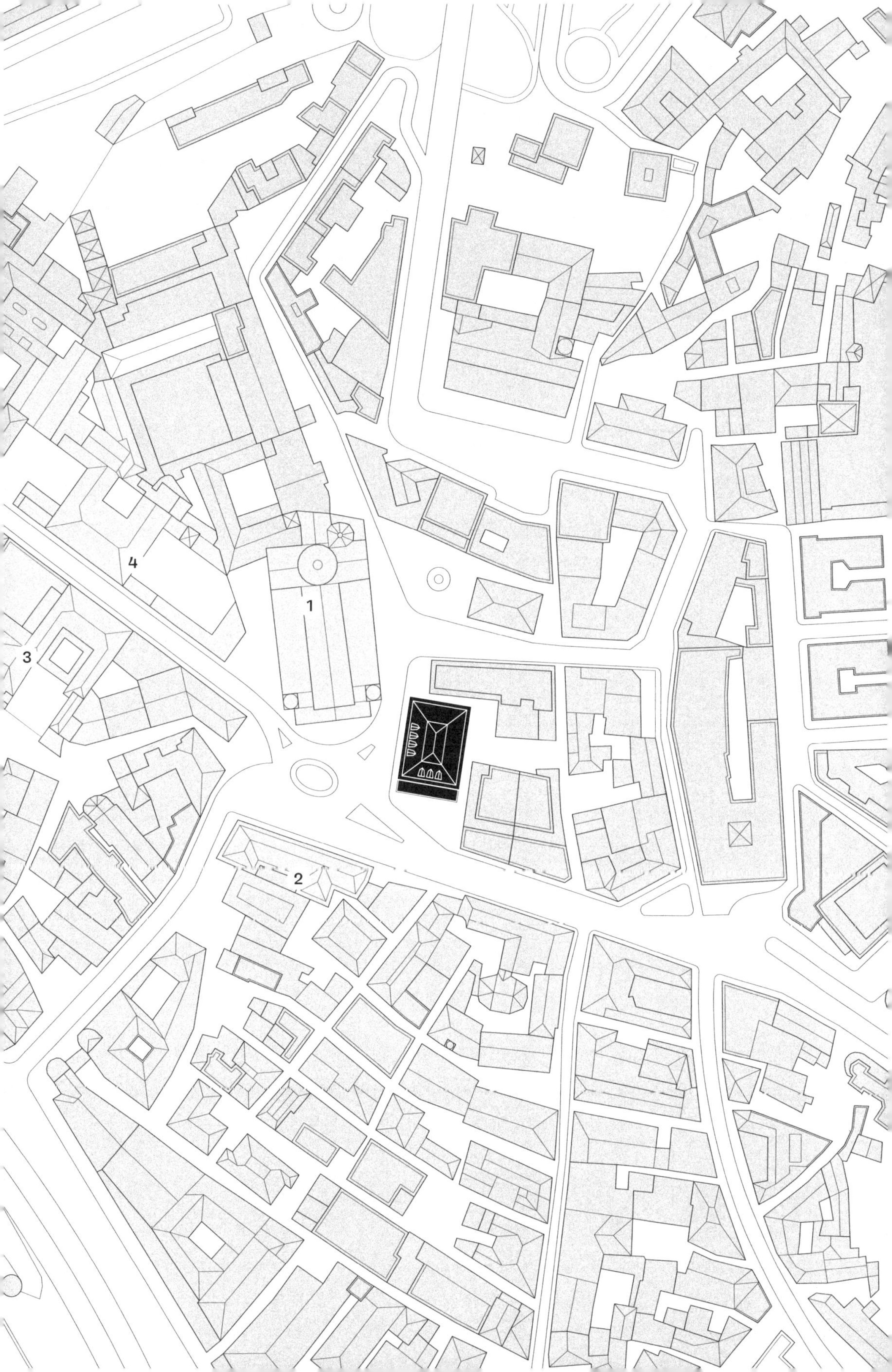
1
2
3
4

Ground floor plan

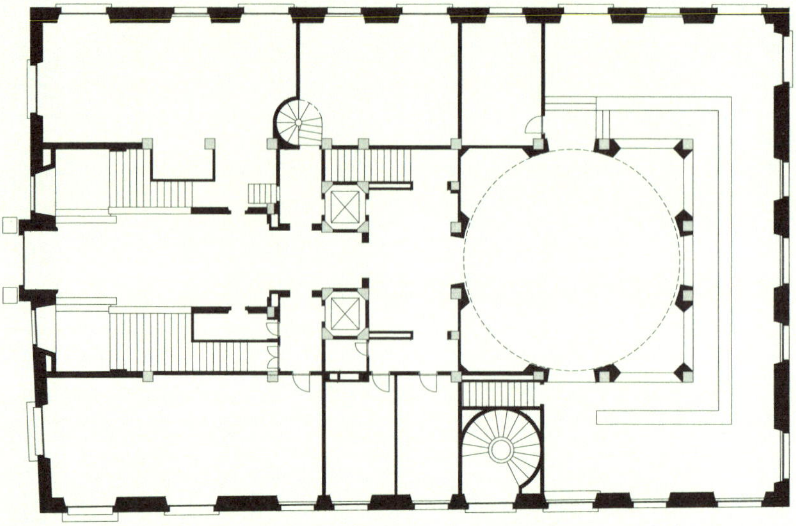

214

Third floor plan

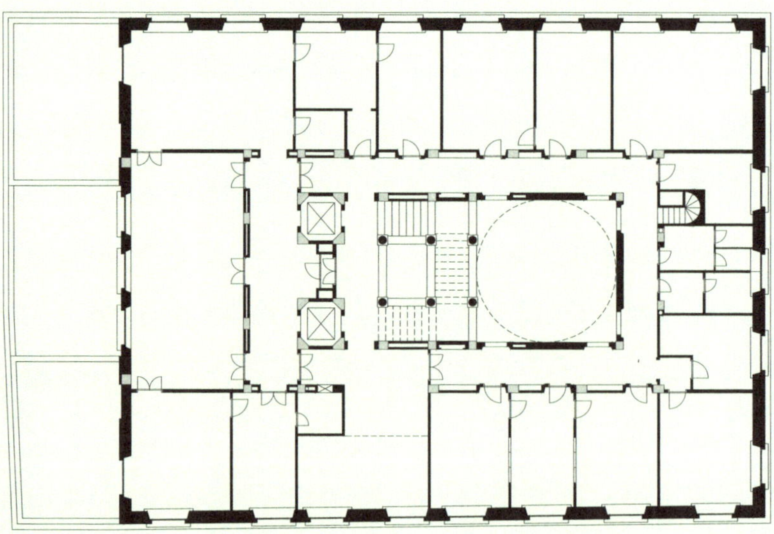

Palazzo della Flotta Lauro

Scale 1:333

West façade

South façade

Scale 1:333

1948–1953 (modified in 1962)
Via Giovanni Amendola, Albaro, Genoa

In 1947, the owner of the area located at the confluence of Via Piave and Via Amendola Guido Jester, commissioned Morozzo to carry out a feasibility study for a residential building. The purpose was to obtain the building permit and sell the area with an authorised project.

Adhering to the provisions of the Albaro Urban Plan and the Building Regulations, Morozzo developed several morphological studies, ultimately opting for a horseshoe-shaped plan. The building unfolds as a solid structure approximately nine metres thick, void at the centre, with a covered area of 375 square metres and a height of 15 metres. Asserting itself with a curvilinear profile, serving as the monumental terminus of the city block to which it belongs, the structure comprises four above-ground floors, with the raised ground floor designed to address the street's slope, and a terrace. The centrally located stair-elevator core serves two apartments per floor, totalling eight residences. These are characterised by a rational organisation of spaces, with the daytime zone adjacent to the core and the nighttime area with amenities along the internal perimeter. The structural framework is composed of reinforced concrete. The initial project included the construction of an underground cinema-theatre, which was never realised.

Morozzo develops various solutions for the street-facing façade as well. The first, presumably inspired by examples from the Genoese tradition, such as the Genoese Stock Exchange building designed by the Coppedè studio, alternates square windows with metopes of varied decoration. In this solution, the "modern" use of decoration exhibits similarities with other 20th-century buildings, particularly in Milan, such as Giovanni Muzio's Cà Brutta or the building on Via Euripide by Asnago and Vender. Another intermediate variant stands out by juxtaposing an opaque solid base with upper registers featuring continuous glass panels.

The area is subsequently sold to the Braggion company, which confirms the professional commission to Morozzo. In the execution phase, the building retains its original horseshoe shape but undergoes a radical transformation in its architectural expression. By 1950, the building is completed with the addition of a continuous perimeter loggia enveloping the entire surface of the upper structure, emphasising the plinth. In 1952, the Braggion company sells the underground garage beneath the building, constructed in place of the theatre, and the ground floor to Boero and Co. Between 1952 and 1953, the Boero company, again based on Morozzo's design, expands the ground floor by creating two wings on either side of the rear courtyard. In 1962, the Italpiave company, the new owner of the premises previously owned by Boero and Co., once again commissions Morozzo to provide a new design for the coverage of the entire courtyard, incorporating the two wings and transforming them from offices into a showroom for displaying automobiles. A glass enclosure is planned for the perimeter closure of the façades of the new wings.

Palazzo del Sole

1. Salvi Roncallo Building
Luigi Carlo Daneri | 1927

1

Mezzanine floor plan

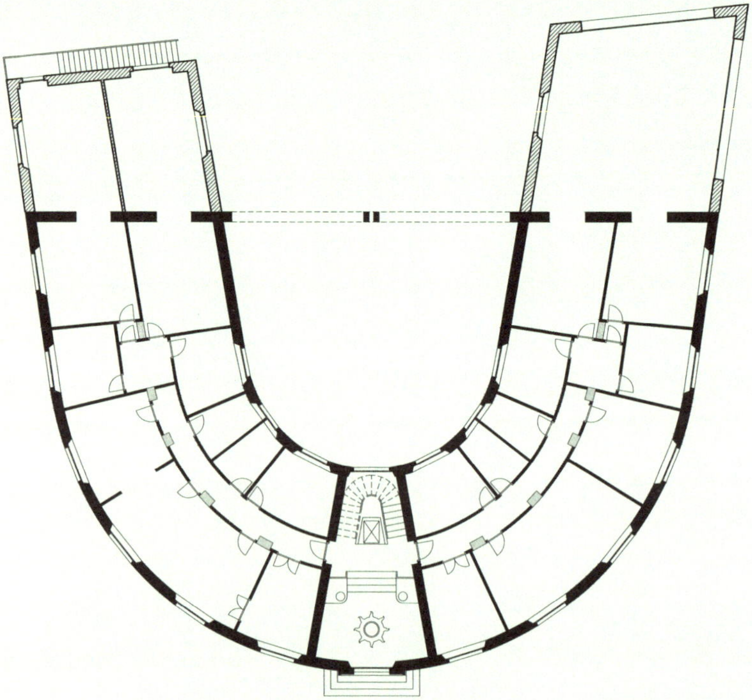

Typical floor plan

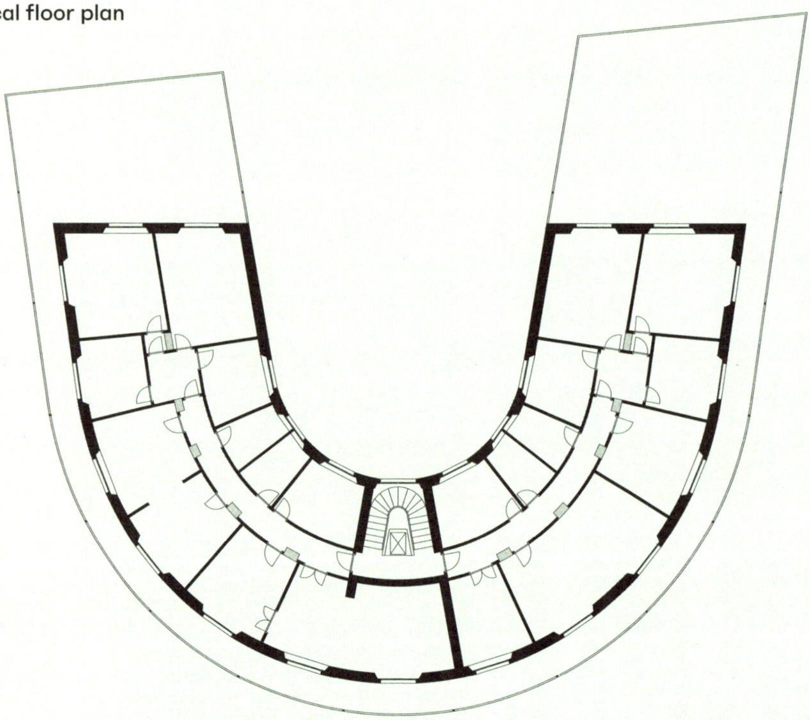

Scale 1:333

North façade

South façade

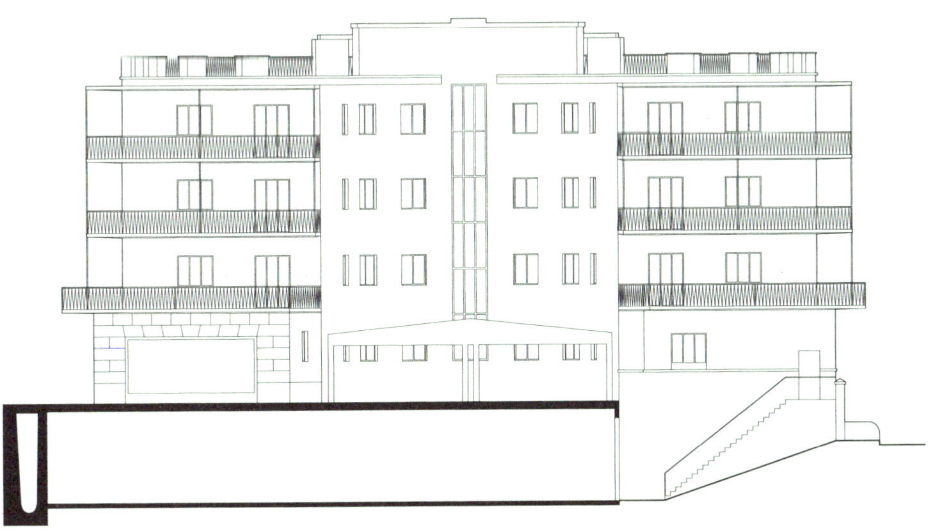

Scale 1:333

INA Casa District on Mura degli Angeli

Via San Bartolomeo del Fossato, San Teodoro, Genoa

1949–1951

The complex is situated on a rocky hillside in the western part of the city, upstream of the Lanterna, on a cliff overlooking the sea between it and the remains of the ancient walls of the last fortification built to defend the city. The site is the result of the cutting through of the San Benigno hill, ensuring the connection between the city and Sampierdarena to the west. In close proximity lies another INA district, Porta degli Angeli, designed by a group of professionals led by Luigi Carlo Daneri (1954–1956). The construction of the complex marks the beginning of Morozzo's work for the National Institute for Public Housing (INA Casa). Initially, the assignment was given to the group of architects composed of Enrico Castiglioni, Giovanni Battista Repetto, Aldo Morbelli, Robaldo Morozzo della Rocca and Gino Levi Montalcini.

Following a preliminary study, the INA Management entrusted only Morozzo and Levi Montalcini to continue the project. The entire complex consists of buildings constructed in two different periods. The project includes a group of buildings on the hillside, particularly exposed to prevailing winds, covering an area of 25,000 square metres for a total of 194 housing units. It comprises two groups of buildings completed at different times: the first, finished in 1951, consists of linear buildings with a maximum height of four floors. The second is characterised by a more articulated urban design, including a square, a church and equipped green areas.

The project is grounded in two fundamental concepts: shielding the area from the prevailing northern winds and preserving and enhancing the precious yet captivating vistas of the harbour and coastline. The final design develops out of these considerations: to safeguard panoramic views and sunlight for the rear buildings, the second phase was conceived with four tower structures, each eight storeys tall, spaced approximately 25 metres apart. The uniquely shaped towers, arranged in a fan-like fashion, gracefully extend towards the outermost edge of the precipice, counterbalanced by the linear building curtain of shorter structures located in the northern part of the plot. The tower arrangement frames picturesque views of the harbour and, from below, defines an iconic skyline that emerges from the surroundings.

The tower buildings, featuring a structural system of reinforced concrete pillars and beams with concrete slabs, adapt to the terrain's morphology, utilising elevation differentials for cellars and partial sub-levels. The row buildings, aside from partial cellar zones, leverage the terrain's slopes to create spaces characterised by pilotis, open to panoramic perspectives of the sea.

Adhering to INA's guidelines, the buildings are constructed with maximum economy in mind. The volumes exhibit articulation with expansive vertical surfaces, both opaque and fenestrated, and loggias to create a play of light and shadow. Areas not occupied by buildings are treated as public green spaces.

1. **Catholic church**
   Cesare Fera and Luciano Grossi Bianchi, | 1959–1965

2. **Housing units**
   Fermi and Felis | 1951

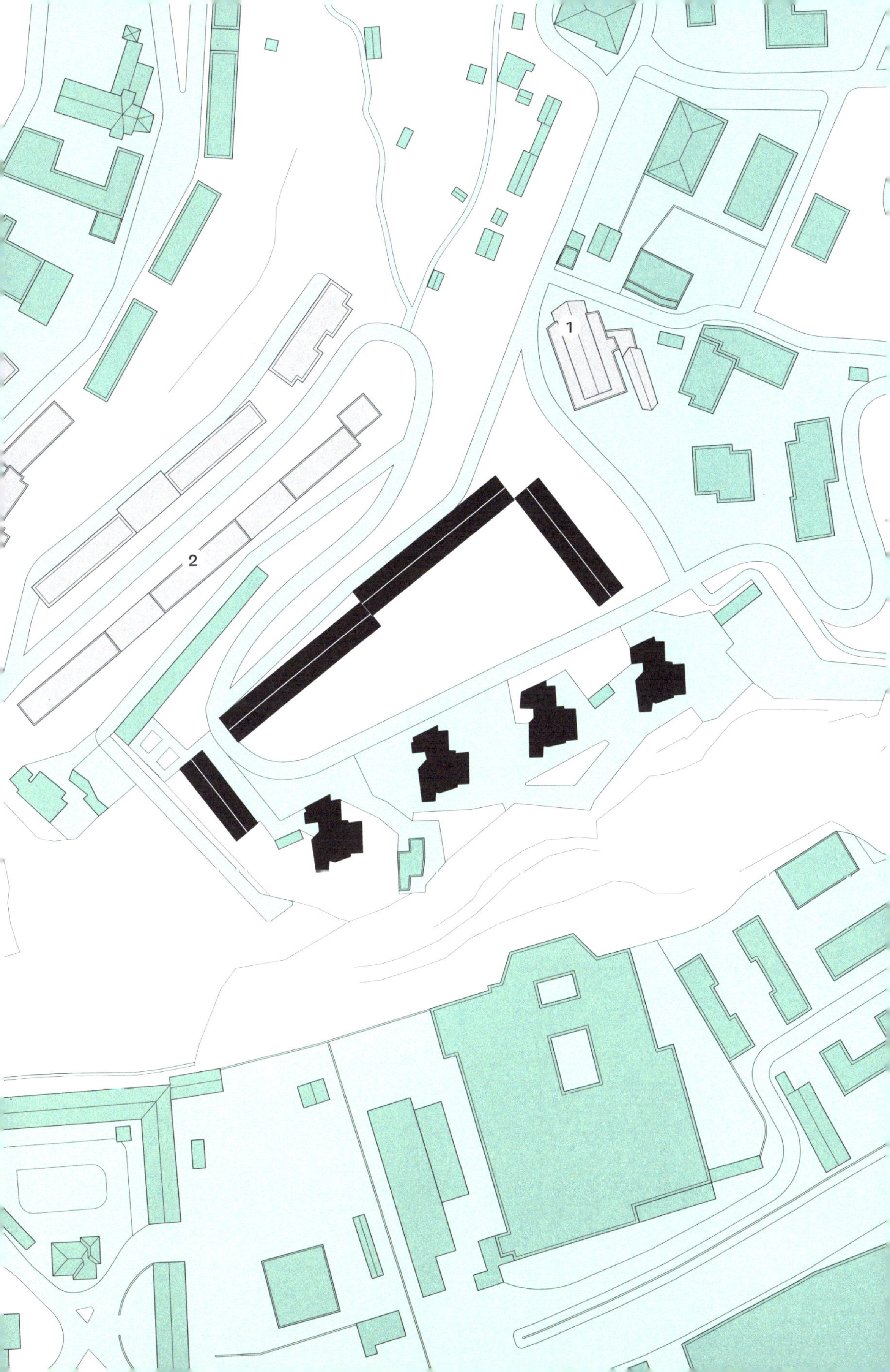
1
2

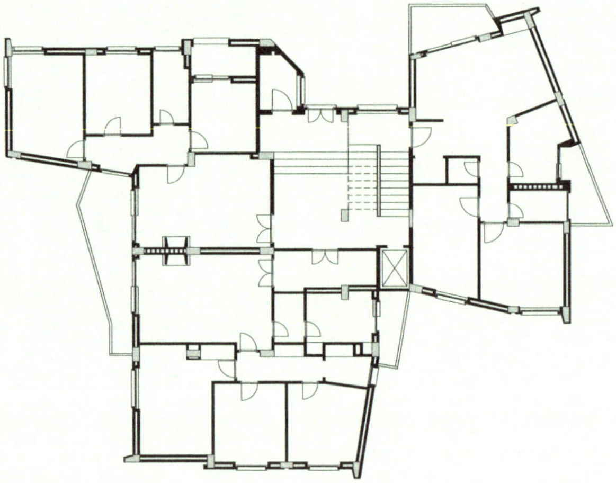

Tower, ground floor plan

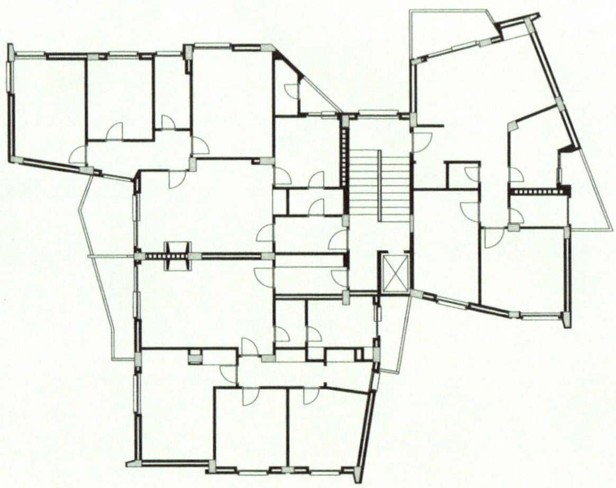

Tower, typical floor plan

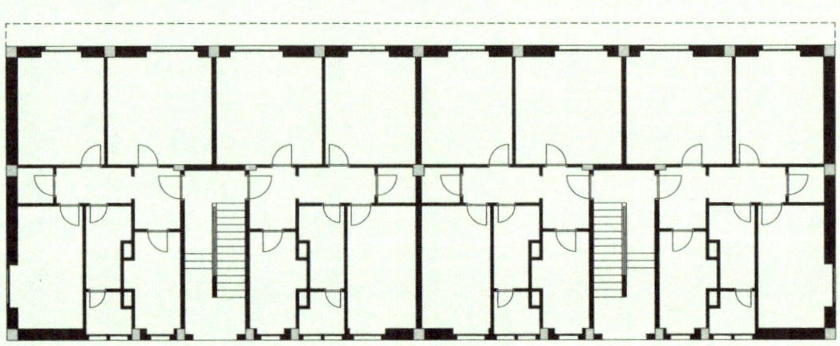

Linear units, typical floor plan

Scale 1:33

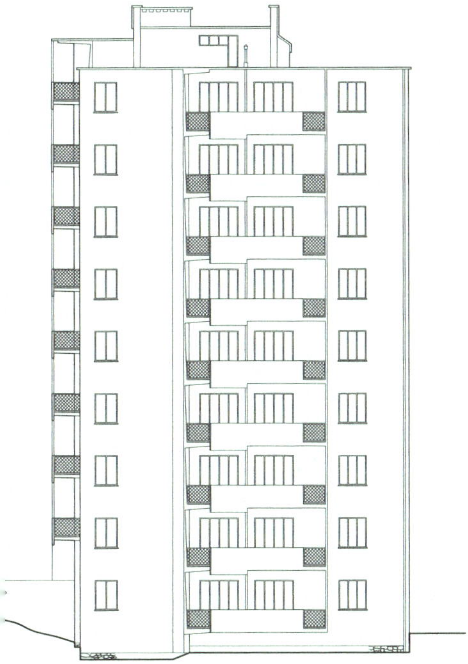

Tower, south façade

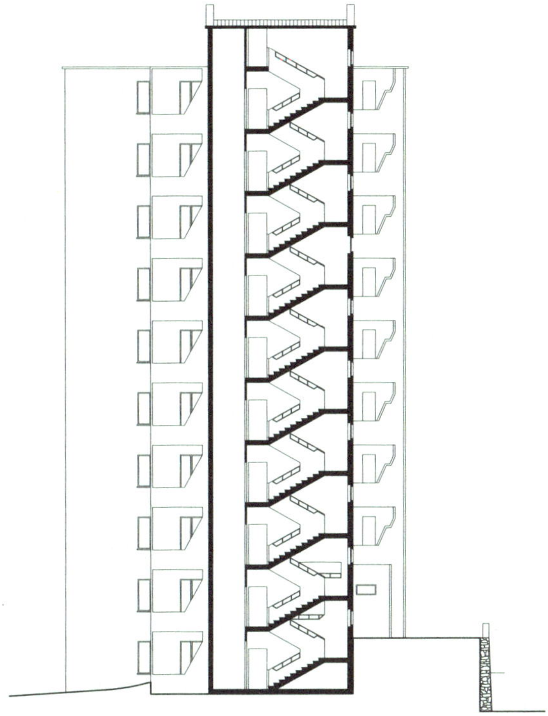

Tower, section

Linear units, south façade

Scale 1:333

Palazzo della Società Attività Ligure

1936 (1st project) – 1949–1952 (2nd project)
Via Mura degli Zingari, San Teodoro, Genoa

The building, subject to multiple internal reconfigurations, was originally conceived to house residences, offices and a hotel. It stands as the concluding backdrop of the parcel bordered by the vehicular routes of Via San Benedetto and Via Adua, adjoining the eastern side with the church of San Benedetto and delineating the western edge of the garden belonging to Palazzo Doria Pamphilj in Fassolo, a late Renaissance architectural structure designed by Perino del Vaga (from 1521, attribution according to Vasari) with transformations by Giovanni Ponzello (1594) and Morozzo (between 1936 and 1962). In this role, it forms an integral part of a unified monumental architectural complex. Morozzo della Rocca undertook the transformation of Palazzo Doria Pamphilj from 1936, with interventions both before and after World War II, aimed in part at addressing the damage incurred during the conflict in 1944. Since the mid-19th century, the surroundings of these buildings have undergone significant changes: the 16th-century walls between the sea and the palace were dismantled to make way for the widening quays of the harbour (1880), resulting in the separation of the palace from the sea and the loss of the garden uphill. The construction of both the railway (1854) and the Maritime Station (1930), along with the opening of Via Adua (1935), further contributed to the transformation of the area. In 1936, the construction company that had owned the area since 1924, Garbarino & Sciaccaluga, sold the plot to entrepreneurs Riccardo Parodi and Giovanni Baj, who commissioned Morozzo for the design of a new building. The final planimetric and volumetric choices were deduced after a prolonged and deliberative approval process, involving, among others, Gustavo Giovannoni (Superior Council of Fine Arts) and Luigi Vietti (Director of the Superintendence for Monuments in Liguria).

Given the numerous manufacturing constraints and the project's economic unsustainability, Parodi sold the area to the company Ansaldo in 1942. The project resumed only after 1945 when the new owner, the Società Attività Ligure, requested an extension of the project and confirmation of the building permit granted in 1939 from the Ministry of Public Education. In the revised design, substantial modifications were introduced compared to the original configuration, yet the concept of a volume characterised by a classical horizontal articulation was retained. Stretching nearly 100 metres, with a height of 20 and a width of over 30, the building consists of a main structure that bends to create a gentle convexity towards the west, and a lower body attached to the east, porticoed and staggered concerning the main façade to recompose a street front.

The austere and compact main volume, clad in pink Verezzi stone and marked by square openings, rests upon a rusticated six-storey basement, three of which are underground, with the others housing offices and residences. A crowning element of two floors concludes the top of the volume covered in White Finale Stone, characterised by an interplay of solids and voids. A terraced area on the north front regulates the relationship between the penthouse of the new building, the loggia of Palazzo Doria, and the church. The layout of the living spaces is resolved with the peripheral positioning of the representative areas and the opening of the deep volume through three small courtyards overlooking the service rooms and bedrooms. Two spiral staircases, similar but not identical, along with a trapezoidal one at the top, disrupt the regularity of the spaces, seemingly evading the rigour of rationalism to become elements of intimate expressive experimentation.

1. **Miramare Hotel**
   Gino Coppedè | 1908–1913
2. **Doria Pamphily palace**
   Perino del Vaga and Giovanni Ponzello | 1521–1594
   Transformations by Morozzo della Rocca | 1936–1962
3. **Church of Saint Benedict**
   Andrea Cerasola (Vannone) | 17th century
4. **Ponte dei Mille ferry terminal**
   Ludovico Biondi | 1924–1930

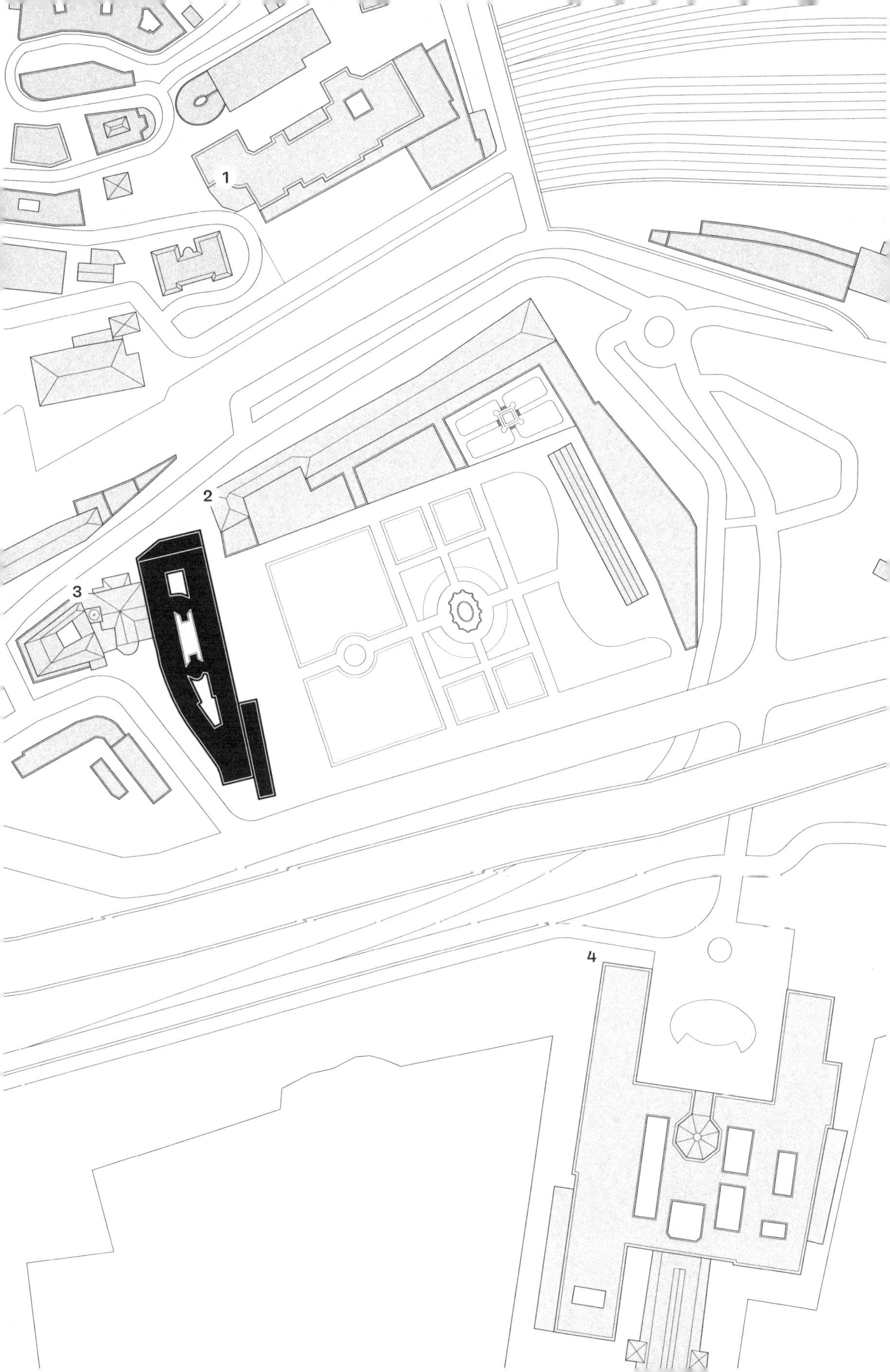
1
2
3
4

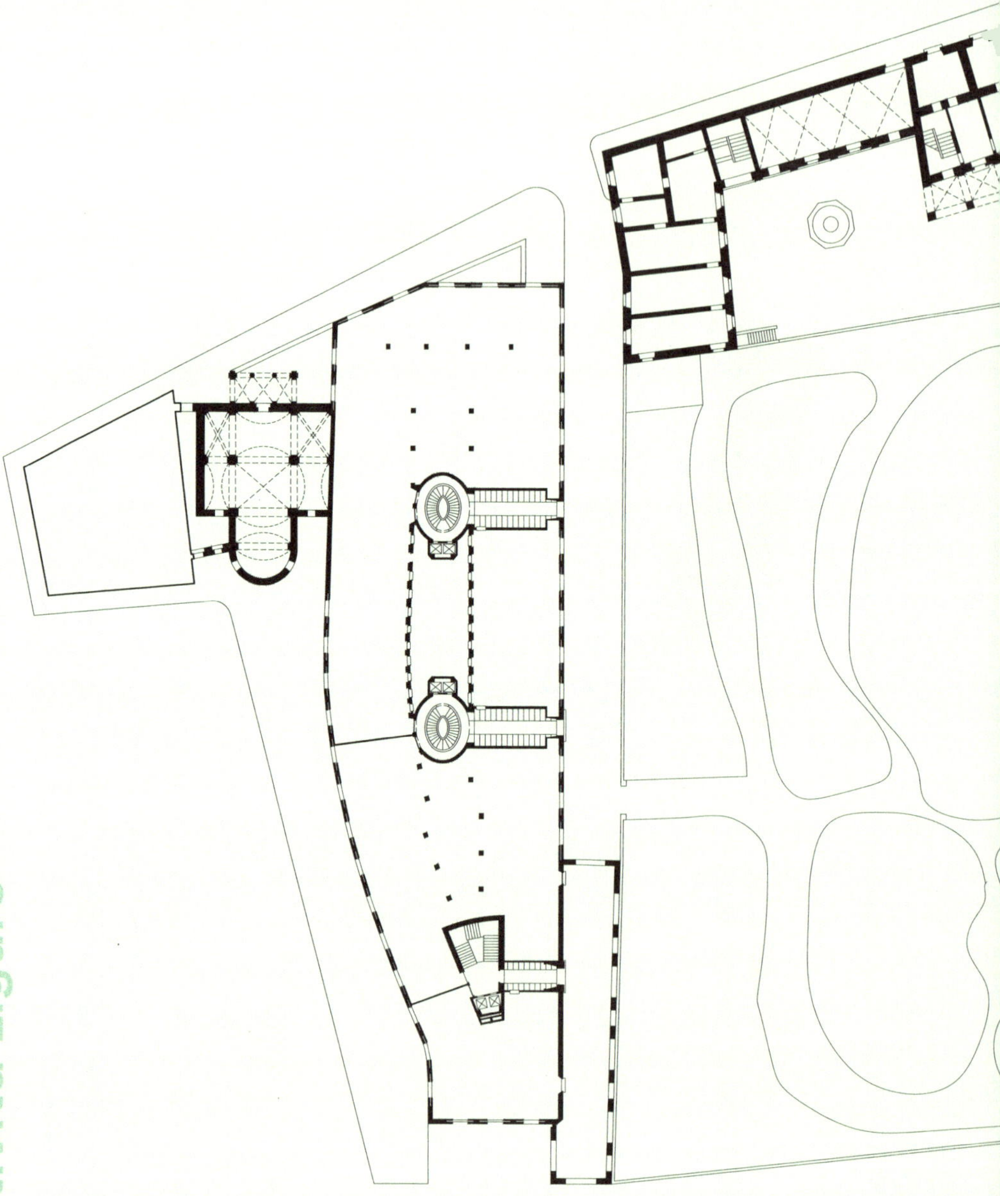

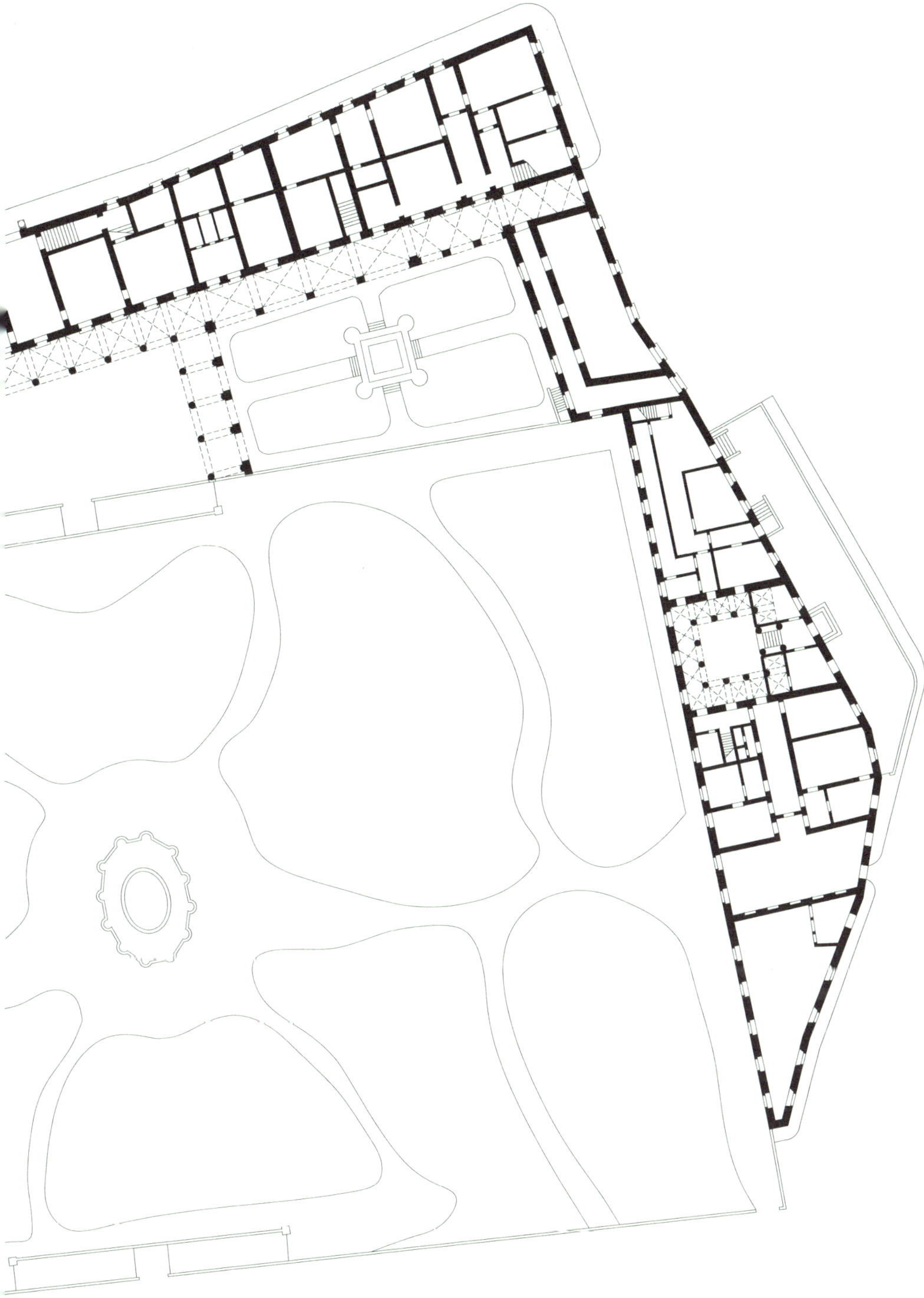

Monumental complex site plan

Scale 1:800

First floor plan

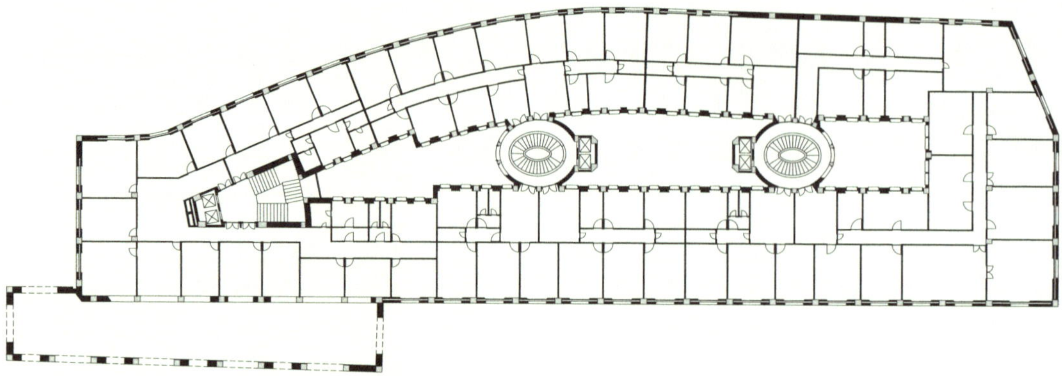

Third floor plan

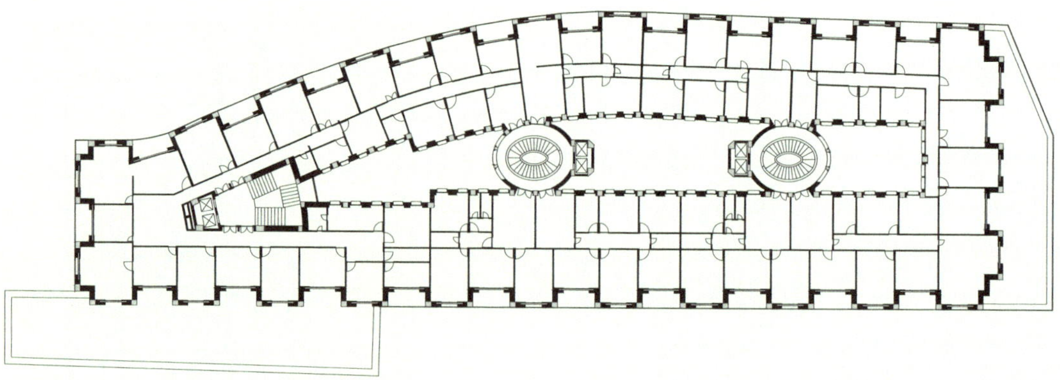

Scale 1:66

Vest façade

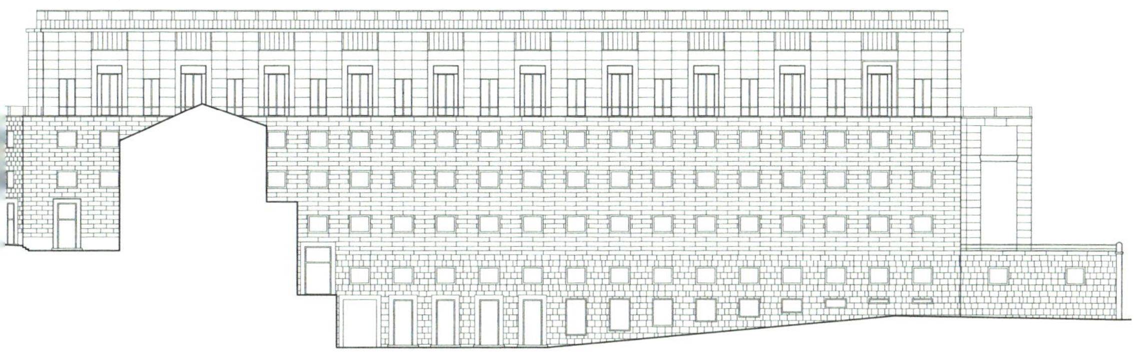

ongitudinal section

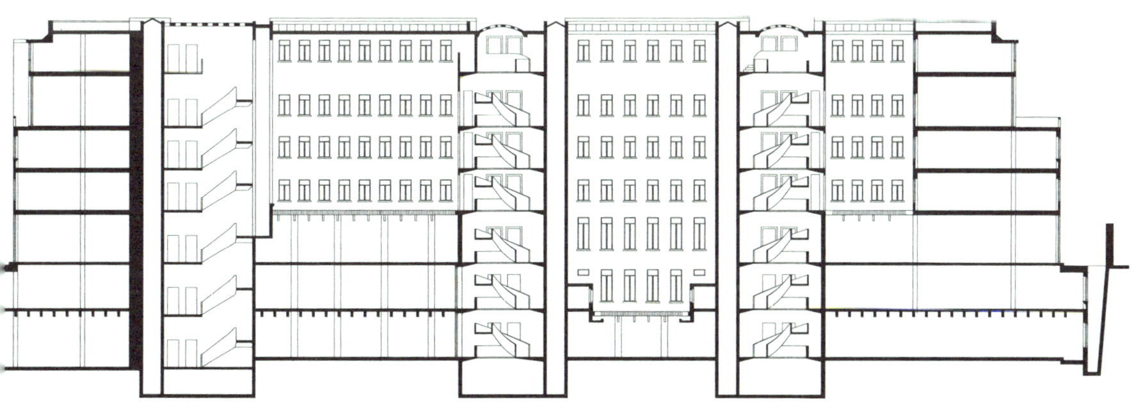

Scale 1:666

Palazzine Braggion

1949–1953 Via V Maggio, Quarto, Genoa

The two residential buildings were conceived for Mario Braggion, a post-war Venetian construction entrepreneur active in Genoa. The urban planning project pertains to an eastern suburban area, previously occupied by villas and gardens, which underwent significant speculative development operations in the post-war period. The two structures occupy an irregular and gently sloping plot. The land is situated opposite the Terme di Quarto, adjacent to the railway line, encompassed by Via Cinque Maggio and Via Carrara, within the vicinity of the former Villa Foroni.

In contrast to the aesthetic-lexical unity pursued by Luigi Carlo Daneri, around the same years, for the complex of buildings at Lido di Albaro (1952–1955), three blocks organised around a central void and adhering to the same syntactic register that imposes itself on the city in its declared rationalist orthodoxy, Morozzo counterposes the concept of *varietas urbana:* two collaborating yet distinct volumes, organised on “common ground”, differing in morphology, three-dimensional development, and façade design. Similar to what will occur later for the two villas in Arenzano, Morozzo intentionally creates a distinction between the two buildings, subtly reflecting the necessary aesthetic diversity of the historic city, producing an effect of variety in line with the aspirations of urban art. Indeed, the two buildings have fundamentally different characters and forms, based on a glossary of elements that make it almost challenging to attribute the authorship of the volumes to the hand of the same creator.

The building located to the north is based on an “absolute” geometric form: a compact volume, delineated from a triangular shape with truncated corners and the hypotenuse facing north, adjacent to the railway. The first building, on the other hand, has a composite form, not reducible to an elementary figure, where the absolute shape is “corrupted” by a series of deformations suggested by the context: a rectangle with a concave southern side and the opposite side “cut” by the railway line, incorporating an octagonal body containing the staircases.

Morozzo designs a single entrance for the complex, situated at the southwest corner of the plot, which, through a walkway and a double-ramped staircase, provides access to both buildings. Despite the speculative nature of the intervention, Morozzo does not forget the “bourgeois” embellishments of the entrances, richly elaborated, where the staircase characterises the perspective backdrop, dominating the “scene”. The west-facing building, positioned at a higher elevation, reaches a height of approximately eleven metres. The centrally located staircase, contained within the building’s “body”, serves two apartments per floor, totalling six residences. In addition to the three above-ground levels, there is a basement level serving as the building”s base. This lower level, housing cellars and technical rooms, protrudes on two sides and is clad in split stone, in contrast to the upper levels finished with plaster.
The eastern building has three above-ground levels that rest on a semi-basement plinth containing garages, annexes and technical rooms. The octagonal staircase serves a single apartment occupying the entire first floor and two separate residences on the upper levels, totalling five apartments. The apartments are characterised by an enclosed loggia with a sinuous bay window, reminiscent of that at Villa Ollandini, artistically carved through the breaching of the façade facing the sea. The buildings, constructed with an in-situ cast reinforced concrete structure, maximise the potential offered by the post-war Italian “craftsman-style” construction site.

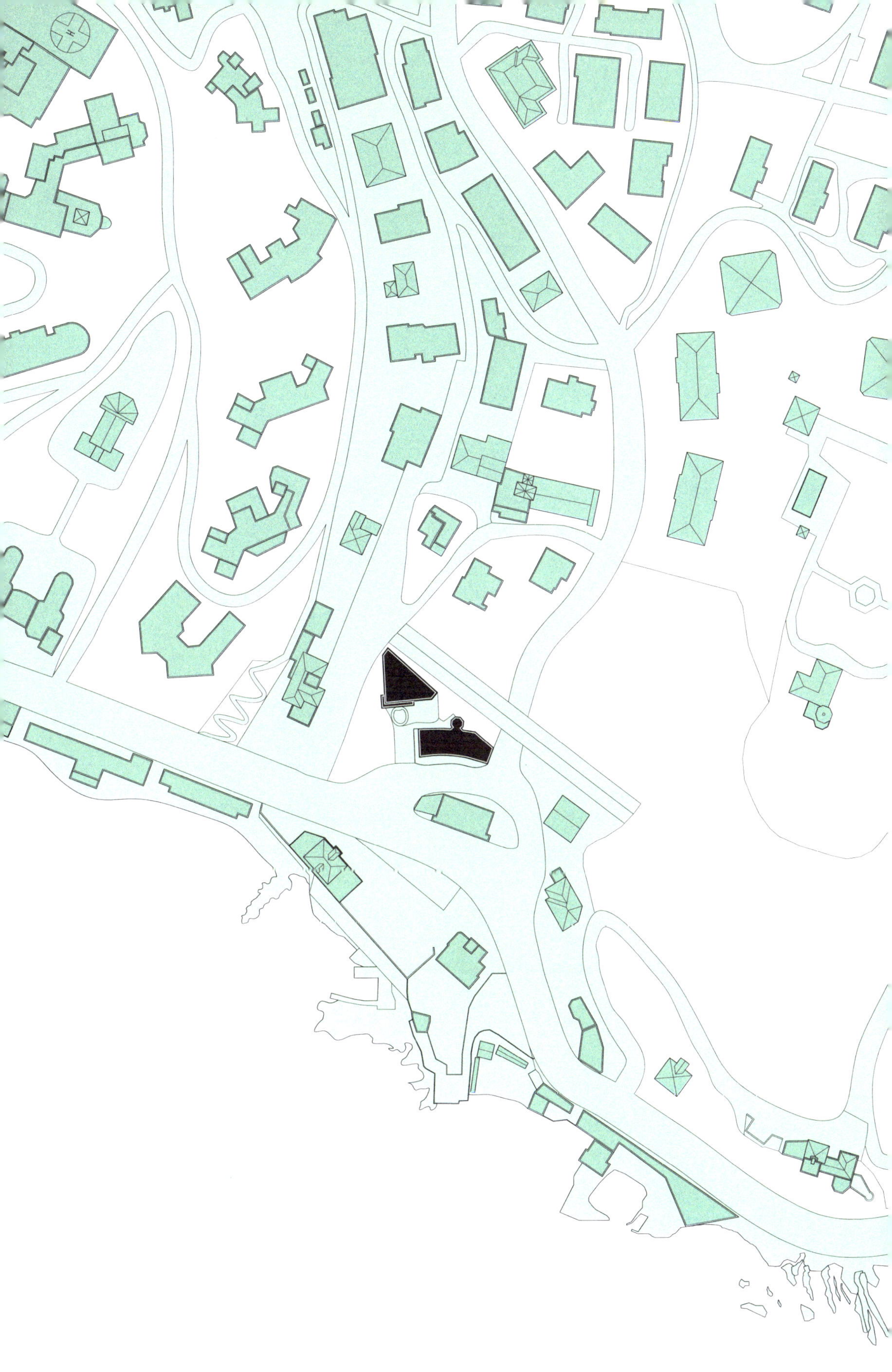

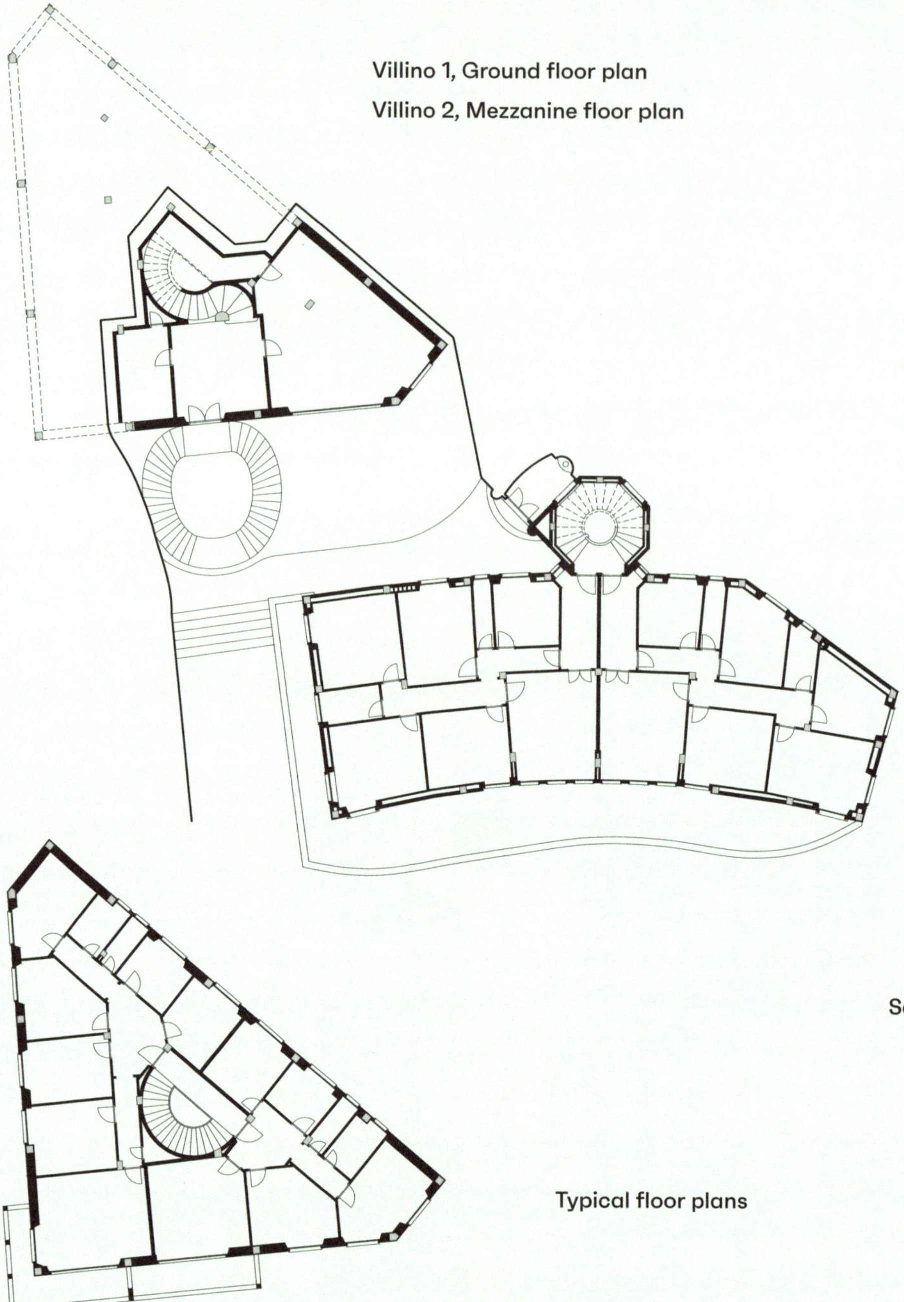

Villino 1, Ground floor plan

Villino 2, Mezzanine floor plan

Scale 1:333

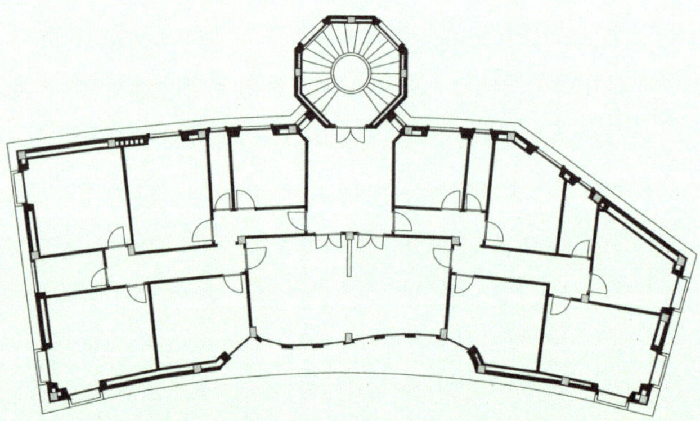

Typical floor plans

Villino 1, South façade

Villino 2, South façade

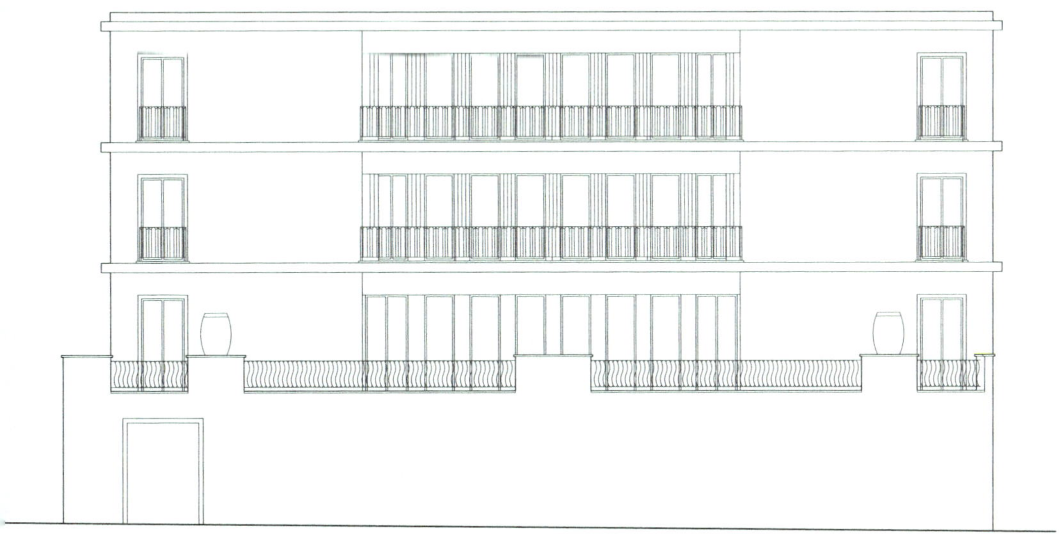

Scale 1:200

Palazzina Vitruvio

The building is situated on the hairpin turn of Via Pozzo, adjacent to the Sanguineti building (1953–1958) designed by Luigi Carlo Daneri, both overseen from above by Paradisetto, the gentrified residence constructed by the same Morozzo Podestà of Genoa, the Marquess Bombrini. The edifice crafted by Morozzo for the Vitruvio Building Society is characterised by a calligraphy that harmonises seamlessly with the surrounding environment. The result of an extended gestation period, during which the rationalist orientation gives way to a neoclassical language, the building references the regulations of the Albaro Urban Plan and mirrors, both in programme and typology, the model of the bourgeois apartment building.

The volume is nestled into the steep profile of the hill through a base that houses the entrance to the residential floors and service functions: an atrium, two lofted garages, one facing north and the other south, warehouses, machine rooms and the porter's apartment. The atrium features a floor of Collemandina red marble; the walls are clad in polished Botticino slabs; the ceiling is plastered with light stucco profiles. Dominating the centre of the entrance is the staircase modulated with treads in Botticino and risers in red Collemandina marble, inlaid within the Botticino framing that extends to the sides. On either side, two bases support ornamental sculptural compositions. The compact base against the hill, containing the entrance, is surmounted by a rectangular body of four floors, with two apartments per floor, each equipped with a balcony. The building is enclosed by a pitched roof. From a planimetric organisation perspective, the sleeping and service areas are distinctly separated from representational areas. Within the volume, following the course of the road, the main bedrooms and service rooms are orientated towards the southeast side, while the living room, lounge and kitchen face northwest.

The apartments feature light marble floors in the entrances, while prestigious rooms boast red, green, or yellow marble. Bedrooms are adorned with wax-polished herringbone-patterned oak parquet floors, while service areas feature large, uniformly grey-toned terrazzo. The bathrooms and toilets are adorned with glass mosaic.
In accordance with the regulations, the building reinterprets traditional Genoese architectural elements, ensuring its appropriate integration into the local urban context. The main façades, in particular, harken back to tradition in terms of layout and materials used for cladding. The main façade is divided into three parts, with double registers of superimposed loggias at the ends, framed by robust corner pilasters. The central zone, punctuated by four windows per floor, contrasts with the shadows cast by the lateral balconies.
Following a scheme deeply rooted in the local villa tradition, the hierarchy of the parts is unified through the use of the same stone favoured by Robaldo Morozzo and extensively employed in both preceding and subsequent works. The plinth and string courses are crafted from slabs of pink Verezzi stone, while the pilasters and lintels forming the lateral loggias are clad in slabs of white Finale stone. The central body's wall and the rear walls of the loggias are coated with "Fulget" plaster, a granulated yellow Siena marble compound.

1. **Villa Il Paradisetto**
   Robaldo Morozzo della Rocca | 1935
2. **Palazzina Sanguineti**
   Luigi Carlo Daneri | 1953–1956
3. **Monastery of the Sacramentine Sisters**
   Giuseppe Crosa di Vergagni | 1955
4. **"Il Paradiso" or Villa Saluzzo Bombrini**
   Andrea Vannoni | late 16th century

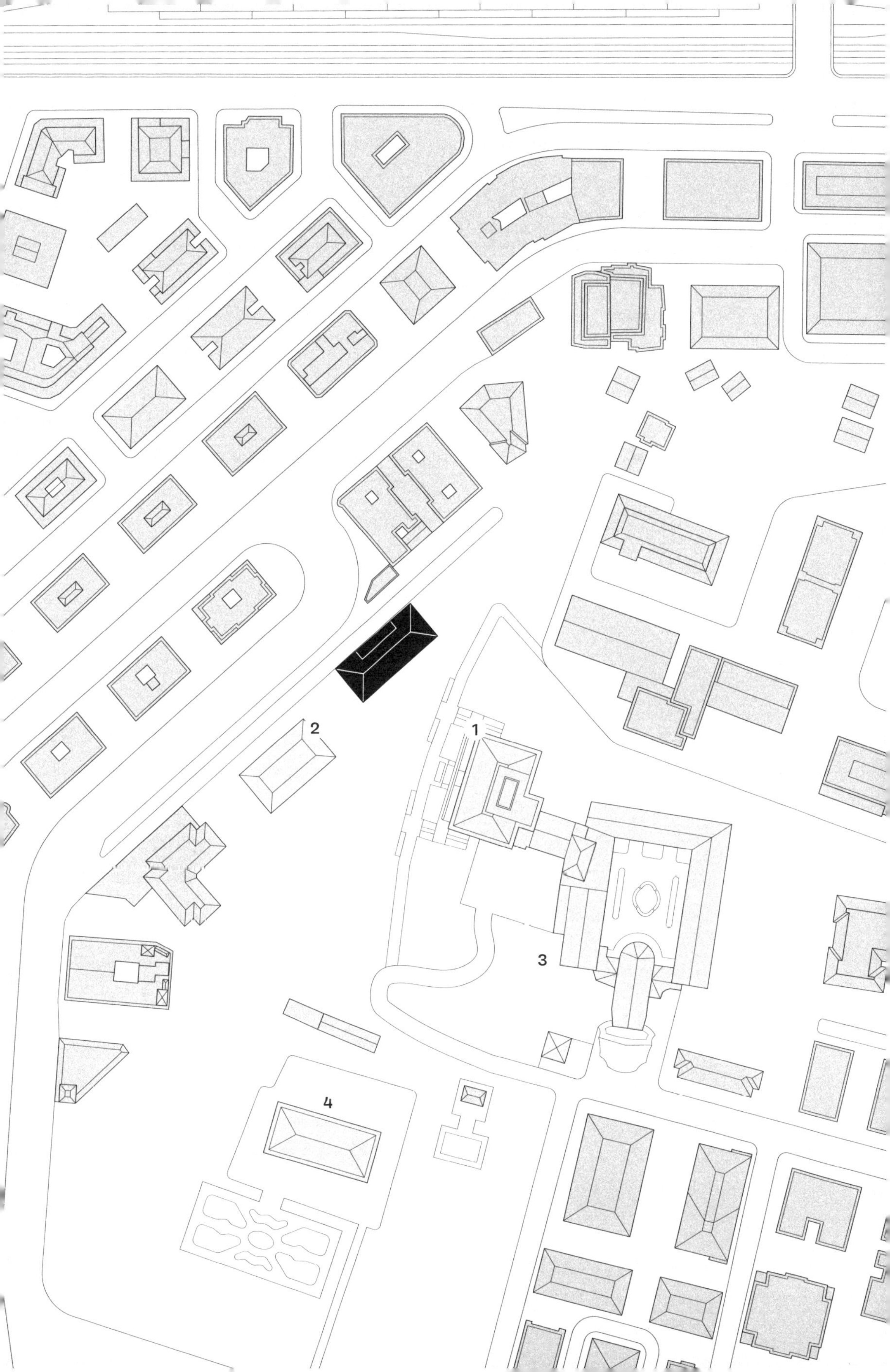
1
2
3
4

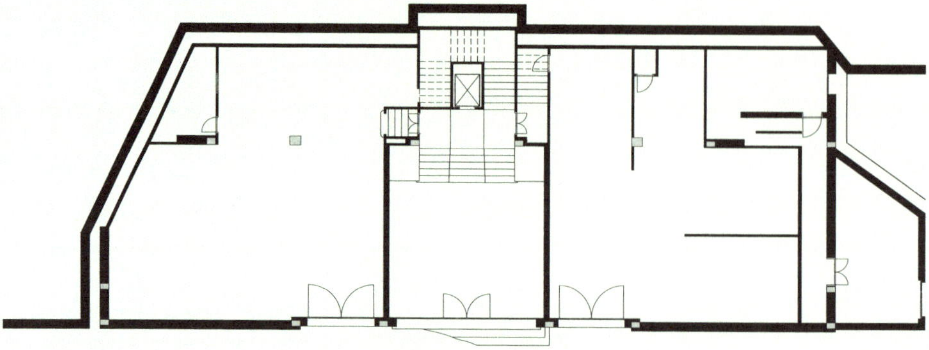

Ground floor plan

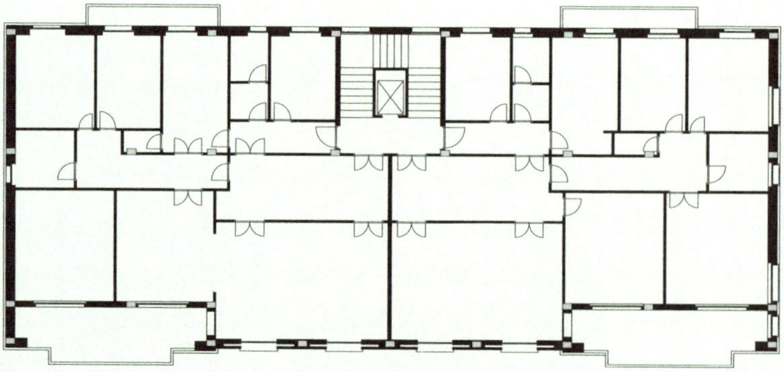

Typical floor plan

Scale 1:333

West façade

East façade

Scale 1:333

Palazzina Ollandini Hoffer (*Pianoforte*)

1953–1956 Via San Vito, Albaro, Genoa

The building stands within a densely populated context, in the late 19th to early 20th-century expansion area of Albaro, a raised plateau in the eastern part of the city sloping towards the sea, beyond the perimeter of the historical walls. It is intricately tied to the traditional representation of a villa residence, a space where the needs of both agrarian and urban life coexist. In the 20th century, with the elitist adaptation of aristocratic vacationing to the real estate market, the area was earmarked for prestigious residences and tourist-sporting infrastructure. The building occupies the site of the Church of San Vito, dating back to the 11th century. After its abandonment in 1879, it was purchased by the Genoese shipowner Raffaele Rubattino and his wife Bianca De Simoni Rebizzo, who transformed it into their residence in a castle-like form, in keeping with the typical Neo-Gothic taste of the period. Following Rubattino's death in 1881, the property passed to his cousin Selene Gavino, the daughter of Rubattino's uncle. She first married Marchese Gerolamo Ollandini and later Rodolfo Hoffer, the financial director of the shipping company. The castle remained unchanged until 1942 when it was destroyed during a bombing raid. In 1948, Marchesa Ollandini and her husband decided to construct a building on the site of the castle, capitalising on the manufacturing opportunities offered by regulations, creating a structure distinct from its predecessor but capable of evoking its memory. The plot falls outside the purview of a Controlled Master Plan but under a deed (Ghersi), as part of the Bonifacini – De Ferrari subdivision, dated 1949 and based on the Gavino-Comune di Genova covenant. The plot concludes the long axis of Via Trento, occupying a prime scenic position with the best exposure to the sea, becoming both the prominent element of a panorama and a vantage point to enjoy the view. The irregular geometry of the area and regulations regarding setbacks in relation to vertical development constrain the planimetric and volumetric characteristics of the project: a seven-storey volume with a surface tapering from bottom to top, featuring two apartments per floor in the lower levels and one on the uppermost floor. Characterised by a distinctive silhouette resembling a grand piano, the building derives from a quadrangular plan with an edge cut by a curved line. In elevation, this gives rise to a sequence of steps, receding upwards, marked by the sole string courses that surpass the glass façade. Two sides of the prism are finished with plaster, and the third exhibits irregular courses of split stone elements resembling strips. The building represents an exceptional achievement, stemming from the villa type and capable of imbuing significance into a speculative model. The dichotomous treatment of the façades, juxtaposing the rusticity of stone against the rationality of the large glass pane, merges antiquity and avant-garde into an unparalleled unity. The stone-clad envelope facing the city suggests an idea of an unfinished ruin that conceals the bedrooms and services, opening up with windows of moderate width. The living spaces face south and west, open to the gulf through the expansive glass surfaces. The reinforced concrete framework is concealed within the walls of Finale's stone quarries, while it is left exposed near the curvilinear façade. Unlike typical buildings, still tethered to the concept of an urban palace with a solid façade, the structure nods to both American models, from which it derives the dynamic use of bay windows, and Renaissance models, not so much in form but in the relationship between the building and nature.

1. **Apartment building with Cinema**
   Luigi Carlo Daneri | 1948–1951
2. **Apartment building**
   Piero Gambacciani | 1954–1956
3. **Church of Saints Peter and Bernard**
   Lorenzo Castello | 1958–1970
4. **Apartment building**
   Angelo Invernizzi-Ettore Fagiuoli | 1930–1935

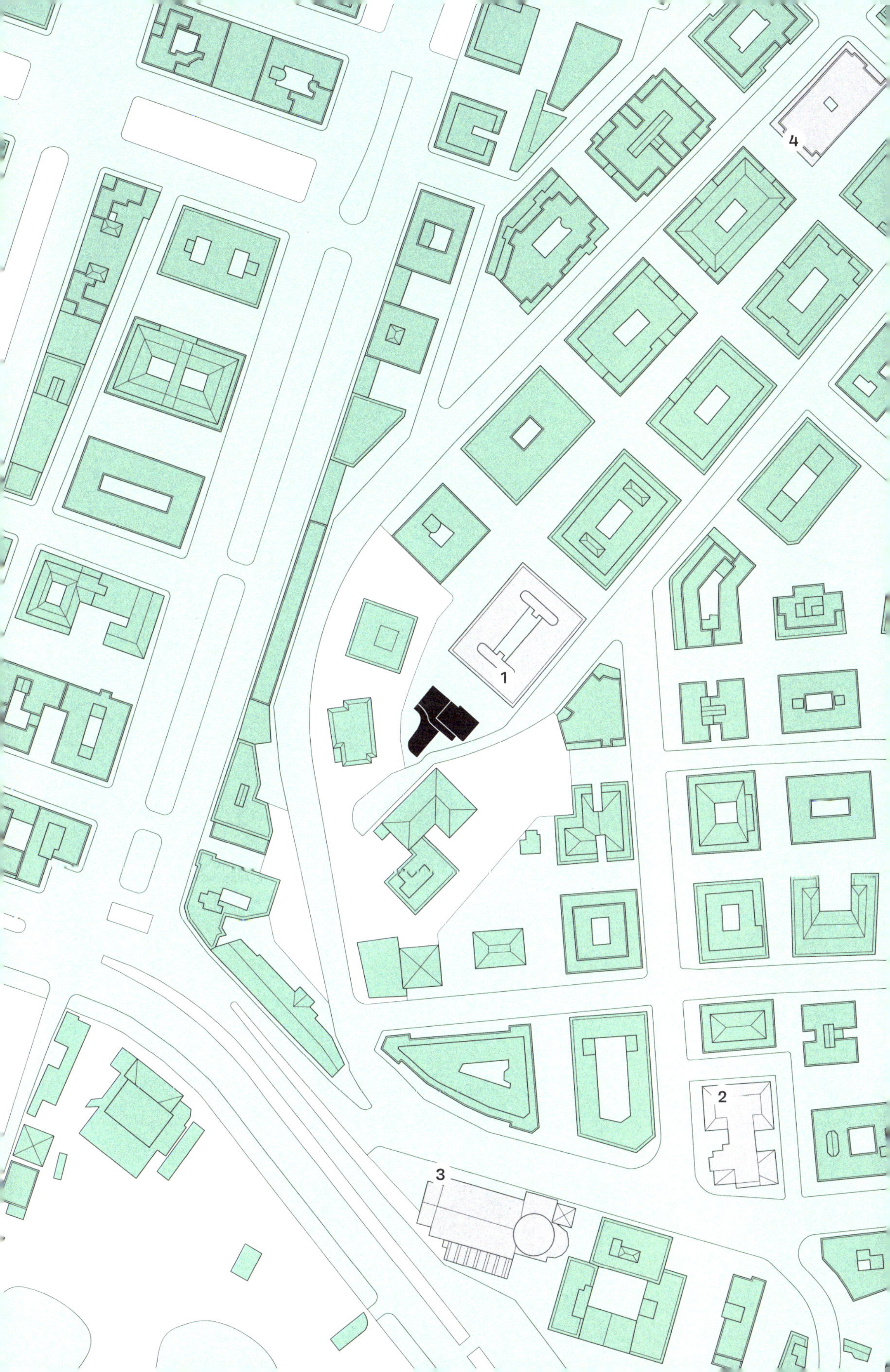

4
1
2
3

Ground floor plan

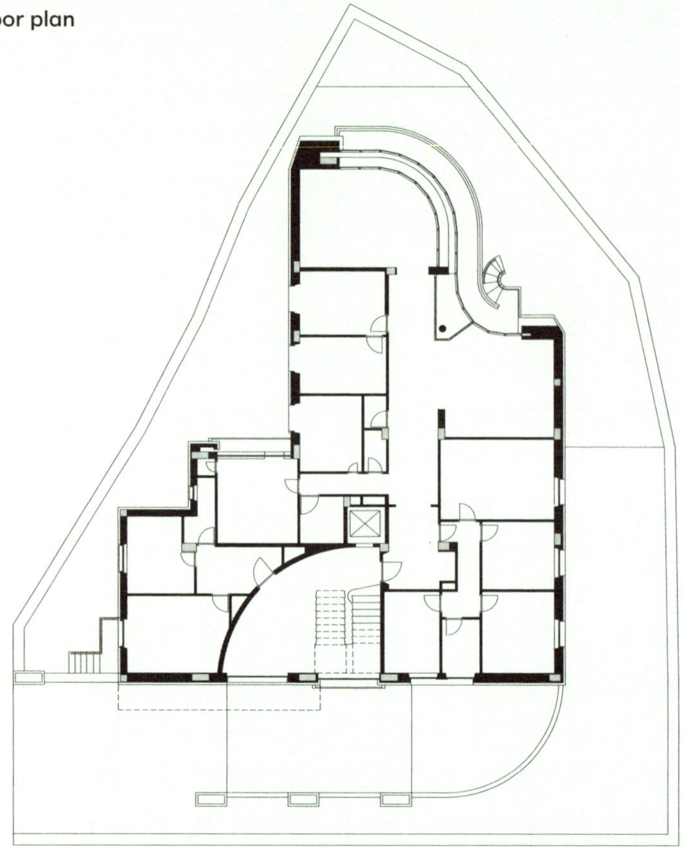

Attic floor plan

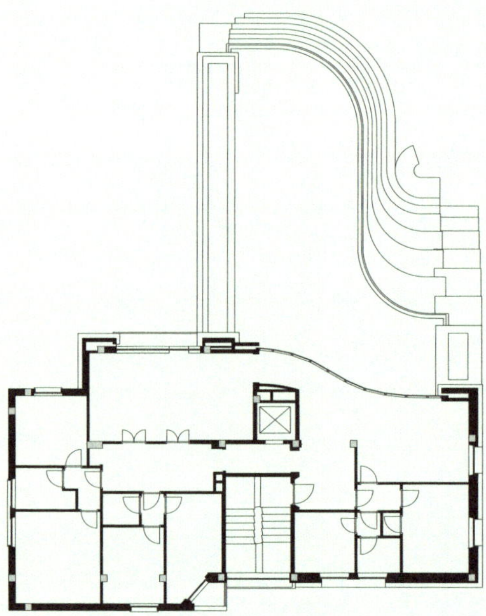

Scale 1:33

outh façade

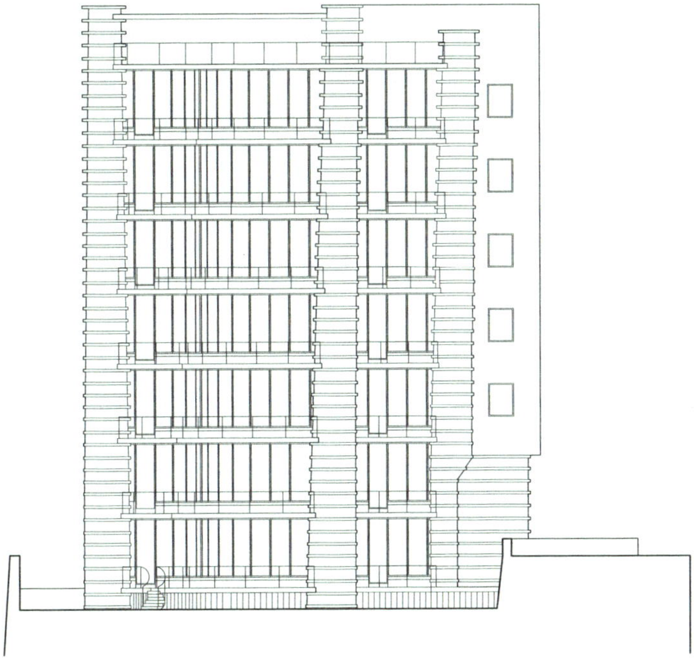

Vest façade

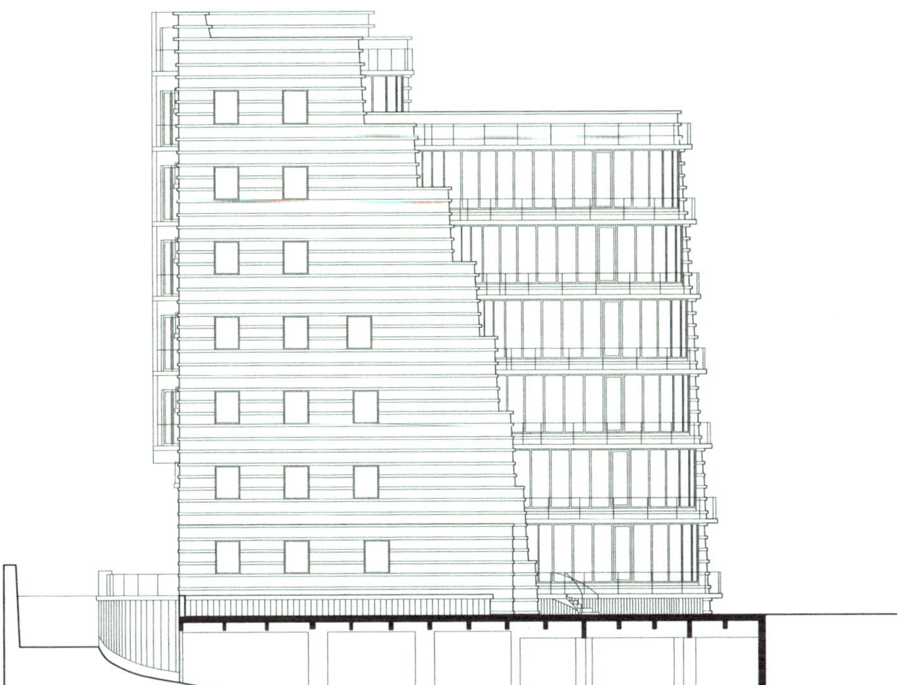

Scale 1:333

Palace of the National Insurance Institute (INA)

The building hosting residences, offices and shops is part of the transformations outlined in the Detailed Plan of Piccapietra, the result of a protracted debate on the redevelopment of this area within the 16th-century walls. The plan envisions the creation of twelve lots, the transformation of certain monumental buildings, and the construction of new mixed-use volumes. In 1955, the National Insurance Institute (INA) announced a competition for the construction of Areas I and IV of the Plan, attracting participants such as Ignazio Gardella and Albini-Helg, the latter emerging as winners of Lot IV. The competition imposed stringent rules regarding location, surfaces, elevations and functions. Morozzo entered the competition for both areas, winning for Area I. For Area IV, he proposed a complex consisting of different volumes: interlocking houses, a lower body and an office base, ground floor shops, and an easternmost body designated for a hotel, small apartments and services. The winning solution for Lot I derived from the rules of the plan but, above all, Morozzo demonstrated the ability to translate regulatory rigidity into a figurative opportunity. He created a plinth composed of a double-height portico for shops, topped by a narrower intermediate section for offices and an upper volume for residences. The schematic nature of the competition proposal, interesting for certain solutions such as the winter garden on the eastern façade, gave way to a more organic solution. The construction, carried out by the Gagliano company from Turin with the collaboration of architect Dante Datta, annexed a hall from the church of Santa Marta. The dichotomy between the main and secondary fronts persists, as does the analogy between the end elevations: the horizontality of the eastern façade is juxtaposed to the grid of the western one. On the short fronts, the two wings are brought close together and inflected, creating a central fissure.

The building's section has a root that extends throughout the lot. The differences in elevation between the opposite ends of the area suggest the introduction of a gallery not prescribed by the plan. This solution draws inspiration from Carlo Barabino's "sulle mura" path, which, through a trench-like staircase, connected the Spianata dell'Acquasola to the Villetta Di Negro and Piazza Fontane Amorose. Barabino's invention is reinterpreted in the passage that links the elevation of Via XII Ottobre to that of Piazza Corvetto, where elements of rationalist origin coexist with neobaroque ones. On the north façade, two openings are carved into the depth of the base: one leads to the gallery, the other introduces the entrance vestibule. The porter's lodge intercepts a luminous corridor, where three staircases, illuminated by pyramid skylights, connect to the upper floors. Each staircase serves two apartments, totalling six units per floor that overlook the gardens of Acquasola through full-height windows and a pass-through typology.

The building features a reinforced concrete load-bearing structure cast in place, organised by connecting two rows of pillars to the stair cores, one internal and the other flush with the façade. In the elevational volume, the cantilever of the floor slabs forms sculpted string courses, clad in marble; among these courses, the metallic elements of the balustrades, integrated into the rhythm of the large openings, accentuate the chiaroscuro vibrations of the eastern elevation. The same string course folds onto the western façade, where vertically textured bocciardato concrete elements delineate the grid of the loggias. Calacatta, black and green Polcevera marbles, azure mosaic tiles, frosted glass balustrades, wooden window frames and shutters, and aluminium fixtures define the material richness of the building.

1. **Offices and multi-family dwellings**
   Franco Albini and Franca Helg | 1955–1962
2. **Office building**
   Dante Datta and Marco Dasso | 1962
3. **Office building**
   Piero Gambacciani | 1964–1966
4. **Rinascente commercial and office building**
   Marco Lavarello with Aldo Molteni | 1960–1961

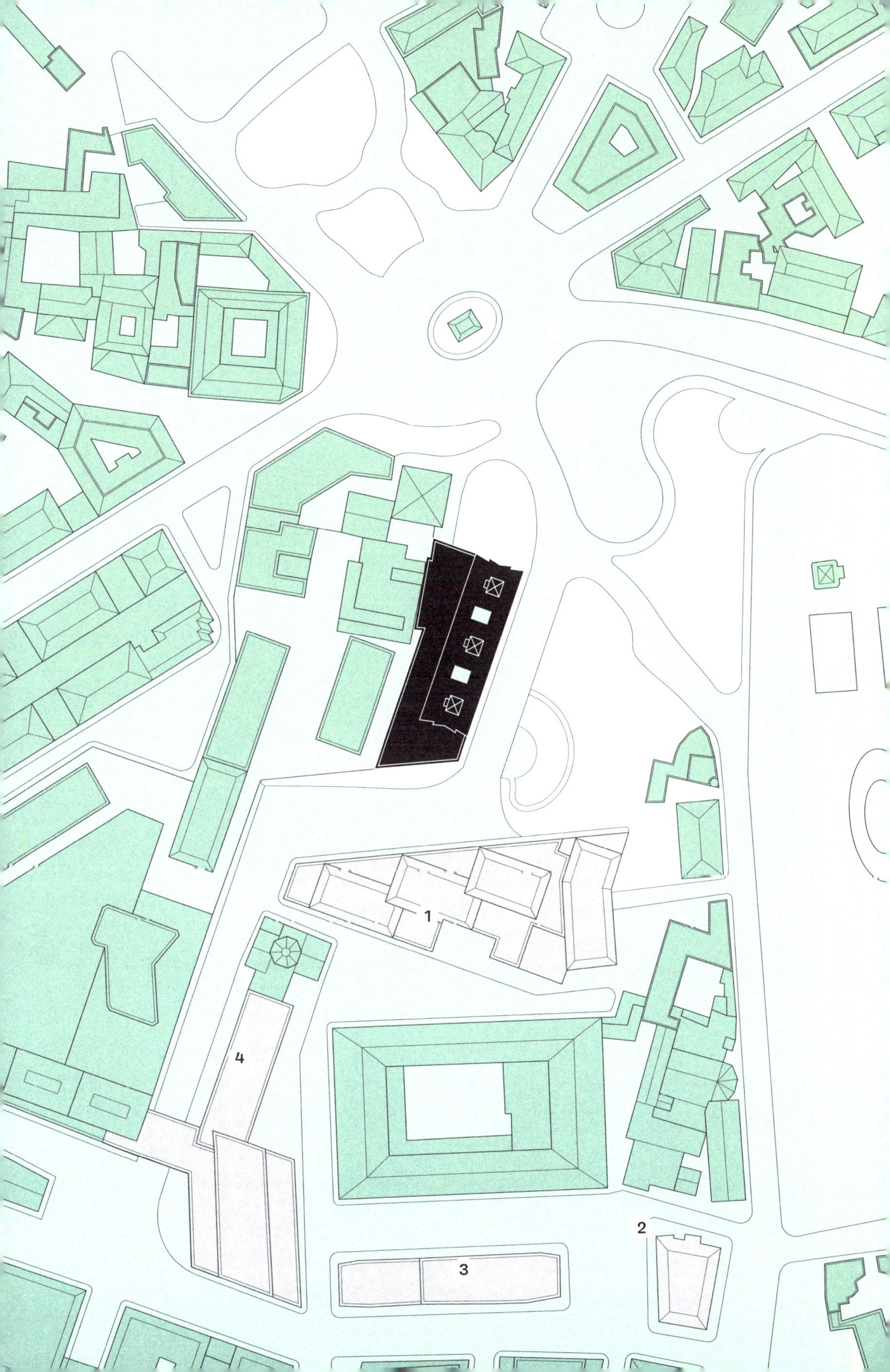
1
2
3
4

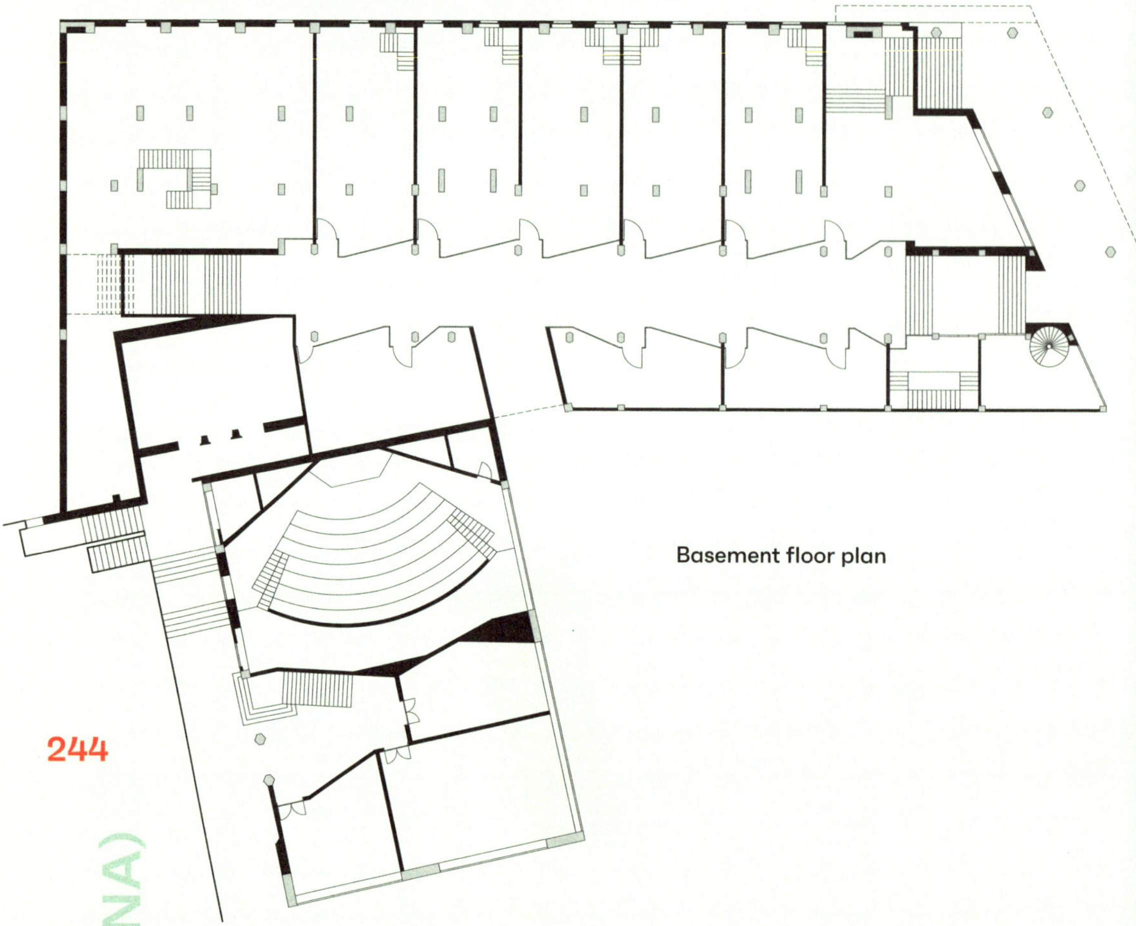

Basement floor plan

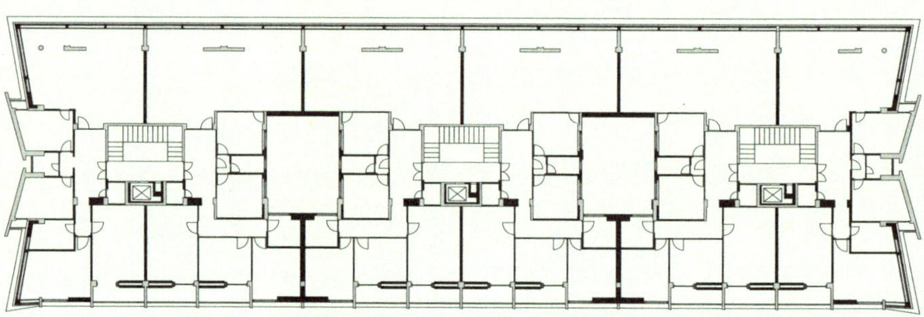

Typical residential floor plan

Scale 1:500

North façade

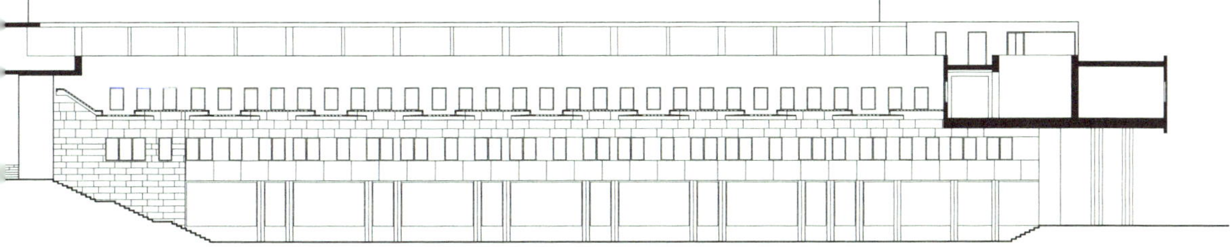

West façade

Scale 1:500

INA Casa Ansaldo *(Interruttori)*

1956–1959 Via Coronata, Cornigliano, Genoa

The building commissioned by the Ansaldo Society and constructed by the Cooperative of the Genoese School of Building is located within the INA complex planned by architect Claudio Andreani, encompassing eleven structures.
The intervention serves as the culmination of the initial seven-year plan of INA Casa, dominated by the challenges of extensive reconstruction and industrialisation. In this context, the abandonment of a representational architectural language, characteristic of the Fascist era, delegates the negotiation directly to professionals within the frameworks of various local institutions.

The site is situated on the Coronata Hill in the western part of Genoa – an erstwhile territory of aristocratic suburban retreats featuring opulent villas and vineyards. Over the course of the 20th century, this landscape underwent a radical transformation with the establishment of an extensive industrial sector. The building emerges on a marginal and sloping plot, usable primarily in its upper portion, situated lower than both the public road and the access road. This topographical condition informs the decision to position entrances at a mid-height level, accessible through walkways. The wooded space beneath enhances the panoramic quality of the structure.

The structure assumes a rectangular footprint, with residences arranged along the north-south axis: the sleeping quarters and amenities positioned uphill and the living areas downhill. Each floor of the building accommodates four residences, served by two stairwells, one for every two apartments. This differentiation manifests in the façades: oblique diaphragms, staggered between one level and the next, unveil the representative, non-load-bearing nature of the loggias shaping the sea-facing façade, defining the architectural expression of the edifice. On the uphill front, contrasting compositional matrices come into play, featuring an abundance of real and faux windows that create an ironic scenic tableau.
The intervention articulates the theme of affordable housing through the utilisation of a rationalist-inspired calligraphy, eschewing neorealist interpretations while encapsulating pseudo-vernacular stimuli. Morozzo synthesises within a singular figurative ambiance the avant-garde aspiration of the grand loggia-clad façade and the peripheral serenity of the posterior domestic prospect. The rigour of the functionalist framework is also contradicted by the asymmetry in the planimetric organisation of the apartments, transforming the parallelepiped into a composite, asymmetric and dynamic form.

Given the limited width in relation to the substantial height, in addition to structural solutions necessitated by the eastern façade – trapezoidal-sectioned pillars with significantly reduced dimensions, a connecting beam embedded in the thickness of the floor slab spanning the entire front – the reinforced concrete structure, engineered by Giovanni Longari, aims to stiffen and interconnect the cast-in-place reinforced concrete framework as much as possible, countering the effects of horizontal forces.

Despite the contingent constraints, Morozzo did not forsake compositional enthusiasm, engaging in a series of "caprices" that underscore the iconic nature of the building in contrast to the subdued tone of its surroundings. Elements such as the stone plinth of uncertain workmanship, the walkways, the inclined loggias and the tightly ordered rear windows, both real and faux, delineate a distinctive character, effectively creating architecture and contributing to the urban fabric even with limited resources.

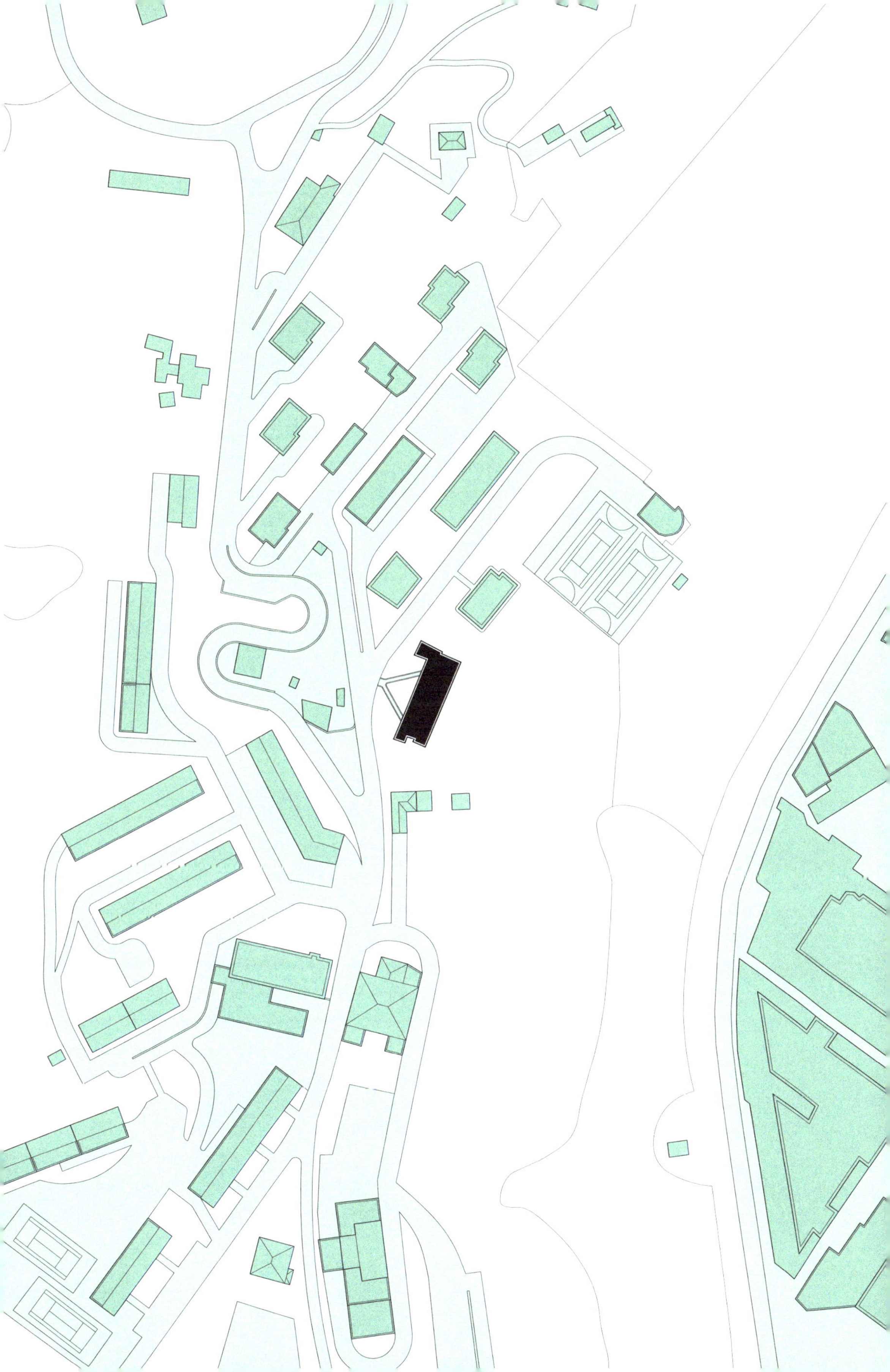

Typical odd floor plan

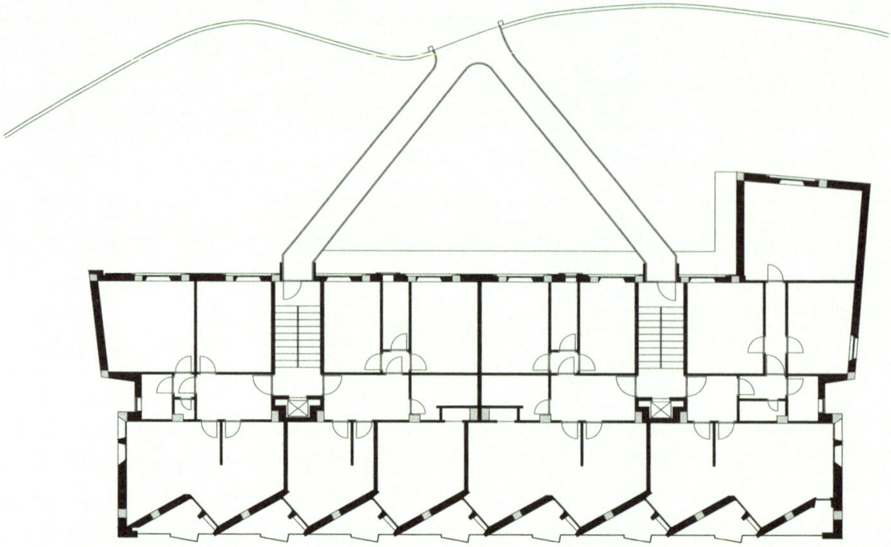

Typical even floor plan

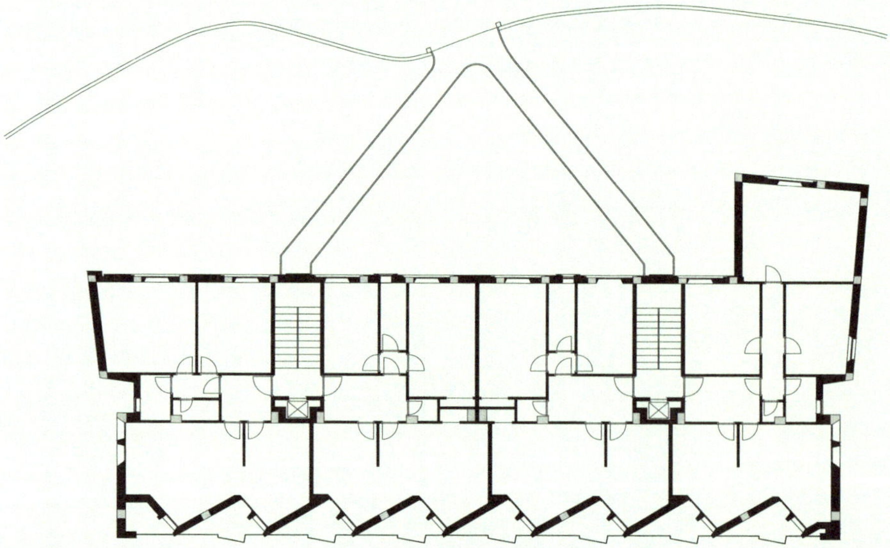

Scale 1:333

East façade

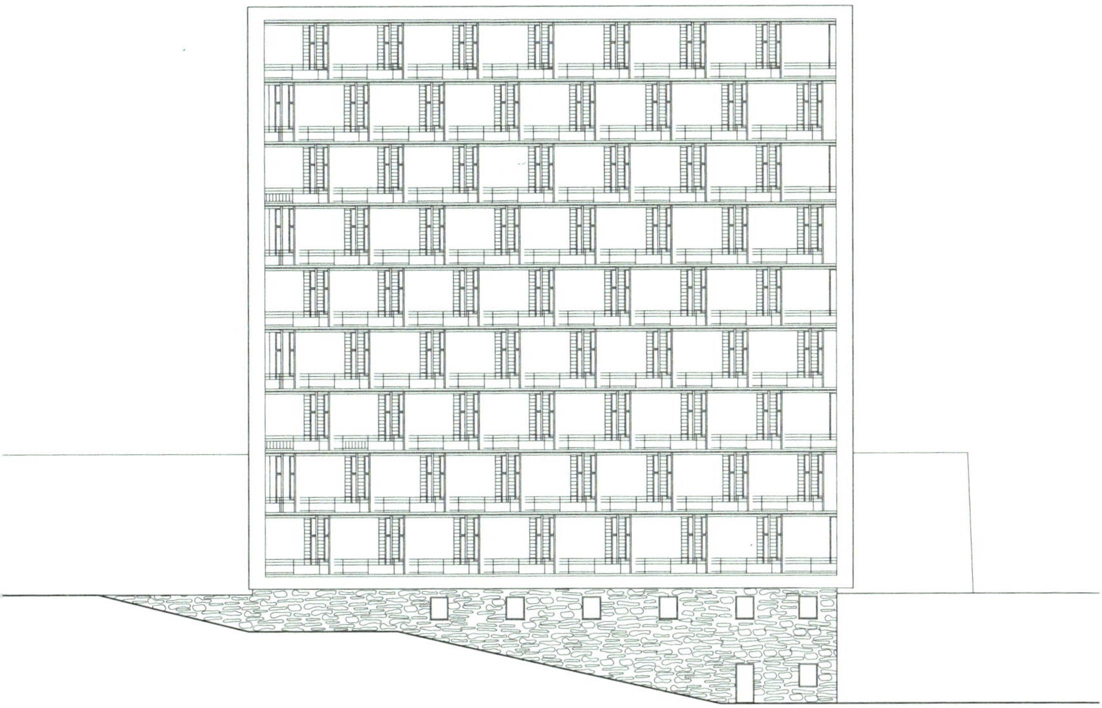

West façade

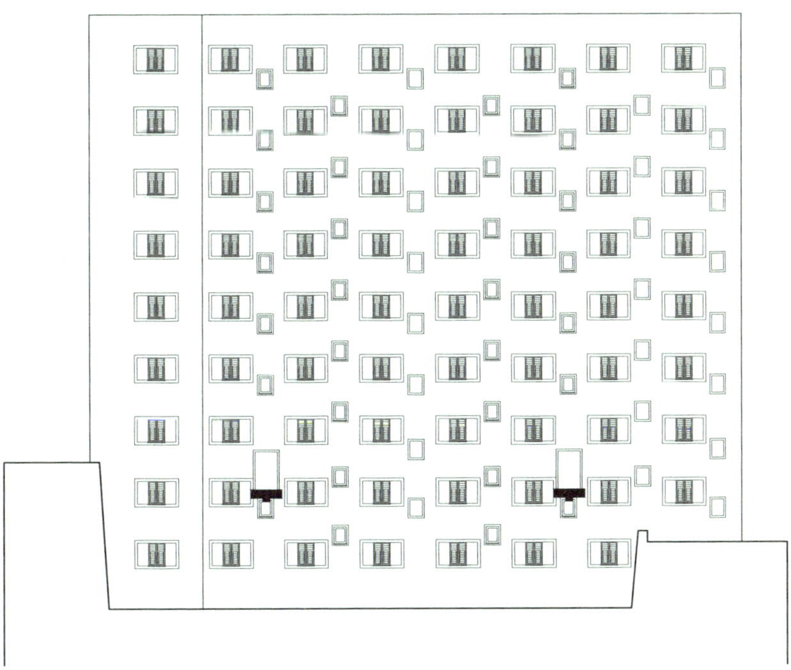

Scale 1:333

C Building of the INA Forte Quezzi District (*Biscionetto*)

A manifesto and a "pioneering" model of intensive mass housing, the district stands as one of the most significant accomplishments of the second INA Casa seven-year plan. Despite a management history that has proven to be unsuccessful over the years, the complex starkly embodies a residential concept that, even today, appears unconventional and of extraordinary value.

The urban design of the district was a collaborative effort involving 35 professionals, each leading the design of a specific building: Luigi Carlo Daneri and Eugenio Fuselli (coordinators, group leaders for Building A); Claudio Andreani (group leader for Building B); Robaldo Morozzo della Rocca (group leader for Building C); Mario Pateri and Angelo Sibilla (group leaders for Building D); Gustavo Pulitzer Finali (group leader for Building E). The expansive planimetric and volumetric articulation of the complex rests on an amphitheatre-like valley nestled against the Marassi district, just below the 19th-century fortifications of Quezzi Hill, overlooking the estuary of the Bisagno River. The peripheral plot sits approximately 200 metres above sea level, boasting an extraordinary view of the gulf. Notably, the high residential density concentrated in five extensive buildings, described as "horizontal skyscrapers", forms a plastic composition that is both monumental and panoramic, commanding and framing a segment of the city.
This iconic project, featuring sinuous modulations designed to be perceived from a considerable distance on a geographic scale, represents a distinct alternative to the neorealist approach proposed by INA Casa elsewhere during the same period. While newspapers criticise the elongated blocks, other perspectives, such as Bruno Zevi's, support the rationale behind choosing these "worm-shaped houses instead of a hundred little houses".

Building C by the Morozzo group (Mario Braccialini, Claudio Spina, Marco Dasso, Dante Datta) consists of three residential floors positioned above a base, organised to contain cellars, garages and shops. The structure is situated on the edge of a level road that follows the sinuosity of the contour lines. The ground-level pavement is covered by the overhang of the portico that runs the entire length of the building on the upper mezzanine floor. The continuous portico is dimensioned and located both thermally and panoramically to facilitate collective living under optimal conditions. Due to the morphology, the apartments feature various configurations that constitute variations of two fundamental models, totalling 144 units, distributed among 24 four-room dwellings, 96 five-room dwellings, and 24 six-room dwellings.

The framework is reinforced concrete cast in-situ, composed of 48 spans. The pillars of the portico have a germinated form, marked with a central low ground to follow the sinuosity of the volume. A superstructure of staggered mesh concrete creates sunbreaks shading the loggias of the apartments, enclosed by a reticulated glass railing.
Material insertions and chromatic variations determine the physiognomy of the building, which, more than any other in the complex, exhibits figurative analogies with the Brazilian Pedregulho model by Affonso Eduardo Reidy (Rio De Janeiro, 1946): the base is clad in rustic masonry, while the end faces feature slate crusts; the parapet of the portico is made of asbestos-cement modules embedded in a concrete hood, while the interior is finished with plaster and ceramic floors. The loggias' louvres are in terracotta and the window frames are made of wood.

1. **Unit A, Ina Forte Quezzi housing**
   Luigi Carlo Daneri and Eugenio Fuselli (coordinators) | 1956–1968
2. **Unit E, Ina Forte Quezzi housing**
   Gustavo Pulitzer | 1956–1964

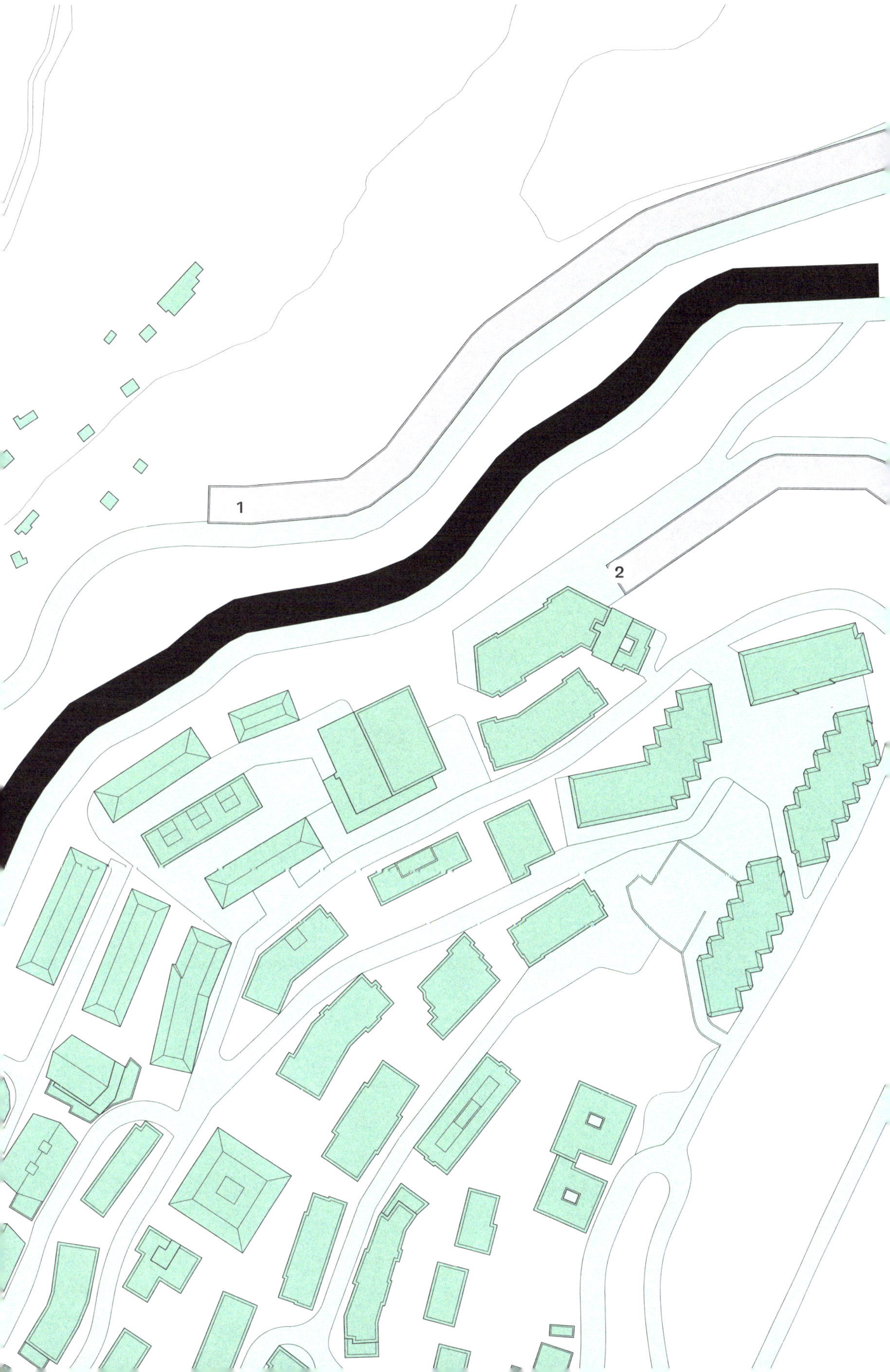
1
2

Scale 1:333

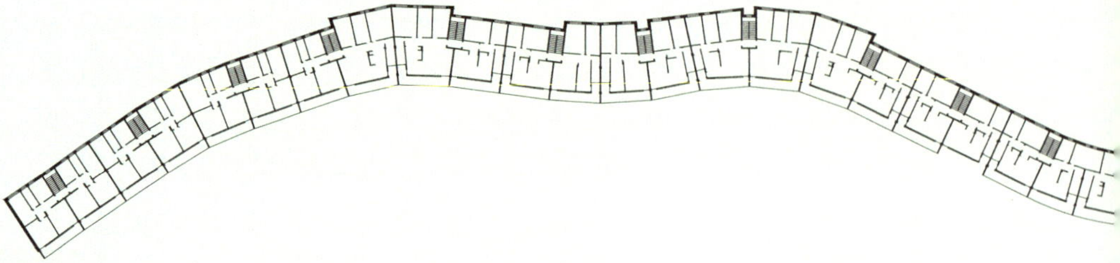

Typical floor plan

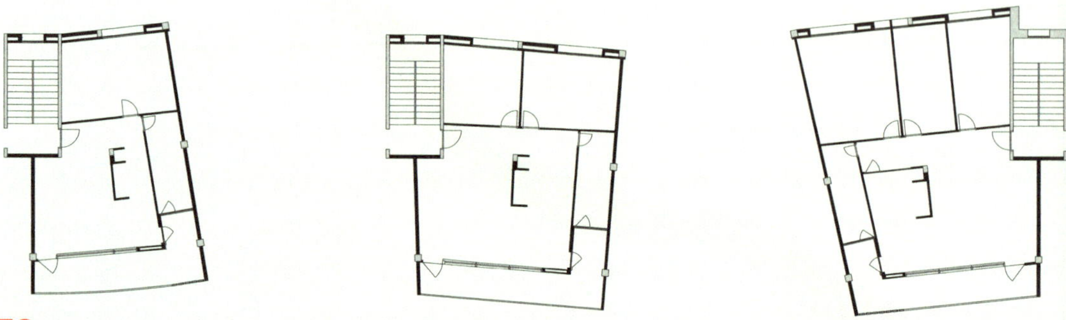

Apartment typologies

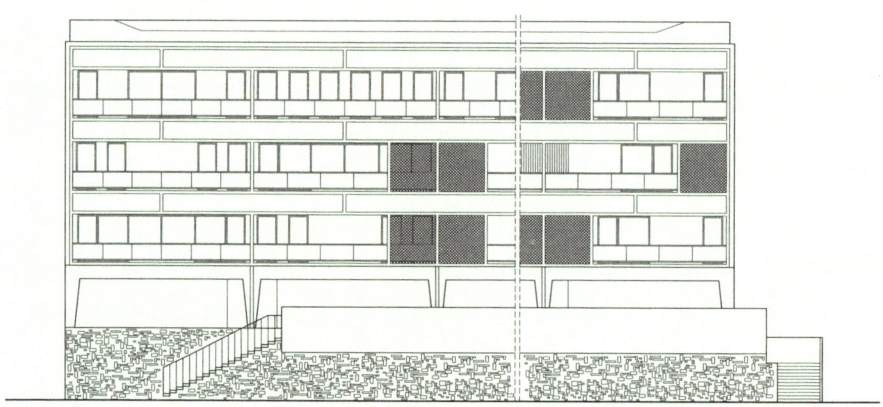

South façade

Scale 1:333

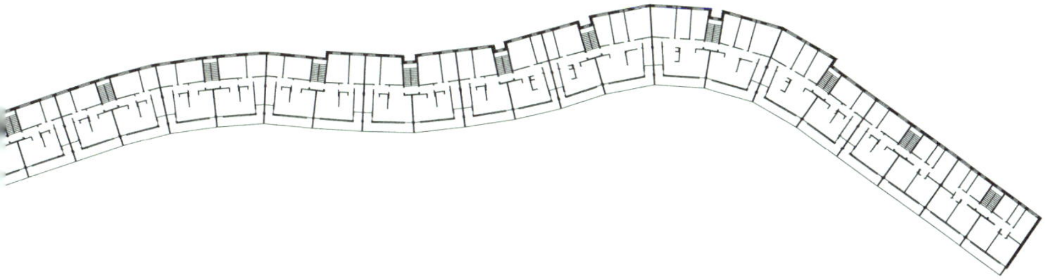

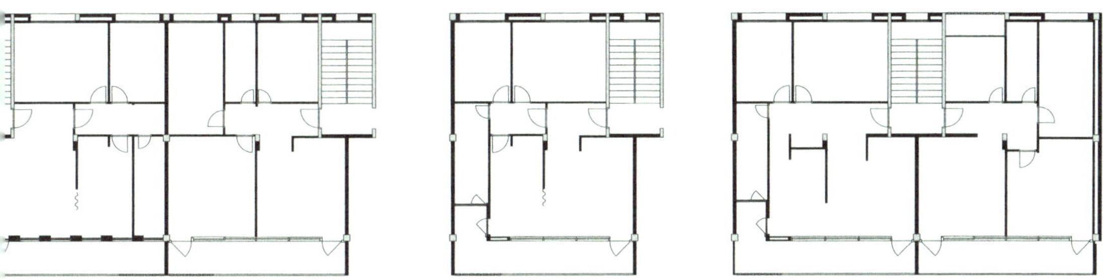

Apartment typologies

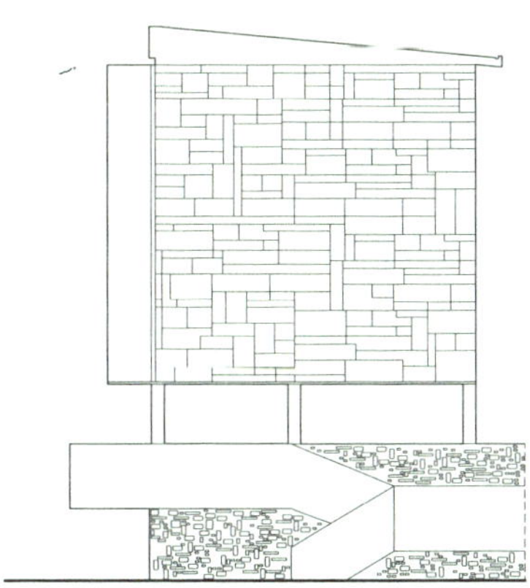

Side façade

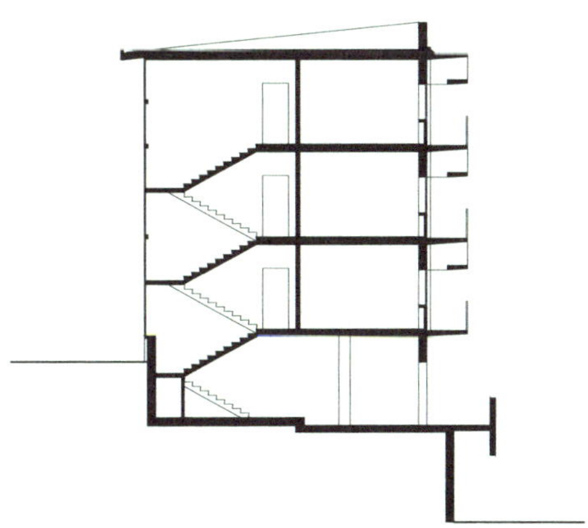

Transversal section

Completion of the Church of the Sacred Heart and St. James

1963–1970 Via Jacopo Ruffini, Carignano, Genoa

The present church replaces the one dedicated to Saint James, founded in 1154 by Ansaldo Spinola as the family's private church, on the edge of the cliffs that bordered the Carignano hill facing the sea. The original core of the current building was constructed in a Neo-Romanesque style, designed by architect Luigi Rovelli, in Piazza Rocco Piaggio (formerly Nino Bixio), a tree-lined square situated midway along Via Corsica, at the heart of the Carignano district, developed in the second half of the 19th century. The original construction, initiated in October 1892, underwent significant modifications during its execution. The first part to be completed was the expansive hall of the crypt (November 1896); in this space, which has housed the Carignano Theatre since 1969, the church temporarily began its functions. In 1902, above the already completed premises, the actual church was erected. The works, continuing after the death of the designer in 1911, were overseen by his son Antonio Rovelli and came to a halt in 1914. Only the altars and pictorial decorations were eventually completed during the Twenties.

Externally, the church presents itself with a Neo-Gothic façade, featuring a central rose window and broad lateral openings, those in the middle register being tripartite, and, in the upper register, with a loggia flanked on either side by two clocks. The surface is entirely composed of exposed, reinforced concrete, crafted in regular horizontal courses, with terracotta finishes. The church is surmounted by a tall octagonal dome that culminates in a lantern and an imposing spire.

Following the bombardment of May 1944, the building suffered substantial damage, necessitating extensive restoration.
In 1966, the parish administration entrusted Morozzo della Rocca with the completion of the building, tasking him to design the scenography of the liturgical reservoir left incomplete by Rovelli. Morozzo designed and constructed a multitude of new elements that integrate with the previous framework, defining the new aesthetic and spatial character of the sacred space: the entrance vestibule, marked by a diaphragm consisting of a wall with doors, both made of glass; the lithic cladding of the wall surfaces and pilasters, using blocks of grey stone and white marble, with various dimensions and cast-in-place installation; the paired confessionals, set against the longitudinal walls, composed of four pilasters supporting two arched openings and a tympanum; the new paired columns, formed from a single piece of granite, with a base in red granite, plinths of green marble (extending from polylobate holy water fonts), and various bronze pulvini; the reconfiguration of the altar through the construction of two ambos flanked by marble slabs with vertical grooves.

Morozzo also intervenes in the main structural components: internally, originally divided into three naves, the lateral nave is covered with a plastered, reinforced-concrete barrel vault, while the side naves feature square-plan cross vaults separated by arches, also in plastered reinforced concrete. The vertical load-bearing structures are made of plastered reinforced concrete.

1. **ILVA building headquarters**
   Giuseppe Crosa di Vergagni | 1929–1930
2. **Palazzo Custo**
   Morozzo della Rocca | 1936–1939
3. **Apartment building**
   Luigi Carlo Daneri | 1937
4. **Villa Croce**
   Giovanni Giacomo Croce | 18th century.

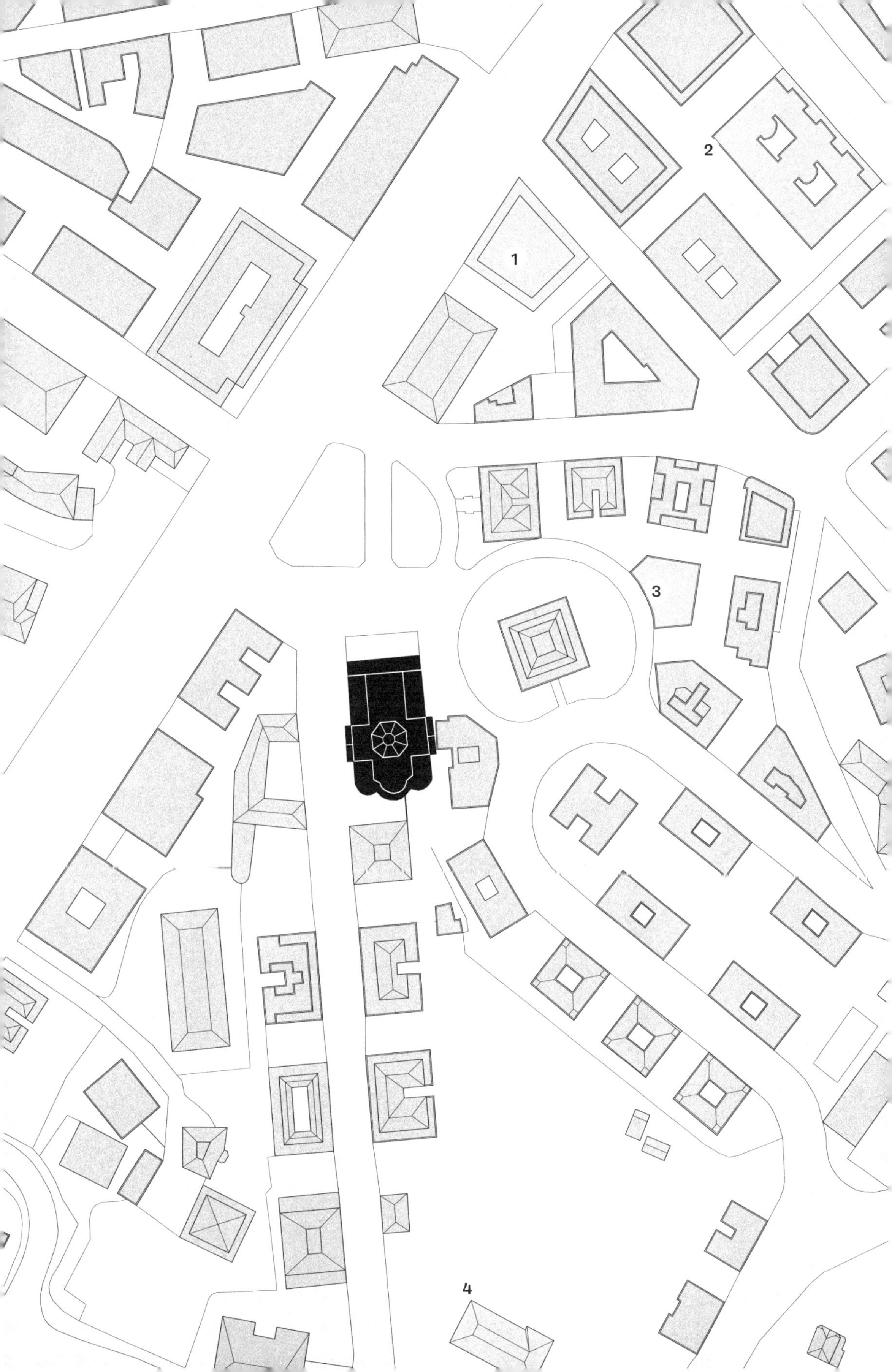
1
2
3
4

Scale 1:333

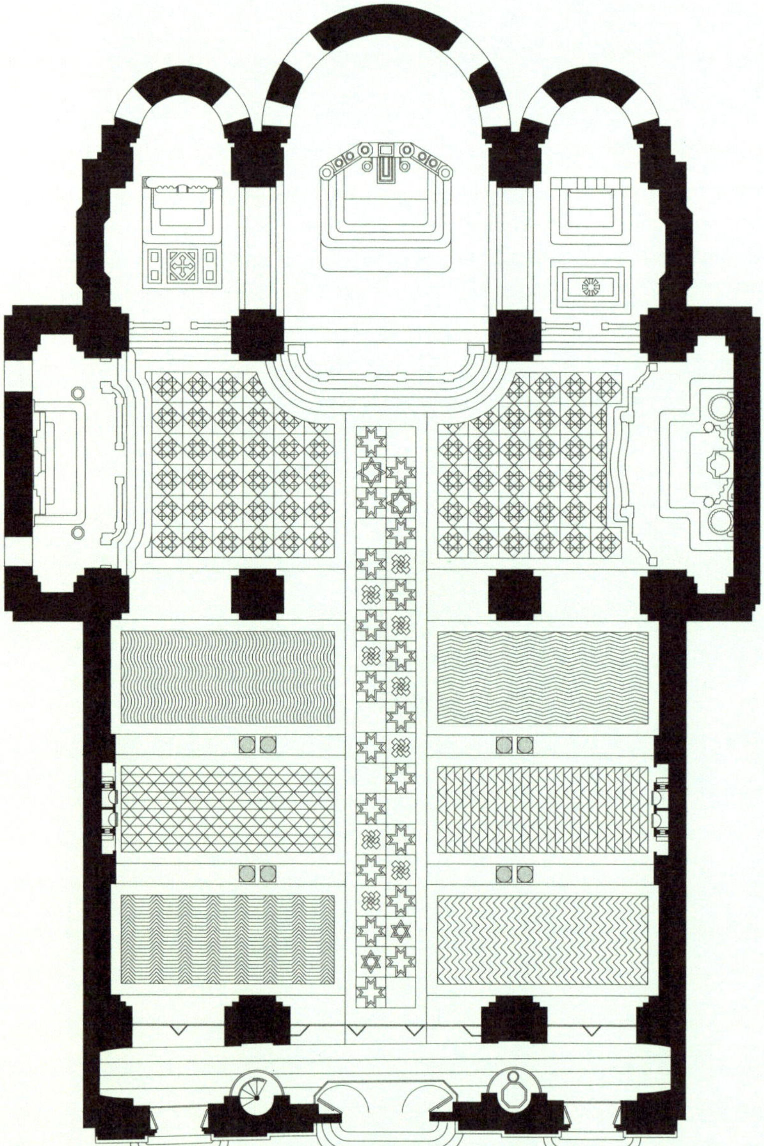

Church floor plan

Scale 1:333

Transversal section

Longitudinal section

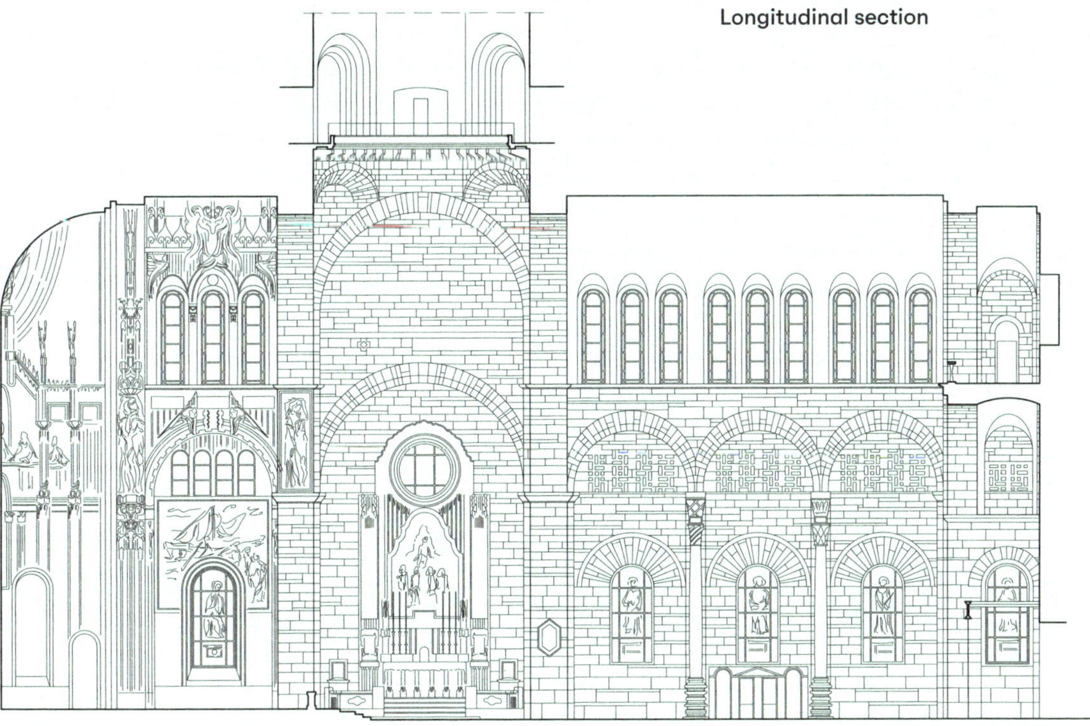

Villini Elios e Selene

The small villas represent the final significant commission in Morozzo's career. The project is situated in the Punta San Martino section of the Arenzano Pine Forest, where Marchesa Matilde Giustiniani Negrotto Cambiaso and her son-in-law Marcello Cattaneo Adorno play leading roles in the real estate development of a vast area around Capo Panaggi. The enterprise, named Centri Marittimi di Soggiorno (Maritime Housing Centres), entrusted the managerial expertise of the Lombard financier and builder Ambrogio Gadola by appointing him as president. Due to his personal connections, the General Plan of Colletta was assigned to Ignazio Gardella, Marco Zanuso and Guido Veneziani in 1956.
The absence of a regulatory plan granted absolute freedom regarding the rules for the construction of the areas: the company owned the lands, acted as the contractor, assessed the quality of the projects and managed the services. Alongside firms associated with Cemadis, such as Mario Valle (owned by Gardella himself), other companies were involved in the area, including the Savona-based Bagnasco Enterprise which commissioned Morozzo.
The settlement principle and layout of the villas constitute a sophisticated exercise in construction, strategically aligning geometric volumes with the landscape and topography. Figurative characterisation, meticulous attention to details and the judicious use of materials define the distinctive relationship between the surrounding nature and the structures. The two volumes perch on the hill within an area with a pronounced slope, subtly weaving through the dense and diverse Mediterranean vegetation, almost concealing their presence. Access to the plot is facilitated by a winding and descending ramp, along which underground garages are ingeniously integrated.

Villa Elios, positioned at the highest elevation, unfolds along a curve that follows the natural terrain, deploying its concavity to embrace the panorama of the riviera. The compact structure comprises two above-ground levels, each accommodating two apartments. Symmetric elliptical staircases lead to the entrances of the residences, where the internal layout is rationally organised: a sleeping area with two or three bedrooms and a bathroom, and a living area with a lounge, kitchenette, study and another bathroom. Two rows of exposed reinforced concrete parapets, rhythmically aligned with the repetition of recast beams, artistically characterise the façade facing downhill. On the upstream side, concrete membranes framing the windows project prominently from the façade, alternating between plastered sections and others left in their natural concrete state.

Villa Selene, situated further downstream, unfolds three parallelepiped volumes along the contours of the terrain. The articulation of the three-storey volumes is orchestrated by a slender point of tangency. Among the three blocks, the one upstream features a gabled roof, while the others boast a flat terrace for the units above, enclosed by reticulated glass balustrades. At the base of the head volume, concrete buttresses elegantly resolve the connection to the ground. Ramped staircases flank the three blocks to facilitate access to the entrances.
Internally, the functional organisation delineates a clear distinction between the living and sleeping areas, with the prestigious spaces orientated towards the sea. The façades alternate between vertical bands finished with rustic and irregular Barge stone courses and compositions of windows with aluminium fixtures, interspersed with masonry and rhythmically punctuated by relief bands crafted from exposed concrete.

1. Sette Sorelle condominium
Marco Zanuso | 1962

2. Punta San Martino Hotel
Ignazio Gardella and Marco Zanuso | 1958

1
2

Scale 1:300

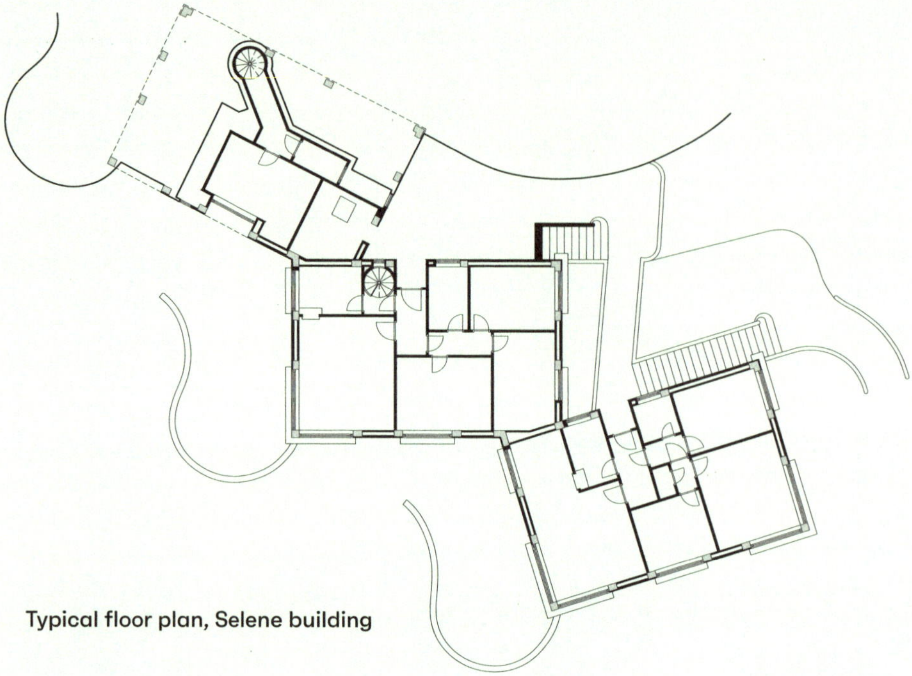

Typical floor plan, Selene building

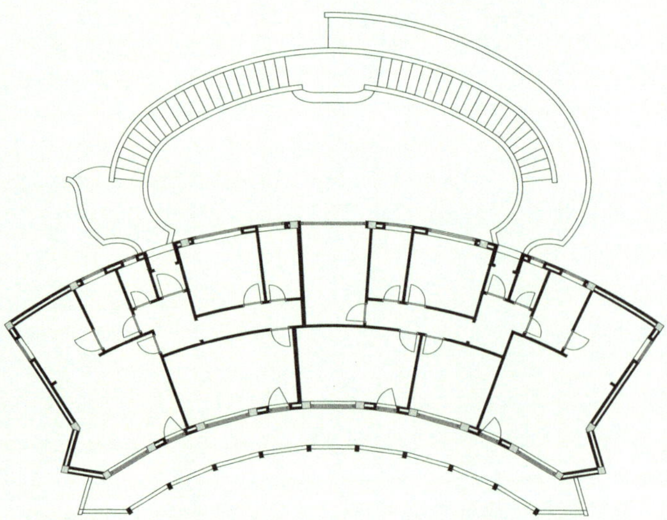

Typical floor plan, Elios building

Scale 1:333

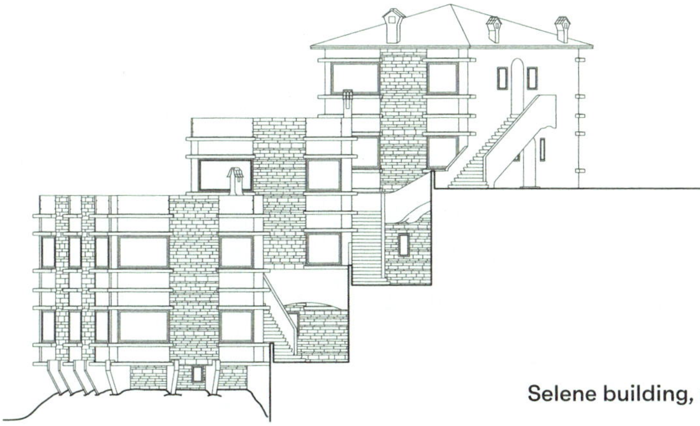

Selene building, north façade

Selene building, east façade

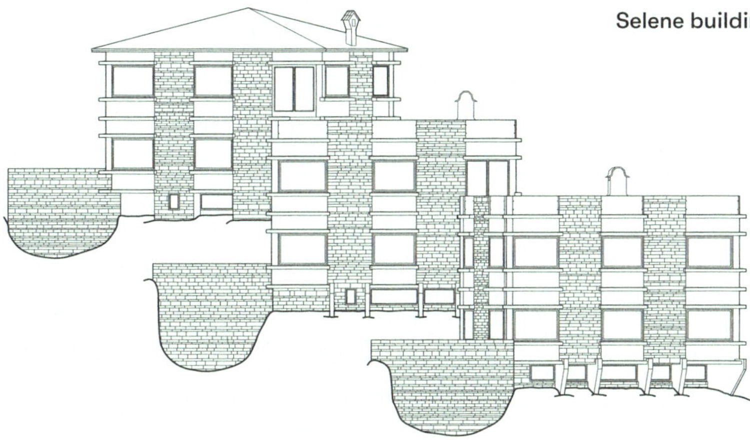

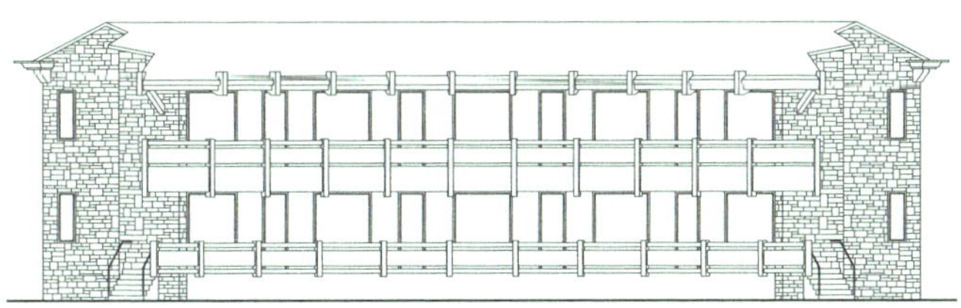

Elios building, south façade

Elios building, west façade

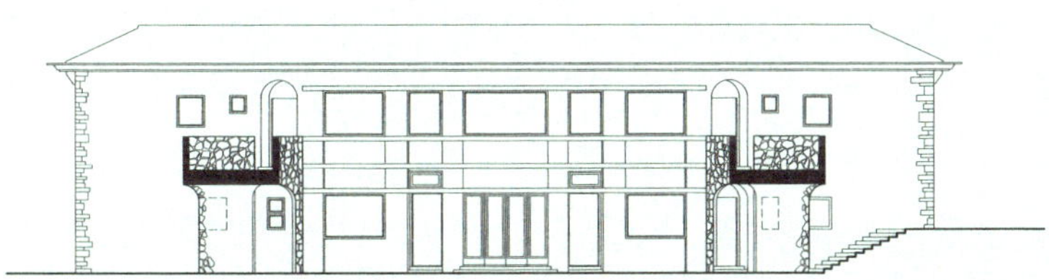

Above: Project for a restaurant on the water
Genoa, undated.

Centre: Villino Daneri
Levanto, undated.

Below: Project for an housing block at the Foce
Genoa, 1931.

PERSPECTIVES

CRITICAL SECTION

Experimenting by doing
Marginal notes on the work of Robaldo Morozzo della Rocca

Carmen Andriani

"Having listened to the norms of the day, we realise that something else is speaking to us at the edges of the day; not having listened to that gives us no peace."[1] With these words, Roberto Gabetti and Aimaro Isola explained some of the motivations behind the controversial project *Bottega d'Erasmo* in Turin. It was 1957 and the pages of Casabella,[2] directed by Ernesto N. Rogers, showed the work alongside an exchange of letters between the two Turinese architects and Vittorio Gregotti. The *Bottega d'Erasmo* was described as a heretical work, the fruit of an exclusive relationship with the delicate sensitivity of the two architects, but, according to Gregotti, far from architecture's mission of *public responsibility*, and consequently that of the magazine, which is generally seen as a vehicle for mainstream doctrinal teachings.

In fact, the *Bottega d'Erasmo* appeared during the process of critical re-examination of the modern movement and its values, until then considered indisputable. This process would continue without interruption until the mid-1970s,[3] although a strong ideological prejudice endured for most of the latter half of the 20th century, influencing critics and reviews, and penalising a widespread fabric of cultured and sensitive professionalism towards the character of the environment in which it operated. *Bottega d'Erasmo* brought to light the *Italian difference*:[4] a polyphonic architectonic culture, of the fragment and multiplicity, anchored to the topography of places, sensitive to geographical and historical character, and fuelled by the great variety of urban and architectonic relationships offered in consolidated cities of any type or size. Besides, Italian specificity was also measured in the capacity to unite technical aspects and a humanist sensibility; with the awareness that the project demanded a high level of attunement with the environment and that *doing*, beyond bureaucratic protocol, was guided by involvement and relationships.

Robaldo Morozzo della Rocca's professional career spanned a good part of the 20th century and was practised in this context; Morozzo was one of the valid cultured professionals somehow left in the background, due to the heedlessness of critics and an excess of reserve in the

1. See: Karl Jaspers, *Philosophie*, Berlin, 1932 (trans. as *Filosofia*, Umberto Galimberti (Ed.), Turin 1978); the quote refers to step 3. "Law of Day vs. Passion for Night", p. 1049.
2. Roberto Gabetti/Aimaro d'Isola, "Bottega d'Erasmo. Un edificio per una libreria antiquaria e per appartamenti a Torino", in: *Casabella*, no. 215, 1957, p. 62; id. "L'impegno della tradizione", in: *Casabella*, op. cit., p. 63.
3. See: Rafael Moneo (Carmen Diez Medina/Orsina Simona Pierini, Eds.), *L'altra Modernità. Considerazioni sul futuro dell'architettura*, Milan, 2012.
4. See: Alberto Ferlenga, *Architettura. La differenza italiana*, op. cit., 2023.

man himself, more given to *making* architecture than *preaching* it. Robaldo was born in Turin in 1904. In 1923, after two years' studying Engineering in Genoa, he requested a transfer to Rome, to the first Scuola Superiore di Architettura Italiana[5] instituted in 1920: here, a group of respected professors[6] involved both in public debate and in the profession, had established a new course to train architects. In the teaching of project design, entrusted to Arnaldo Foschini,[7] there was nothing imposed in terms of style and no other formal restrictions. The method was highly appreciated by students, and Foschini himself defined it as "monitored self-training". The figure of the *integral architect* was brought into being: a balance between tradition and innovation, and a perfect synthesis of technical knowledge and humanist culture.

Robaldo Morozzo della Rocca was a contemporary, among others, of Adalberto Libera, Mario Ridolfi[8] and Luigi Moretti. They all converged at Rome's School of Architecture and they trained, as Luigi Vagnetti recounted as an intense witness,[9] in a climate where students were left free to shape the individual trajectories that, for the more talented, would be seen over time as mature and well identified poetics. From Libera's lyrical purism to the expressive texture of Ridolfi's[10] architecture, from the troubled and brilliant spatiality of Moretti[11] to the concrete and polysemic realism of Morozzo della Rocca, such poetics express an unorthodox modernity that was anachronistic and therefore misunderstood for a long time; without doubt fostered by Rome's cultural climate, so resistant to the Modern and its illusions.

Robaldo Morozzo della Rocca was a *integral architect* in the best tradition of 20th-century Italian architecture. Although many projects did not come to fruition, his whole activity showed a continual creative tension. Every design was rooted in the place for which it was destined, absorbing its character and

5. See: Nulio Pirazzoli (Ed.), *Arnaldo Foschini / Didattica e Gestione dell'Architettura in Italia nella prima metà del Novecento* (Conference Proceedings), Faenza,1979, p. 19–20 ff.
   After a debate lasting almost a quarter of a century (from 1873), the teaching of architecture, thus far entrusted to Fine Art Studies and confined to Architectonic styles, became autonomous and academic in nature.
6. Numbered among the teachers taking part in this renewal were Manfredo Manfredi, the young Arnaldo Foschini, Gustavo Giovannoni, Marcello Piacentini, Enrico Del Debbio, Vincenzo Fasolo, and later Saverio Muratori and others. The ongoing reconstruction of events relating to both lecturers and students at the first Scuola Superiore di Architettura Italiana is accessible at the Biblioteca Centrale Facoltà di Architettura, Fondi Archivistici; in particular all documents relating to the educational background of Robaldo Morozzo della Rocca, matriculation no. 148.
7. Arnaldo Foschini, who became a professor in 1924–1925, lectured on Elements of Composition from 1920 to 1936 and Architectonic Design from 1928 to 1954.

   At least five generations of students took his Project Design courses; including Mario De Renzi, Luigi Moretti, Adalberto Libera, Mario Ridolfi, Robaldo Morozzo della Rocca, Ludovico Quaroni and Saverio Muratori, later his controversial successor.

   See: Luigi Vagnetti, "Arnaldo Foschini, 1884–1968", in: *Arnaldo Foschini / Didattica e Gestione dell'Architettura in Italia nella prima metà del Novecento*, op.cit.
8. Mario Ridolfi (1904–1984). Mario Ridolfi's entire oeuvre was reassessed towards the end of the 1970s by Paolo Portoghesi, flanked by a working group made up of the lecturers Cellini, D'Amato, Valeriani and, in the capacity of collaborators, by Andriani, Avagnina, Guccione and Lazzarini. The first monographic exhibition was held at Palazzo Mazzancolli, Terni, in 1979. See the exhibition catalogue: Francesco Cellini/Claudio D'Amato/Enrico Valeriani (Ed.), *Le Architetture di Ridolfi e Frankl*, Rome, 1979.
9. See: Luigi Vagnetti, *Arnaldo Foschini, 1884–1968*, op. cit.
10. Carmen Andriani, "Realismo visionario. Mario Ridolfi, progetto per il Motel Agip a Settebagni, Roma", in: *Firenze Architettura*, Vol. 21, no. 1, Florence, 2017, p. 128–137; id. "Palazzine Romane di Mario Ridolfi: dalla Rea alla Zaccardi, alterazione, distorsione e corruzione della figura razionalista", in: *Rassegna di Architettura e Urbanistica. La Palazzina nel paesaggio urbano contemporaneo*, no. 89–90, op.cit.
11. Luigi Moretti (1906–1973) was a controversial figure in the Italian 20th-century panorama. Manfredo Tafuri's *Storia dell'Architettura Italiana. 1944–1985*, a seminal text in the critical historiography of the second half of the 20th century, includes some brief observations on the Roman architect spread over a few pages. See: Carmen Andriani, "Spazialità e Struttura di una architettura inquieta", in: *AR Magazine*, no. 125–126, *Luigi Moretti. Forma struttura, poetica della modernità*, Rome, 2021, p. 290–303.

bringing together client aspirations, dialogue with the context, and the practicality of construction. Each project was exclusively given over to the specific circumstance that generated it and to which it responded with realistic imagination. The complex geometry of Palazzina Ollandini Hofer, for example, was nothing if not the handling of restrictions and limitations dictated by existing structures; the plan to maintain the echo of the old, ruined dwelling generated the powerful juxtaposition between the stone shell delineating the house towards the city and the unexpected recurrent wave design of the large windows that look out towards the sea. Capturing the light is one of the motifs that recalls the Baroque atmosphere of the years when he trained in Rome. It can be seen in the supple articulation of the façades, in the search for contrasts of light and dark, and in the choice of orientations creating different sides, as well as the singularity of the window spaces opening like petals in search of daylight.[12] However, this does not preclude an equally rational approach, as indeed Morozzo himself explained in an article in 1931, pointing out how Rational Art feeds on the clarity of geometric relationships[13] and what he defines as the Mediterranean Style. This reference to the geographical context, and in this specific case the topographical context, embraces one of the peculiarities of Italian architectonic culture mentioned above, which is present in some of our best architectures. In a Genoese context, topography, more even than architecture, is the zero degree of the city's *forma urbis*.[14] The tight sequence of level curves descending to the sea conditions any planning for habitation. This is the case at Unit C of the INA Forte Quezzi neighbourhood, Genoa, 1957–1966, where Robaldo Morozzo designed one of the five units; and also the case for the INA complex at the Former Building for the National Insurance Institute in Piccapietra, Genoa, 1955–1962, can, in my opinion, be considered one of his masterpieces. Forte Quezzi is an orographical gathering of parallel lines: the horizontals of the string courses prevail, layered in varied rhythm, as do the contrasts and deep lines of shadow that lift the overlying volumes; as well as the ever changing shadows stamped on the façade's plans of different depths. The design principle follows the sinuous line of the terracing, while in some of his choices of detail, Morozzo is more autonomous, beyond the orthodox observance of Le Corbusier suggested by Daneri, as per his natural approach of experimenting by doing.

For the complex at Piccapietra, being a consolidated part of the city, he creates an out and out urban palimpsest. The layering of floors, functions, materials and the linguistic arrangement render the complex recognisable in its every part. Combined with the varying slope of the plot, this produces an extraordinarily efficacious urban sequence. The logic of the fragment and multiplicity mentioned above finds one of its most eloquent examples in this complex;

12. The motif recalls Luigi Moretti's fanned opening on the side elevations of Palazzina Girasole in Rome, which also generates a Baroque spatiality obtained through the movement of volumes rather than style. See: Carmen Andriani, "Spazialità e Struttura di una architettura inquieta", op.cit.

13. Morozzo writes "Rational Art is no less emotional and spiritual than what makes the grand architecture of the past beautiful". See: Robaldo Morozzo della Rocca, "Architettura Razionale. Valore di una parola", in: *Il Giornale di Genova*, op.cit. Moreover, in 1933 Morozzo set out his design for a *Typical Steel Structure House* at the V Triennale di Milano, dedicated to modern architecture and Italian Rationalism.

14. See: Piero Barbieri, *Forma Genuae*, op.cit.

the urban scale can be reinterpreted in the capacity to create connections in a register of multiple perspectives (the arcade on the one hand and the portico on the other, located at different heights); the meaning of the city itself can be read in the sophistication of detail created with loving care, worthy of Italy's best architecture. We might call it *Topographical Rationalism*, emotional certainly, as evidence of what Morozzo had affirmed at the age of 27. Here, architecture is not delivered in a single, static vision, but is expressed through the fabric connecting its parts, the materials of which they are made, the geometric relations governing their composition, the light that shapes them, and above all the space they create.

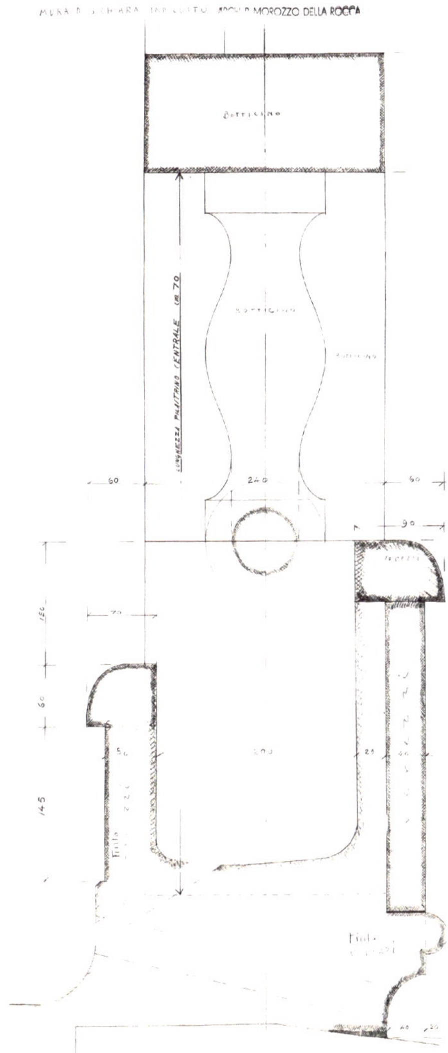

Construction detail for the façade of Palazzo Custo, 1937.

Unit C of the INA Forte Quezzi neighbourhood
Genoa, 1957–1966.

Artists, engineers, and architects:
Renewed professionalism in 20th-century Italy

Maria Carola Morozzo della Rocca

The modern conception of the architect in Italy took shape between 1919 and 1920 in Rome, with the establishment of the first Royal Higher School of Architecture, recognized as a university-level institution, by Royal Decree No. 2593 on October 31, 1919. The foundation of the Roman School, occurring between the two world wars and coinciding with the rise of the Fascist regime, resolved long-standing issues of education and accreditation that had been ongoing among French-derived specialized schools, polytechnics and fine arts academies. This resolution simultaneously sparked broad debate on the definition of the so-called "integral architect", his societal role and, indirectly, the necessity of establishing compositional principles for a national style, which would become a symbol and emblem of the nation first and the regime thereafter.

Before the Royal Decree, architects were trained either at polytechnics, which provided a predominantly technical education, or at fine arts academies, which offered a decidedly artistic training. This dichotomy resulted in two distinct professional profiles, each with different preparations and competencies.

The Roman School was intended to address the issue by creating a singular figure who, as Camillo Boito eloquently put it, needed to be "a most skilled builder... and moreover a wise and imaginative artist".[1] Giovannoni's speech at the School's inauguration stands as a true programmatic manifesto, reiterating key concepts such as the precarious state of architectural education in Italy until then, which he famously described as "a ship without a helmsman in a great storm". He delved into the well-known myth of the *Integral architect* and the perhaps less renowned *Integral history of architecture*.

The orator immediately emphasized one of the new School's goals: to find a line of contact and balance between academic artistic knowledge and technical engineering expertise. Giovannoni also defined the professional profile of the future architect, a notion he had introduced years earlier in the 1908 report of the Commission for the Schools of Architecture.[2]

The didactic organization under the stewardship of Manfredo Manfredi emerged through a series of meetings of

1. See: Camillo Boito, "Architettura odierna e l'insegnamento di essa", in: *Giornale dell'Ingegnere – Architetto e Agronomo*, Milan, 1860 [trans.].
2. See: Gustavo Giovannoni, "Relazione della Commissione per le Scuole di Architettura", in: Guido Zucconi, *Dal Capitello alla città*, Milan, 1997, p. 127.

the faculty in anticipation of the official commencement of courses in January 1921, which saw 55 enrolled students. On this topic, Giovannoni provides direct testimony of these meetings,[3] which were moderated by the *rector seraphicus*, Manfredo Manfredi, and attended by professors such as *Gino Navoni* (Gustavo Giovannoni), *Arnaldi* (Arnaldo Foschini), *Vincenzi* (Vincenzo Fasolo), *Marcelli* (Marcello Piacentini), *Battisti* (G. Battista Milani), *Giulii* (Giulio Magni), *Fausti* (Fausto Vagnetti), and *Santi* (possibly Bargellini).

The discussions revolved around three interrelated issues: the methods and approaches for teaching architectural composition to novices, directly involving the yet-to-be-codified National style and the appropriate stance towards modernism; the role and significance to be attributed to the history of architecture; and, finally, the architectural themes to be tackled with the students.

Regarding the instruction of composition, Foschini appears to have triumphed over Milani. With the mediating intervention of Giovannoni, Foschini successfully imposed the notion that the instructor must cultivate in students a spirit of observation and introduce them to relatively simple design themes, especially in the early years. This approach was at odds with Vagnetti, who advocated a grandiose, academically styled thesis topic. The dispute was ultimately resolved by Manfredi's mediating intervention.[4]

In contrast, the clash between Fasolo and Piacentini regarding the role and teaching of history was more vehement. This quarrel concluded with Giovannoni's mediation favouring Fasolo, aligning more closely with the conservative, tradition-orientated ethos that characterised the initial framework of the Roman School, a stark divergence from the contemporaneous manifesto of the Bauhaus School in Germany.

Within this context, the figure of Morozzo della Rocca serves as a pivotal reference for tracing the evolving landscape of Italian architecture and appreciating the distinctive education that characterises the "first generation" of Italian architects.

Having completed his classical studies, Morozzo continued his education in Genoa, straddling the traditions of the Accademie di Belle Arti and the Physical-Mathematical Biennium of the Faculty of Engineering. He then relocated to the capital to graduate from the newly established Regia Scuola Superiore di Architettura, thus becoming an artist and mathematician, historian and physicist, engineer and architect simultaneously.

His training at the Accademia Ligustica imbued him with a graphic sensitivity, making his drawings and project models easily distinguishable. Meanwhile, his time at the Faculty of Engineering drove him to delve into both purely theoretical physical-mathematical subjects, such as the hypothesis of motion unity,[5] and more exquisitely practical topics such as sound, visual and architectural modulation.[6]

3. See: Gustavo Giovannoni, "Discussioni didattiche", in: *Questioni di architettura nella storia e nella vita*, Rome, 1925, p.39.
4. Ibid., p.75.
5. See: Robaldo Morozzo della Rocca, *La unità del moto*, op.cit; id., *Memorie intorno alla ipotesi di unità del moto*, op.cit.
6. See: Robaldo Morozzo della Rocca, "La Modulazione Architettonica nella Proiezione Ortogonale e nella Prospettiva", op.cit.

Following this rich educational journey, Morozzo demonstrated an ability to amalgamate all his studies into his professional life, channelling a multifaceted array of interests and skills into his projects. This synthesis of diverse disciplines, while not unique, is at least exceptional in its breadth.

Morozzo epitomises the characteristics of a cohort of 20th-century architects marked by a broad and intricate education, albeit not without its contradictions. This type of education has waned and been lost amid a series of university reforms that have led to the fragmentation of knowledge and the emergence of professionals with specific qualifications, where once there existed a singular, comprehensive professional identity.

During his Roman period, certain teachings and professors became pivotal to Morozzo's personal development: Foschini, Manfredi, Milani and Giovannoni in the realm of project design, and Fasolo in the study of architectural styles. Fasolo imparted to Morozzo the principle that history is the master of all arts and the cultural foundation of any architectural or epistemological endeavour, with drawing as the primary instrument of any discourse.

Architectural drawing, as an expressive language and tool of knowledge – applied by Fasolo in the teaching of History and Styles of Architecture – provided Morozzo with a comprehensive understanding of historical architecture. This was not solely for cultural enrichment but to elevate classical architecture as a model for reinterpretation in the design phase.

Fasolo's words are unequivocal: "We believe that the knowledge derived from the experience of ancient architectures constitutes a necessary foundation for ensuring that the new creations, which are the aspirations of young architects, can integrate into an uninterrupted tradition."[7] Elsewhere, he clarifies: "A rational orientation in the successful pursuit of new structural forms, logically aligned with both the new guiding principles of modern architecture and a high sense of healthy classicism, which must and always will warm the heart of the Italian architect, cannot be realised without a profound understanding, by those embarking on this path, of the evolutions that these forms have undergone in past epochs."[8]

Morozzo della Rocca applied Fasolo's teachings both in the reinterpretation and restoration of existing architectures and in the design of new structures. His approach to historical constructs was never trivial, always showcasing a deep understanding and mastery of the architectural field. This capacity for interpretation and re-elaboration was evident in the diverse projects he undertook.

Fasolo's influence drove Morozzo to become his assistant during his Roman period, and later, Morozzo continued Fasolo's teachings at the University of Genoa. Upon returning to Liguria, he balanced his professional practice with teaching Scenography, rekindling his early interests from the Accademia Ligustica di Belle Arti. In the 1950s, he resumed university teaching, focusing on Drawing and the History and Styles of Architecture.

7. See: Vincenzo Fasolo, *Guida metodica per lo studio della storia dell'architettura*, Rome, 1948, p. 5.
8. See: Vincenzo Fasolo/Giovanni Battista Milani, *Le forme architettoniche dall'antichità classica al medio evo*, Milan, 1931

Morozzo earned his free teaching qualifications in Drawing in 1958 and in Architectural Composition in 1959. His university career culminated between 1965 and 1971 when he served as Director of the Drawing School at the Faculty of Engineering and as a Professor of Life Drawing at the Faculty of Architecture. In 1969, he secured the position of Associate Professor in Drawing, and in 1970, he was poised for a chair in Architectural Composition.

He concluded his academic tenure by integrating his previous teaching spheres into a comprehensive course on Drawing and Design for fourth-year Architecture students between 1975 and 1976.

Concomitantly with his academic responsibilities, Robaldo Morozzo maintained an active professional practice with a remarkably prolific output. The study of Morozzo's works and archives not only delineates the cultural milieu within which the architect operated, but also attests to his vibrant role as a scholar and designer. It underscores his keen attention and interest in diverse currents of thought and design that influenced Italy and Europe throughout the 20th century. Morozzo critically reinterpreted their foundational principles, offering personal solutions and shaping his own intellectual framework, not merely through journals but also through direct observation during frequent cultural excursions.

Left: Drawing of Silenus in the form of Plato, from the Faun Relief of Villa Albani by Julius Thumann, undated.

Right: School project for a building, 1928.

Moderno genovese

Valter Scelsi

The impression conjured by Genoa as seen from the hilltop vistas is Paris projected onto a dishevelled bed. This Paris, indeed a slender one, is a city that hastens to conclude upon the harbour quays, plunging into them. A city composed of fragments that 20th-century urban planning endeavoured to stitch together, continually revealing its own fortuitousness: patches of fabric, masses of architecture, emergences of residential blocks from the ancient city's tapestry, and special buildings from the veil of speculative hillside developments. In the quest for an origin point – not so much chronological as narrative – from which to commence the tale of Genoese modernity, we encounter Orlando Grosso,[1] who in 1946 wrote on Genoese architecture's dependencies on the Roman school, and subsequently described Luigi Carlo Daneri as "inspired by the pure ideals of Le Corbusier."[2] These are the two trends we endeavour to trace.

The reference to Le Corbusier's oeuvre, constantly evoked by Daneri's architectures, delineates a contiguity that is not merely cultural, but also geographical and thus physical. In the immediate post-war years, the nearby city of Marseille drew labourers to the grand construction site of the Unité d'Habitation, initiated in 1947 and completed on October 14, 1952. At least two accounts attest to this influx. The first concerns Carlo Giulio Barberis,[3] who grew up in Genoa and trained there as a carpenter and joiner. Naturalised as a French citizen, Barberis won the contract for the entire wooden fittings of the Cité Radieuse in the late 1940s. From that point onwards, he became a dedicated and recognised collaborator of Le Corbusier, culminating in the construction of the *Cabanon* at his workshop in Salines, Corsica. The *Cabanon* was transported and assembled in the summer of 1952 at Roquebrune Cap-Martin, adjacent to the tavern *L'Etoile de Mer.*[4] It is there that Barberis is photographed at the architect's table on August 11, 1965, and captured in a film likely made by his wife, Delleda Barberis.[5] These colour frames contain the last known images of Le Corbusier, who would pass away just sixteen days later.

1. Orlando Grosso (Genoa, 1882 – Bonassola, 1968) was a conservator, museologist and art historian. After graduating in Law, he was appointed as the secretary of the artistic section of the Office of Fine Arts in the Municipality of Genoa in 1909. Established in 1905, this office was responsible for the administration and management of Genoa's artistic, archaeological, historical and scientific heritage, including its galleries and museums, acquired palaces and other artefacts.
2. Orlando Grosso, *All'ombra della Lanterna. Genova nell'arte e nella storia*, Milan /Genoa, 1946.
3. Carlo Giulio Barberis, later known as *Charles Barberis*, was born in Acqui Terme on March 31, 1908 and died in Ajaccio on October 31, 1980. See: Felice Ragazzo, "Charles Jules (Carlo Giulio) Barberis, da Menuisier a precursore della prefabbricazione architettonica, al seguito di Le Corbusier", in: *Abitare la Terra*, no. 51, 2019, p. 32–35.
4. Tommaso Rebutato (known as Robert) was born in 1907 to a modest Italian family in Beausoleil, near Monaco. A plumber by trade, he opened a business in Nice in 1940, which he abandoned in 1949 to enter the burgeoning tourism industry on the Côte d'Azur. He purchased a small plot of land in Roquebrune-Cap-Martin and, together with his wife Marguerite, opened the restaurant *L'Étoile de Mer Chez Robert* in the summer of 1949. That same year, he met Le Corbusier, a guest of his neighbour Jean Badovici.
5. Amateur silent colour film shot in 8 millimetre format (Archives Départementales des Alpes-Maritimes). In the film, Le Corbusier dines on the veranda of Robert Rebutato's L'Etoile de Mer in Roquebrune, accompanied by friends and collaborators, including Guy Rottier and Charles Barberis.

The second story connects the emblematic site of the Modern Movement to the personal history of Caterina Marcenaro, the driving force behind the significant museological and museographic developments in 20th-century Genoa. Marcenaro, who would later organise the civic galleries[6] of Palazzo Bianco and Palazzo Rosso, lost her father at the age of two and saw her only brother, Bartolomeo (known as Mario), move to Marseille in 1947 to work on the Unité. This separation would only heal with their reunion at the end of the 1960s.[7]

The Roman influence on the references of key figures in Genoa's architectural scene appears self-evident, particularly when considering their educational trajectories. Indeed, two major works by the Roman architect Marcello Piacentini,[8] a dominant figure in Italian architecture from 1910 to 1940, significantly shape modern Genoa. These are the master plan for Piazza della Vittoria – around which Piacentini designed the Palazzo INFPS and the buildings known as Garbarino & Sciaccaluga, and where, between 1924 and 1931, he created, alongside artists Arturo Dazzi, Giovanni Prini and Edoardo De Albertis, the Great War Memorial in the form of the Victory Arch[9] – and the skyscraper in Piazza Dante. The latter, designed with Angelo Invernizzi and completed in 1940, remained the tallest building in Italy until the construction of the Torre Breda in Milan in 1954.

The grand architectural projects in Genoa during the 1930s engaged a significant portion of the local architectural culture in collaborations with Piacentini. Eugenio Fuselli[10] – an architect, urban theorist and professor – having passed the state examination in Engineering in 1929 and the state examination in Architecture the following year, first established connections with the Roman Urbanist Group[11] and subsequently with Piacentini himself. Piacentini appointed Fuselli as his assistant at the Faculty of Architecture and collaborator in his studio, where projects such as the expansion of the Casa Madre dei Mutilati in Rome were underway. Fuselli would later apply this expertise in Genoa with the construction of the Casa del Mutilato in 1938.

Concurrently with Robaldo Morozzo della Rocca, born in Turin on May 6, 1904, another figure emerged with distinct characteristics shaped by Roman training and a subsequent career marked by significant architectural opportunities in the Ligurian territory. This figure is Luigi Vietti, born in Canobbio on February 13, 1903.

6. In 1949, the mayor of Genoa, Gelasio Adamoli, appointed a commission for the reorganisation of the municipal collections. Members included Orlando Grosso, director of the Office of Fine Arts, Antonio Morassi, superintendent of the Galleries and Artworks of Liguria, and Mario Labò, president of the Academy of Fine Arts Linguistics, along with Franco Albini as external consultant and Caterina Marcenaro, who officially succeeded Grosso in April 1950.

7. Raffaella Fontanarossa, *La capostipite di sé. Una donna alla guida dei musei. Caterina Marcenaro a Genova 1948–71*, Rome, 2015.

8. Born in Rome on December 8, 1881 to Teresa Stefani and Pio Piacentini, he was the architect responsible for the Palazzo delle Esposizioni on Via Nazionale (1882). He died in Rome on May 18, 1960.

9. References in: Giuliano Forno, "La sistemazione della Piazza della Vittoria", in: Giuseppe Marceraro (Ed.) *Genova, Il Novecento*, op. cit., p.320–334; Silvia Barisione et al., *Architetture in Liguria dagli anni Venti agli anni Cinquanta*, op. cit.; Giorgio Rossini (Ed.), *Da Baroni a Piacentini. Immagini e memoria della Grande Guerra a Genova e in Liguria*, Milan, 2009; Mario Lupano, *Marcello Piacentini*, op. cit.

10. Born in 1903 in Varallo Sesia, in the province of Vercelli, to Carlo Fuselli, an engineer known for numerous Genoese buildings blending Art Nouveau and Baroque styles. He passed away in Genoa on March 18, 2003.

11. The Group of Urbanists of Rome (GUR) consisted of Luigi Piccinato, Gino Cancellotti, Mario Dabbeni, Roberto Lavagnino, Luigi Lenzi, Giuseppe Nicolosi, Marcello Piacentini, Alfredo Scalpelli and Cesare Valle. Eugenio Fuselli is also credited in the proposal for the Territorial Plan and Municipal Urban Plan of Rome in 1929.

Morozzo graduated in Rome in 1929, completing his university education that commenced with a "biennium of physics and mathematical studies" at the University of Genoa. In the same year, he qualified as an architect in Milan. Vietti, having graduated from Rome a year earlier, registered with the Order of Architects of Genoa in 1929. In the Ligurian capital, he was appointed to head the Detached Office of the Superintendency of Turin for the Monuments of Liguria, a position he held from 1931 to 1933. This was a period of profound transformation for the city – Italy's foremost port and a pivotal vertex of the national industrial triangle – stemming from the administrative creation of Greater Genoa, a metropolis born from the union of the central city with its delegations and 19 smaller adjacent municipalities.

In the 1950s, freed from the monumental pre-war emphasis, the reference to Rome for Genoese architects began to transform into a narrative *topos*, akin to the literary debut of Giovanni Arpino. Written in only 20 days in a boarding house on Via Prè, Arpino's work exudes the grim and desperate flavour of the port's alleys, mirroring their essence in its pages. The protagonist of *Sei stato felice, Giovanni*[12] departs from the belly of Genoa, leaving behind the wine, hunger, taverns, violence, memories of war and impossible loves, ultimately heading to Rome in the book's closing lines.

For Morozzo, the processes of assimilating elements from his education and integrating those from his subsequent practice found their full realisatio in the complex[13] designed and buil between 1955 and 1964 for the Istitut Nazionale delle Assicurazioni in the Pic capietra area, along Via XII Ottobre an at its juncture with Viale IV Novembre.

The transcendence of Roman-derive monumental models is epitomised i Morozzo's unwavering commitmen to proposing a new civic architectur The Piccapietra building is conceive with a complex foundational structur that adeptly accommodates the site' varying elevations through a perimete colonnade and a network of commercial *passages*. These galleries embrace novel model, reminiscent of the covere corridors of the monumental cemetery o Staglieno, designed by Carlo Barabin the foremost architect of Genoa's urba design in the 19th -century, and his disciple Giovanni Battista Resasco. The became integral to an intricate urba system of covered walkways, whic sought to delineate a new commercia city in the Genoa of the economic boom intertwining structures from variou eras – the 19th-century Galleria Mazzin the portico of the Teatro Carlo Felic modern arcades and underpasses, an the commercial spaces of departmen stores.

The connection to the adjacent religious complex of Santa Marta unveil the historical depth of the cultura journey from Genoa to Rome an back. The statue of the Glory of Sant Marta, crafted by Filippo Parod within a Baroque architectural spac constructed in the church's presbyter

12. Giovanni Arpino (Pola, 27 January 1927 – Turin, 10 December 1987) published *Sei stato felice, Giovanni* in 1952 by Einaudi. Arpin won the Strega Prize in 1964 and the Campiello Prize in 1980.

13. Information in: Stefano Passamonti, *Ex Palazzo INA Piccapietra. Robaldo Morozzo della Rocca*, op. cit.

n the final decade of the 17th-century, ›mbodies this revelation. Parodi, a ›upil of Bernini,[14] chisels in stone the ›ssence of his Roman sojourn and the visdom acquired there, rendering it a ›onsummate symbol in the elevation of ›he saint's figure, reaching beyond the ›helter of architecture.

Both images: Multipurpose buildings for the National Insurance Institute in Piccapietra.
Genoa, 1955–1964
Invited competition, 1st Prize for Plot IV.

14. "he carried with him a letter of introduction to Cavalier Bernino (sic), who, in good faith, received him as a disciple." See: Raffaele Soprani. *Vite de' Pittori, Scultori, ed Architetti Genovesi*. Genoa. 1768. Vol. 1. p. 54 [trans.].

Robaldo Morozzo della Rocca: One of many brave ones

Adam Štěch

I encountered the work of Robaldo Morozzo Della Rocca during my first trip to Genoa in 2011. I discovered his masterpiece – the Palazzina Ollandini – in a book and seized the chance to see it in person. At that time, I was mainly interested in the work of lesser-known Italian postwar organic architects, so the Palazzina, designed by an unheard-of architect on the fringes of architectural history, was a perfect fit for what would later become my research focus. I visited it and, kindly invited by the owners, toured one of the apartments. It was only later that I discovered Morozzo's extensive and varied oeuvre, spanning different architectural approaches and styles of the 20th century, including Neo-Classicism, Art Deco, Novecento, Rationalism, Organic Architecture, Postwar Modernism, Brutalism and sculptural tendencies. Together with other unsung architects, Morozzo represents a timeline of architectural modernity and the historical events he lived through, making him an "architect-chameleon". Since that visit, I have documented the work of those architects who, like Morozzo, remained outside mainstream architectural discourse and were overlooked by retrospective interpretation despite their innovative, contextualized and exciting work. This is common in architectural history: many architects worked locally with a specific geographic focus and created a diverse and surprising body of work that is hard to categorize. To illustrate this, I have chosen five examples of other international architects whose work parallels and mirrors the themes and challenges of Morozzo's multifaceted career and the abundance of his oeuvre. Through these little-known architects, I intend to retrieve some of the complexity of the historical context of 20th-century architecture, challenging past generations of historians and going beyond their sole focus on Modernism. Our generation of researchers must uncover these outsiders' work, fill the gaps and create new layers of 20th-century architectural history.

Elio Luzi and Sergio Jaretti: Same story, different city

The work of the Turin architects Elio Luzi and Sergio Jaretti parallels that of Morozzo in being associated with one specific city. It is no coincidence that the first comprehensive monograph on them by Bernd Schmutz is also being published this year. Their unorthodox creations, which were until recently a hidden treasure of mid-century Modernism in Turin, combined Modernism, Mannerist Eclecticism and even Radical Design. As pupils of Carlo Mollino at the Polytechnic of Turin, they embraced free architectural expression in the 1950s, notably in Casa Obelisco, one of their first projects. This eclectic apartment building, inspired by Antonio Gaudi, is characterised by overflowing organic shapes and expressive decora-

-tive elements. The result – mirroring Morozzo's palazzina Ollandini – a symbiosis of Modernism and organic Art Nouveau, earned the name "Neoliberty". Casa Obelisco is an unparalleled example of quirky architectural formalism, celebrating fluid forms and rich decor at the peak of modernity and standardisation. In the 1960s and 1970s, Luzi and Jaretti's work evolved to feature concrete and brick, with massive geometric volumes replacing organic forms, a shift also seen in Morozzo's 1960s projects. Torre Pitagora and Torre Mirafiori are examples of large residential projects where this shift can be seen. Despite the quality of their work, local architects like Luzi & Jaretti and Morozzo were often overlooked by mainstream critics and journalists with national and international readerships.

Jaretti & Luzi, Casa dell'Obelisco, Turin 1954–1959
Picture by Adam Štěch

Henry Lacoste: Amazed by ancient history

The Belgian architect Henry Lacoste gained prominence in the 1930s with his Art Deco churches and public buildings. Initially influenced by his father's blacksmith forge, Lacoste developed an early fascination with ancient civilizations, classical art and architectural history, setting himself apart from the high Modernism trend. After studying under Ernest Acker at the Royal Academy of Fine Arts in Brussels, he continued his education at the National School of Fine Arts in Paris. Graduating in 1913, Lacoste participated in archaeological excavations in Greece, returning after World War I. By 1923, he settled in Brussels and was appointed professor at the Higher Institute of Art History and Archaeology and the Academy of Fine Arts in 1926.

Lacoste's work, deeply rooted in his archaeological interests, is refined, eclectic, historicist and unconventional, similar to Morozzo's approach to heritage. In an era dominated by Modernism and standardization, he boldly designed churches echoing the late Belgian Gothic style. His artistic expression aligns with Slovenian architect Jože Plečnik and Italian Novecento architects. Using historical elements contextually decades before Postmodernism emerged, he can be seen as a "proto-Postmodernist."

The Queen Elizabeth Foundation building (1930s) exemplifies his approach with its unique Belgian interior decorations. The brick structure, adorned with colorful materials and ornaments, features vibrant glass panels and a grand library, creating an eclectic design. Custom-designed lamps on faceted pillars mimic Egyptian papyrus columns, showcasing Lacoste's artistic freedom in a period dominated by Modernism.

Conversely, Lacoste's late 1940s reconstruction of the Leuven University Library replaced vibrant Art Deco elements with the purity of solid wood and a monumental style. The library now includes two levels of horizontal balconies with triangular alcoves and smoothly integrated oak paneling and balustrades. Like Morozzo, Lacoste remains relatively unknown outside his country.

Sybold Van Ravesteyn: Baroque fusion

Located in Utrecht, just metres away from the notoriously famous Schröder House by Gerrit Rietveld, the house by the Dutch Modernist architect Sybold van Ravesteyn is still a well-kept secret of European interwar architecture. Small, refined and unusual, the house is the manifesto of "Other Modernism" developed by Van Ravesteyn as an almost obscure synthesis of Functionalism and Baroque architecture. Van Ravesteyn's bold career can be described as transiting from strict rationalism to neo-Baroque fantasies. This prominent architect worked extensively, designing train stations for the Dutch railway system, including Utrecht (1940), Rotterdam (1957) and Nijmegen (1954) stations. By the late 1930s and 1940s, his austere formal language evolved into organic, curved forms and developed a distinctive personal style. A driving force for this change was a trip to Rome in 1936, exposing him to the curves of the Italian Baroque churches. As he wrote: "Ornaments fulfil a spiritual need to give our environment a more natural shape, to resolve and display scale... Sometimes the function of ornaments is very specific. Ornamentation on a building can complete it and allow a natural transition to the cityscape. Humanity has formal needs that cannot be explained by reason and that remain unsatisfied by overly puritanical and functional architecture. The ban on ornamentation pronounced by the new functionalist trends was an attempt to mask its spiritual poverty." Ravesteyn went even further and the integrated decorative vocabulary of historical styles into his Modernist structures. His notable projects include the Theater Kunstmin in Dordrecht (1940) and Rotterdam Zoo (1941). His De Holland van 1859 administrative building in Dordrecht (1939), reminiscent of Morozzo's 1930s palaces, highlights his Baroque approach.

Togo Murano: Samurai of Japanese architecture

Togo Murano's remarkable buildings radiate creative energy through decoration, historical references, and glamorous monumentality. He founded his studio in Osaka in 1929. His early works, influenced by German Modernism (offices and Sogo department store, 1939) and Scandinavian Modern Classicism (Town Hall in Ube, 1937), evolved into a rich, eclectic style. These projects honed his attention to detail and delicate decorative style, which defined much of his later work. His buildings resemble elementary forms adorned with ornate, attractive details. Traditional structural elements were transformed into richly decorated shrines with numerous historical and artistic references.

In the 1950s and 1960s, despite a range of influences, Murano consistently referenced ancient Japanese architecture. He believed Modern and innovative features should follow mastery of traditional principles. His eclecticism is evident in the Roman-inspired Hiroshima Peace Cathedral, the Brutalist Nishinomiya convent for the Trappists, and the organic Takarazuka church (1966).

Murano's mature style is highlighted in projects for the Grand Prince hotel chain. The New Takanawa Hotel in Tokyo (1982) is a large complex with a conference centre; though many original interiors are lost, some remain intact. The Hakone Hotel (1972) elegantly blends with its landscape, resembling scenes from a Studio Ghibli animated film. Structured with circular pavilions on the lake shore, the well-preserved hotel features a long hall with windows, intimate seating, and Murano's acrylic decorations. Its interiors mix materials and architectural styles, combining Art Nouveau with medieval masonry and iron fittings. Chandeliers shaped like horses, paper sculptures, and carnival masks add to the whimsical atmosphere. Murano never aligned with any Japanese Modern architecture school, reflecting an artistic and stylistic freedom similar to Morozzo's approach.

Cäsar Pinnau: Squeezed by ideaologies

The German architect Cäsar Pinnau's career was shaped by dramatic political changes. Born in Hamburg in 1906, he initially apprenticed as a carpenter before studying Architecture and Interior Design in Berlin and at the State School of Applied Arts in Munich under Richard Berndl, Emil Preetorius, and Joseph Wackerle. Before opening his own office, he worked for Fritz August Breuhaus de Groot in Berlin, designing villas and luxurious interiors for the airship LZ 129 Hindenburg. In these projects, Modernism, banned in Germany by Adolf Hitler, was adapted into a more traditional style. In the late 1930s, Pinnau joined the NSDAP, which allowed him to work closely with the government. He renovated the Reich President's Palace for Mussolini's visit, the interior of the Reich Chancellery, and the Japanese Embassy in the Tiergarten. During the war, he served as a professor at the Academy of Fine Arts in Berlin. Despite his regime involvement, his career thrived after World War II, as the Neo-Classical style gave way to refined Modernism. Although he failed to secure state commissions, Pinnau became popular with the new capitalist elite, including Rudolf-August Oetker, designing villas, administrative headquarters, and factories. Among his postwar projects, the Hamburg Süd Gebäude skyscraper, built for Oetker in 1964, exemplifies refined Modernism. Its pure, simple glass and steel curtain façade, inspired by American postwar corporate architecture, reflects Morozzo's Palazzo INA in Genoa, which can be considered the "most modern" of his works. In the 1960s, Pinnau focused on maritime architecture. The Cap San Diego cargo ship, commissioned by Aristotle Onassis, features highly elegant design and has been converted into a museum in Hamburg Harbour. Pinnau's career, deeply influenced by political shifts, is a dramatic story. His varied and sometimes contradictory projects reveal new layers of architectural history.

NOTE ON SOURCES.
What is missing ?

The extensive literature on 20th-century architecture has been a crucial resource for this work. It includes seminal works of Italian critical historiography by Bruno Zevi Zevi (*Storia dell'Architettura Moderna*, 1950), Gillo Dorfles (*L'architettura moderna*, 1954), Leonardo Benevolo (*Storia dell'architettura moderna*, 1960), Manfredo Tafuri (*Storia dell'architettura italiana 1944–1985*, 1986) and Renato De Fusco (*Storia dell'architettura contemporanea*, 1977), as well as international research by George Everard Kidder Smith (*Italy Builds. Its Modern Architecture and Native Inheritance*, 1955), Nikolaus Pevsner (*An Outline of European Architecture*, 1975) and Richard Etlin (*Modernism in Italian Architecture, 1890–1940*, 1991). Recent texts have also been highly significant, such as those by Giorgio Ciucci and Francesco Dal Co (*Architettura Italiana del Novecento*, 1990), Luca Molinari (*Between Continuity and Crisis: History and Project in Italian Architectural Culture of the Postwar Period*, 2000), Kenneth Frampton (*The Other Modern Movement: Architecture, 1920–1970*, 2021) and Roberto Gargiani (*Eretici italiani dell'architettura razionalista*, 2021).

The research has been enriched by more specialised volumes, including those by Cesare De Seta (*La cultura architettonica in Italia tra le due guerre*, 1972), Giorgio Ciucci (*Gli architetti e il Fascismo. Architettura e città*, 1989; *Figure e temi nell'architettura italiana del Novecento*, 2023) and Vittorio Magnago Lampugnani (Ed. – *L'Avventura delle Idee*, 1985). In these texts Morozzo is always mentioned "on the sidelines", due to his political stance and love of risk. This obscurity is only lifted, as seen in works by Silvia Danesi and Luciano Patetta (*Il Razionalismo e l'architettura in Italia durante il Fascismo*, 1976), Michele Cennamo (Ed. – *Il Miar. Materiali per l'analisi dell'architettura moderna*, 1976) and Ezio Godoli (*Il Futurismo*, 1983). In regional literature, Morozzo's significance is more pronounced: in texts by Paolo Cevini (*Genova Anni '30. Da Labò a Daneri*, 1989), Franca Balletti e Bruno Giontoni (*Una città fra le due guerre*, 1990), Giovanna Franco e Stefano Musso (*Architetture in Liguria dopo il 1945*, 2016) and in the exhibition catalogue *Architettura in Liguria dagli anni Venti agli anni Cinquanta* (Silvia Barisione, et al., 2004), Morozzo's work is recognised as significant in the construction of the modern city.

Regarding magazines, another significant source, the dissemination of Morozzo's work can be divided into two distinct periods: from the mid-1920s until the outbreak of World War II, and the post-war period. There is a substantial difference in his historiographical fortune between these phases. During the 1930s, Morozzo's work was featured in *Architettura*, *L'Architettura Italiana*. In the post-war period, his "success" experienced a setback, except for Bruno Zevi's magazine, *L'Architettura. Cronache e storia*, and for the very few quotes that appeared in *Casabella*, *Domus* and *L'Architecture d'aujour d'hui*.

Among posthumous sources, notable mentions include the doctoral thesis by Maria Carola Morozzo della Rocca (Vol.1-*L'architetto e il suo archivio*; Vol.2-*L'architetto e il disegno*) and her book with Carlotta Fierro et al. (*Robaldo Morozzo della Rocca architetto. Frammenti d'archivio*, Vols. 1 and 2, 2013), as well as the book by Giovanni Duranti (*Robaldo Morozzo della Rocca*, 2005).

So, what is missing? In an age in which the reputations of the majority of architects were sustained by appeals and manifestos, Morozzo did not write or lecture about his work, nor did he theorize about architecture or enter into the debates that were preoccupying architects from Italy. This book aims to showcase the richness of Morozzo's work, but it is as much about Genoa. The book gathers a collection of architectural attempts, highlighting the significant work still needed to fully capture the complexity and legacy of the 20th-century Italian architectural landscape.